SOUR

MY STORY

A troubled girl
from a broken home.

The Brixton gang
she nearly died for.

The baby she fought
to live for.

Tracey Miller
with Lucy Bannerman

HARPER
element

Certain details in this book, including names, places and dates,
have been changed to protect those concerned.
Some events have been dramatised.

HarperElement
An Imprint of HarperCollins*Publishers*
77–85 Fulham Palace Road,
Hammersmith, London W6 8JB

www.harpercollins.co.uk

First published by HarperElement 2014

1 3 5 7 9 10 8 6 4 2

© Tracey Miller and Lucy Bannerman 2014

Tracey Miller and Lucy Bannerman assert the moral
right to be identified as the authors of this work

A catalogue record of this book is
available from the British Library

ISBN 978-0-00-756504-7

Printed and bound in Great Britain by
Clays Ltd, St Ives plc

MIX
Paper from
responsible sources

FSC
www.fsc.org

FSC™ C007454

Acknowledgements

A big thank-you to my editors Vicky Eribo and Carolyn Thorne; my literary agent Jessie Botterill; my wonderful co-author Lucy Bannerman and the rest of the team at HarperCollins.

A special thank-you to my mum, for giving me life – I Love You! My brother, my sisters, my nieces, my family, who have always been there for me. My two daughters who keep me focused – I love you both dearly. Not forgetting my close friends who have kept me strong in one way or another.

A final thank-you to Brooke Kinsella, Hellie Ogden, Temi Mwale, Elijah 'Jaja' Kerr and Saadiya Ahmed.

Introduction

They call me Sour. The opposite of sweet. Shanking, steaming, robbing – I did it all, rolling with the Man Dem.

I did it because I was bad. I did it because I had heart. And the reason I reckon I got away with it for so long? Because I was a girl.

Sour was my brand-name. How should I put this? I was quite influential round my endz. In my tiny, warped world, where rude boys were the good boys and exit routes non-existent, I was top dog. I want to give people outside the lifestyle some insight into lives like mine. I want parents to think about what their kids really get up to. For them, let this be an education, an eye-opener.

I want to lay myself bare to all the people who knew me when I was bad. I am not offering this as an excuse. I'm offering an explanation.

Above all, for all the youngers like me, the kids without a home who become kids without a conscience, the ones living the streetlife who know the thrill of likking the tills or steaming a shop, the young bucks who don't need to be told how easily a blade slides out of punctured flesh, let this be a warning.

Youth workers could argue I had no chance. Politicians could blame my parents. Others might say the choices I made were mine and mine alone. Maybe they're all right.

Tracey Miller

Me? I think badness is genetic. With a manic depressive for a mother and a convicted rapist for a father, I ain't never gonna be Little Bo Peep.

So this is my story, the real story of how I fell down the rabbit hole of gangland. There are no real excuses. I did what I did and I live with what happened. I have a lot to be thankful for.

The hard part is not working out where it all went wrong. The hard part is making it right.

Mum and Dad

My mum's first memory of her childhood in Jamaica begins with a broom. Mum was eight; her little sister, Rosie, must have been five. They lived in Kingston, in a one-bedroom shack with their nana.

"Yuh pickney have tings easy," she always used to tell us. "When we did young we had to work fucking hard to keep the yard clean bwoy, wash fi we own clothes and dem ting dere, cook our own food and ting. None ah dis mordern shit, yuh ah gwarn wid."

It was the day before Christmas. Mum was outside, scrubbing the yard. She had left Rosie dancing in the dust by the stove, a skinny girl grappling with a broom twice her size. Mum was down on her knees with a scrubbing brush, when she heard the screams.

She'd knocked over the pot of bubbling oil that had been cooking on the stove.

"Burned all the hair clean aff her head," she'd say. "Her little dress stuck to her skin."

Mum, still such a small child herself, rushed for scissors to cut the cotton from the blistering skin and tried to calm the hysterical girl, but it was too late. Boiling oil is too strong an adversary for five-year-old girls.

At the funeral, she arranged the pillow in her coffin to make sure she was comfortable.

"Me did do her hair real nice fi church, well, what was left ah it," she said.

They buried her on Christmas Day.

Her own mother didn't make it to the church that day. She had already long left Kingston, leaving behind her daughters with their grandmother, to chase the tailwinds of the Windrush Generation to the UK.

No one had heard from her mother, but there was a rumour she'd found a job in an office. Mum said she spent years in that old, broken-down yard, waiting for the day she would send for her to join her.

While she waited, her grandmother started taking on lodgers.

That's her other memory – of the lodger. He worked in the garage during the day, and drank beer from his bed by night. He persuaded her to go away with him one afternoon after school, and took her to the cemetery.

"The bloodclart smelled of grease and chicken fat. Laid me on a tombstone and put his finger up me."

Lord have mercy, things weren't right in that house. I never met Mum's grandmother, but maybe that's for the best – I have a feeling me and her wouldn't have got on.

She was too strict for a start. No loitering after school, no free time, no fun.

She would tell my poor mum, "When school done, if mi spit pon de floor, yuh better reach home before it dry."

If not, a beating was waiting. I didn't believe Mum when she told me about the grater.

"She put a grater in the yard, till it got hot, hot, hot in di sun."

2

Then she'd make Mum kneel on it. Oh my days, what a wicked witch! I'd have put that grater where the sun don't shine.

Weird thing is, my mum still sticks up for the woman who raised her.

"Cha man, her heart did inna di right place."

And where exactly would that be?

Still, I'll give her something. She taught my mum to cook all the hardcore soul food that me and my brother love. Chicken, rice and peas, all the meats – no one cooks it better than my mum.

Aged 12, Mum finally got the call. Her mother finally sent a plane ticket for London. She said in the letter she was doing well and life was good. Mum dreamed of a big house with servants. She dreamed of the high life, in a country where people drove shining cars, girls wore short skirts and their wallets overflowed with Queen's head.

But Brixton in the early 1970s wasn't quite the paradise she'd imagined. For starters, she stepped off the plane in a cheap, yellow dress and was welcomed by snow. It pretty much got worse from there.

"In Jamaica we went to church because we suffered so much," she said. "When we came to London, nobody went to church no more."

"Me did know seh dere was a God in Kingston, becah he used to answer my prayers. Nobody nah answer no prayers inna Brixton."

Oh yeah, quite a character, my mum. On her good days, she likes watching EastEnders, Coronation Street and Al Jazeera.

Whenever there's something on the news about "feral youths", as all those suited-and-tied BBC broadcasters like to call 'em, she always shakes her head and mutters, "Yuh pickney haffi learn to rass."

Or, in other words, people's kids need to learn to behave.

She loves baking, and makes a mean Jamaican punch. Oh my days! Nestlé milk mixed with pineapple juice, nutmeg, vanilla, ice cubes. Mix in rum or brandy and you've got a wicked pineapple punch. And a good chance of getting Type 2 diabetes, just like her.

I know I shouldn't laugh, because of her illness, but there were wild times too.

Like that time she insisted on driving me and my brother to school in her speedy little Ford Capri, instead of letting us take the bus.

"Hold on!" she screamed, leaning back and putting one arm across my brother in the front seat and one arm on the steering wheel, as she slammed down her foot on the accelerator.

"Me taking di kids to school!"

She whizzed down Coldharbour Lane that day like she was bloody Nigel Mansell, cutting up cars and swerving wildly down the street. I remember screaming as we jumped the red lights and brought a big-assed bus screeching to a halt. She crashed into a van and folded up the front of the car. Mum didn't even notice.

She just turned the radio up full volume and started chanting whatever weird shit came into her head. Oh my days, it was like Mrs Doubtfire meets Grand Theft Auto.

Yusuf and I clung on to our seatbelts and just prayed to God to get there safely. I swear I've never been so happy to get to school.

"Me go pick yuh up later," she shouted, depositing the pair of us, shaking, traumatised heaps at the no-parking zone by the gates. "Make sure yuh did deh when me reach at tree tirty!"

With that, we heard the wheels spin, the engine roar, then she was gone.

Lo and behold, 3.30pm came and went, but Mum and her Ford Capri were nowhere to be seen.

The policeman told us later they had to give high-speed chase through Brixton.

"Rassclat!" she said, when we told her what happened. "Me did what? Yuh sure? I just remember seh me ah drive tru traffic, me put dung me foot annah drive fast, one minute me ah get weh, next minute dem got me."

We tried not to giggle.

"Den I had to fight a whole heap ah policeman, and dem fling me down inna dem bloodclart van and take me down the station, bastards. Den dem take me go ahahspital."

That was my first day at a police station. We spent the whole day there. They fed us, showed us the horses, the police cars. I'm not gonna lie – it was like a fun day out.

It was less fun, I imagine, for that poor Ford Capri.

She was remorseful about some things. Like the time she dangled my sister off the balcony.

"Me can't believe seh mi woulda do dat to yuh," she told Althea, once she came back down to earth. "I'm so sorry, girl, please forgive me, yuh mum wasn't well."

Althea and her always had problems after that.

Then there were the afternoons she used to pick up her baseball bat and walk through the streets, speaking to herself. Or the time she stripped stark naked and walked calmly down the road at rush hour. Or the time – this is my favourite – when she brought an elderly Russian lady home, and held her hostage.

How many other kids come home from school to find a confused and frail old woman perched on the settee, saying they've been kidnapped by your mum?

"Mum, what you doing?" we screamed.

"Me ah ask de woman, where ye live? And she come with me. Me haffi look after her."

I looked at the frail old woman, clutching an untouched plate of rice and peas in her trembling hands.

Mum came into the front room, brandishing more food.

"Yuh hungry? Eat dis cake, it's nice. Drink some tea. If yuh want, gwarn go sleep and drink."

The sweet old lady reached up for my hand.

"Please," she whispered, "I want to go home."

Yusuf helped her escape, while I kept Mum distracted. She was horrified when she found the front room empty.

"Which one ah yuh let her out? Where's she gaarn? I'm looking after her!"

Oh yeah, every year it was something, and it always seemed to be round Christmas.

You know that song, "Love and only love will solve your problems" by Fred Locks?

That's the one she liked to listen to during her episodes. That's the one she'd listen to over and over again and all through the night. The bass would shake the house.

Whenever that came on, and the volume was turned up, we knew to brace ourselves.

As for my dad, well, he was a proper little bad boy.

Mum's first two babydaddies had been and gone before she met the man I have the misfortune to call my dad.

I've only ever known my mum as a medicated woman but she must have been an attractive lady. She could get the boys.

Sour

Althea's dad was young too. His family were having none of it, and he soon scarpered.

Melanie's dad, he was rich. He had money, but he was married, so Mum was his sidepiece. Not that she knew that at the time. He left her heartbroken and went back to the wife.

But me and Yusuf's dad? Woah, Mum really hit the jackpot there.

In Brixton they called his crowd the "Dirty Dozen". They travelled in a pack.

Marmite liked to play dominoes. Runner, Sanchez and the rest liked drinking. Irie was a school bus driver by day, getaway driver by night. There were rumours he used to lock up girls in the bathroom at parties and assault them. Charmer. Monk was sweet, the quietest of the lot, so it took them by surprise when he ran his babymother down and stabbed her one night on the way home.

Then there was 'Mingo. Short for Flamingo – when things got naughty, that man could fly away and never get caught. And, finally, in his knitted Rasta hat and moccasins was Pedro, aka Wellington Augustus Miller. Or, as I no longer call him: Dad.

He'd break Mum's nose and black out her eyes, gamble away the wages she earned as an admin clerk in an office. He lost me a baby sister too. Kicked Mum in the belly till she dropped her in a toilet. She once ended up jumping through a glass door to escape him. Doctors said she only had a 50–50 chance if they tried to remove the shards from her skull, so they left them inside. They must have done the right thing, coz she's still here.

The X-rays revealed a freshly fractured skull, and a long, unhappy marriage's worth of broken bones and damaged organs. I was six weeks old.

Oh yeah, he was a proper nuisance, my dad. And you know the irony? With the stepdads who followed, I still remember Mum as being the violent one.

She was working in two jobs – clerk during the day, a cleaner in the evenings – living for the weekends when she and her friends would follow the sound systems round south London, stealing drinks and befriending bouncers.

The Dirty Dozen weren't Yardies. They weren't in that league. Sure, they'd beat up an ice-cream van man with a chain, but their crime wasn't organised, not in the way the Yardies' was.

Still, anywhere they got to was pure war.

The first night my parents met, Mum watched Dad beat up a bouncer so bad they took him to the hospital. He had taken offence at being asked to pay an entry fee.

Next time they met in the Four Aces nightclub in north London.

"He had cut off his locks, he looked like a proper gentleman," she recalled.

Not quite gentlemanly enough, of course, to hang around for my birth.

"Not one of those fathers was by my side when I was pushing dem babies out," she still complains, as if that was the worst they did.

He popped in and out of our lives.

We lived in and out of mother and baby units, as she moved in with him and moved out again. I remember a garden, a Housing Association house in Tooting, with pears and apples and strawberries. But the council got a bit fed up with Mr Miller's illegal gambling nights in the front room, so we lost that too.

Sour

The punches went both ways. Dad was once lay waited outside a club, after bursting a chain off this girl's neck. Her friends tried to attack him with a samurai sword. They were the ones who ended up in the dock. Would you believe that it was poor, innocent Wellington who took to the witness stand to testify as the victim?

It wasn't long before he was in court again.

I still remember the day those blueshirts stampeded into our house to take him away.

"BATH RAPIST GETS JAIL TERM" it said later in the *News of the World*.

Let me share it with you. It's enough to make you proud.

"A man was jailed yesterday for raping a woman in her home, after a court heard his victim was so terrified she allowed him to have a bath and scrubbed his back. Wellington Miller, 33, unemployed of Dulwich, denied raping the woman."

She was 24. It was a summer's day in June, 1983, when my dad broke into her home in Tooting.

He told the Old Bailey he only intended to rob the place, but insisted that this kindly housewife had offered him a coffee and ran him a bath.

Because that's what women do when men's robbing them, ain't it? Offer them a bath!

What actually happened was that he forced the woman to scrub his back then raped her once in the bathroom and again in the bedroom, in front of her four-year-old son. His defence lawyer blamed his drinking.

You know what he said?

"When he drinks, he goes for walks early in the morning and can't remember what he's done."

I ain't never heard of that drink – y'know, the one that turns you into an amnesiac rapist.

The judge called him an "insensitive bulldozer".

I can think of other words. He got three years and three months.

So why is he still in prison now? Because two weeks after being released on parole, no word of a lie, he left his bail hostel in Islington and in the early hours of the morning battered down the door of a house just a few yards away, and tried to rape the mother and three girls who had barricaded themselves in a bedroom. The police arrived just in time.

He's still in jail for that one. I've lost track where – he's been moved around that much.

He got life. Could have been out by now if he'd admitted his guilt. He still insists he is innocent. Deep down I think he's scared. I don't think he wants to come out.

He wouldn't be able to use a mobile phone. He wouldn't be able to drive, or use a computer. Hell, the year my dad went down, Alan Sugar was bringing out his Amstrads. The first cool ones with the computer games, remember them? But the world has moved on while he's been inside and my dad knows it.

So maybe it's easier to lie about being innocent, than face the world outside.

He wrote to me when I became a bad girl. "Heard you become a gangster," he said. "Whassat all about?"

There was no lecture. No judgement. Not even disappointment. It sounded like he was simply curious. Maybe he wanted to know what kind of gangster his daughter had become.

If I'm totally honest, for most of my young life it felt glamorous to have an incarcerated dad. No one said "rapist", of course. It would be a long time before I found out exactly what he had done. I didn't trouble myself to find out. All I knew was that having a dad in prison felt like something to boast about. It felt cool and rebellious. It felt like an assertion of status.

The last time I went to visit him, he claimed I wasn't his. Said he had something to tell me, a secret he'd been keeping. He said he was convinced I must be Marmite's. I never saw him again after that. One day, I'll take that DNA test, but not now. Truth is, I'm scared to find out. Which result would be worse? Finding out you do have a rapist for a father. Or discovering you'd wasted all those tears and anger on a rapist who was no relation at all?

So, that's me – a by-product of fuckery. Beyond those black marks, my past is blank. Or maybe there are no good bits to know about. As they say, badness is genetic. I think they might be right.

The Estate

They call it bipolar now, but it was manic depression back then. Mum's episodes meant my brother and I would be shipped out around foster carers and care homes a couple times every year, a few months here, six months there, but we always ended up back in the same place in south London: the Roupell Park estate.

Althea was nine years older than me. I'll be honest, there were times that she got on my nerves, but sometimes she could be a cool sister to have. She didn't take no shit. Her hair was always nice. She wore beehives, French plaits and Cain rows and had a nice boyfriend. She had a good job in WH Smith and went to work every day. When Mum was ill, she had our backs. She wasn't afraid to cuss people off, tell them to mind their own business. But as Mum's episodes became more frequent, Althea's patience ran out. Then of course, there was the balcony incident.

Besides, she was pregnant. Did I mention that? Not heavily – can't imagine Mum would have had the strength to dangle two – but it was enough to make her pack her bags. I couldn't blame her for getting out when she did. She left home early, coming back to visit now and then.

We'd started fighting a lot by that point, so can't say I missed her.

Sour

Now Melanie. She was a different story. Mel was seven years older, and a virtual stranger. Althea he could cope with, but my dad took a dislike to this younger child taking all Mum's attention away from him, so she was sent to live with her dad. He had married this white lady in Clapham, so yeah, Mel got lucky.

When she walked back into our lives as a teenager, after a fight with her dad, it was like having Naomi Campbell coming to visit. I remember when I first set eyes on her I couldn't believe it.

She was modelesque, man. She had long, glossy hair and pale skin. She was tall and slim and beautiful. Nothing like Althea in her WH Smith shirt with her silver name tag. I liked the swagger of this new person I was going to have to get to know.

At last, a breath of fresh air in our claustrophobic yard. Best of all, she worked in fashion. OK, so she was a sales assistant at an Army and Navy surplus store, but don't matter if it's camouflage gear. Clothes are fashion, innit?

She had her own money and her uniform, man, I'll never forget it – she had sexy tops and pencil skirts that were cowled round the waist. I thought, wow, this looks exciting. She seemed like girly fun.

Boy, was I wrong. Melanie liked partying, she liked her freedom, and she didn't have no time for irritating siblings. Most of all, she really didn't appreciate taking orders from an unhinged reggae fan who liked to walk round the estate naked. Her rows with Mum were vicious. She might not have been dangled off a balcony, but soon Melanie too realised Roupell Park was not for her. She lasted about six months before storming out and slamming the door behind her, without so much as a goodbye.

13

"Two bulls cyaan't live inna one pen."

That was all I remember Mum saying about the matter of another lost daughter, and Mel was soon forgotten as quickly as she had appeared. Thankfully, she left behind at least one spangly top in the washing machine.

I'd pose in front of the mirror, with socks stuffed down my front, looking forward to the day I'd be able to get dressed, look fly and hit the dancehall scene.

"You was such a lovely-looking baby," she used to tell us at least once a day.

I preferred Yusuf's company to the girls'. He should have been a comedian, man. We would stay up and talk all goddamn night. When we got the car bed – all red wooden wheels and a spoiler instead of a headboard – we'd spend so long wrestling over the quilt, we'd end up falling asleep in it together. Eventually, we forgot about the nightly fight for the driver's pillow, and just topped and tailed it together.

As all baby brothers should, he worshipped his big sister. Quite right too. Anything I did, he wanted to do too.

If I wanted to take conkers and throw them at passers-by from the balcony, he would join in.

Ice cubes, eggs, anything we could get our hands on. What's the point of having a balcony, if you can't throw shit at people walking by?

We'd wait for the distant explosion of rage to come from the kitchen – "Where's my fucking eggs?" – then hightail it to the caged football pitch area we called the Pen.

Ivy, the old Jamaican lady who was our first foster carer, was a spiteful old witch. She lived in Peckham, and looked elderly and sweet like somebody's nan, but truly was the meanest woman I'd ever met. She salted our food to stop us eating too much and keep the food bills down – even over-salted the Wotsits, the bitch.

Her house smelled medieval, like the scent of an old woman, with everything velvet. Velvet curtains, velvet table-cloth, velvet wallpaper. She beat up her grandson, poor kid. He could barely look you in the eye. Made him hoover the house every day, the mad old bat. Once he made the mistake of using the hoover to try and remove a stain from her precious velvet wallpaper, so she caught him and beat him with a stick.

I ain't letting my little brother stay some place like this, I decided. So we packed our bags and got ready to escape. Her poor grandkid pleaded to come with us.

"Please," he said. "I don't have money now, but when I do, I'll pay you, hand up to God."

He held his right hand up to the wallpapered ceiling, just in case we didn't believe him.

"We don't want to leave you here, honest we don't, but we can't take you with us."

I told him we had to think about ourselves. He didn't argue much after that.

We must have told the social workers about it, because later we heard that Ivy had been shut down. Wonder what happened to that poor kid. I hope he strangled the old witch and buried her in a velvet coffin in the back garden.

The next time we were sent to Birmingham to stay with a nice Muslim family, that was much more like it.

The woman's husband looked like a real-life gorilla, big and fat and hairy, but he was lovely. They had twin daughters who they treated real nice. It felt like the middle of nowhere, though, and we couldn't understand a word anyone was saying, so we were glad to get back home, where we understood people. Still, I missed their garden and the pistachio cakes the mother made.

Yusuf liked the residential care home the best, well, until, that is, the others discovered he still sucked his thumb. It was just like the "Dumping Ground" in the Tracy Beaker books, but with a lot more toast. Toast, toast, toast – that was all there was to eat in between meals, but at least they let you make your own meals and do your own thing. Felt like a proper little adult.

It wasn't perfect, but it was better than living on eggshells, waiting for that music to be cranked up.

Sure, there were other angry kids raging against the system and setting off the alarms, but mostly it was just peace and quiet, innit. I was disappointed the day they came to take us home from there, but like it or not all roads led back to Roupell Park.

Mum was standing in the front room waiting for us. On the glass table was a bumper pack of Squares, and steaming plates of chicken, rice and plantain. I could see she'd spent the day cleaning. The whole house was shining.

"My babies!" She put an arm round each of us and pulled us close. "De doctors say I'm better. Gonna take my medication and mi ago do much better this time."

She hugged us tight, and pressed her face into our hair.

"What you smelling us for?"

"I missed your smell."

It wasn't long after we returned from the care home that Mum made her big announcement.

We were going to move. Our eyes lit up.

"For real?"

"For real."

Sour

We spent the whole day packing up our stuff, asking questions about our new home.

"You'll see," said Mum, with a smile on her lips.

"How are we going to take the car bed? We can't go without the car bed," said Yusuf, sensibly.

"Don't worry about dem things. Removal men will pick 'em up later."

We took our bags outside.

"Please, please," we begged. "Tell us where we're going."

"OK. You ready?"

She pointed across the Pen.

"Tird floor. Block D."

Our hearts sank. So much for the Big Move. We weren't even making it out of the estate. We carried our stuff in boxes 100 metres across the grass of the courtyard, to the opposite block on the other side of the estate. We were moving from the ground floor of Elmstead House to the third floor of Deepdene House. We were moving up in the world, if only literally.

No removal van ever did pick up the car bed.

Gangland

You see, gangland is a small, claustrophobic place. It exists in small, sealed bubbles, squatting in boarded-up worlds no bigger than a postcode. It doesn't like big, wide battlefields. It's the smallness it likes, lurking in the dead ends and shadows of shortened ambitions, conducting its business underneath stunted horizons.

No shit. They don't call them "the endz" for nothing.

For me, gangland began in that third floor flat, flanked by the concrete blocks of Roupell Park estate.

Later, my mental map would expand along the south London bus routes to include the lawless walkways and basement garages of the Angell Town estate, and the bored evenings making trouble around Myatt's Fields and Brockwell Park. Feuds would stretch to Peckham and Stockwell, New Cross and Brixton.

But as a young teenager, the meaning of those postcodes beyond Roupell Park simply didn't exist. I had not yet learned that language. They were not yet "territories". They were still simply postcodes.

I liked Roupell Park. It didn't feel like complete poverty, not like some of the slums in Peckham and Stockwell, the ones with the dark, dismal feeling that you're too scared to walk through.

Sour

In Roupell Park, there was still a mixture of cultures, black and white. Some people still took pride in their window boxes, spiking them with those windmill sticks and dangling chimes from their doors. A caretaker kept the Pen tidy, and the Quaker meeting house round the corner gave us a spiritual veneer.

Less than two miles away was the house where David Bowie was born. Half a mile further, Vincent Van Gogh (both ears still intact) fell in love with a South London girl, while living briefly in a house in SW9.

Even closer was Electric Avenue, the first market street to have the luxury of lighting. "Now in the street, there is violence." That's how the song starts. Sounds so upbeat, but listen to it properly next time. It's about poverty and anger and taking to the street. People forget that. They think it's about bloody lampposts.

I remember a poster campaign during the General Election, just as I was beginning life on the road. It must have been 1992. The posters showed a smiling John Major.

"What does the Conservative Party offer a working-class kid from Brixton?" they asked.

"They made him Prime Minister."

Good for him, innit. But I couldn't see anyone boasting about what they were offering a cute black girl, like me.

My parents had divorced in 1981, the same year Brixton went up in flames. A decade later, a new generation had grown up to hate the boydem.

Brixton had already been bombed and blasted and cleared of slums. By the time I was growing up, it was all about failed social housing and plain-clothes policemen and their hated campaign of stop and search.

Of course, I didn't care about any of that. I had my mum to worry about.

I would learn three important lessons living on Roupell Park. First, Fireworks Night is always the best time to buss a ting in the air. Second, getting caught ain't cool. And third, one day your luck is going to run out.

Everyone knew us as the madwoman's kids.

There was the white kids, who lived in a smelly flat on the fifth floor. We felt sorry for them coz their place stank, man, but they was nice kids. Then there was lovely Peggy next door, always willing to lend a bag of sugar, and Shelley and Andrew, the mixed-race kids on the fifth floor. They were popular. Everyone liked Shelley and Axe, as he'd later be known. People knew each other and helped each other when they could.

There was one newsagent who served the estate. We'd go there for ice poles in the summer. We never stole from Jay. No need. He was a good guy. If you went in there and said you were a little bit short, he would say bring it in next time. There was no point defrauding him.

He got robbed once or twice. Soon after he got a big Alsatian. No one bothered Jay after that.

At night, we'd watch the flashing lights from our window. There was always running kids and commotion. It was usually Tiefing Timmy, an Irish boy with lips like a duck, who'd speed his stolen cars around the courtyard.

Datsuns, Nissans, motorbikes. There was nothing that guy couldn't lift. When it was dark, that's when Tiefing Timmy and his boys would come out to play. We'd watch the nightly blue light show as the boydem chased Tiefing Timmy round the Pen. We'd laugh when he got away, and we'd throw coins at the Feds when they hauled him out and handcuffed him over the battered front of whatever car he'd stolen this time.

Obviously, some of the neighbours didn't like us. Mum took pride in her music system. The Abyssinians, Frankie

Sour

Paul, Dennis Brown, Marcia Griffiths. Old skool Jamaican reggae. She played it loud and she played it proud.

It wasn't all bad. There were the prison visits to look forward to. They were our holiday. As soon as a letter came through the post with HMPS on the envelope we got excited: it meant there was going to be a bus journey or coach trip and a fun day out to the Isle of Wight or Dartmoor or wherever Dad had been moved to this time. We'd always get a tray of cakes. Oh yeah, it was delightful.

Depending on how recently Mum had folded up the car, sometimes we would drive.

They lay waited him in the Upper Cuts barber shop in West Norwood. Yeah, people was real upset when Axe died.

They said it was a drugs connection but Axe wasn't one of the naughty ones. Rafik Alleyne was the guy who did it. He was 21. Axe was 25. They knew each other. People saw them knocking knuckles outside before Andrew went into Upper Cuts on Norwood High Street to get his hair cut.

Guy pulled a gun from a takeaway box and shot him in the back of the head as he sat in the barber's chair. He went running to a minicab office in a panic looking for a getaway car, begging a driver to take him to Stockwell. He got 22 years.

His mum wrote a really sad poem for the funeral. They said she stood up, wearing big dark sunglasses, to recite it.

Who is the one that took my son,
do you really know what you have done?
This is a wake-up call to all of you,
who wants to belong to the devil's crew.

21

The devil's crew indeed. I wished I had listened to her. It would be a long time before I truly understood what she meant.

One afternoon, I had been sitting by the Pen, probably not far from Shelley's and Andrew's flat. I'd bunked off school as usual, and had grown bored of hopscotch and the games we drew in chalk on the crumbling surface of the court. The goal nets and basketball rings were long gone – that is, if they'd ever been there in the first place – so we used to entertain ourselves inside the cage.

The only other kid kicking around that day was Jerome. He was just one of the kids around the way. I didn't much like him, but beggars, choosers and all that.

Was it the first time I'd ever been stabbed? I honestly can't remember. Getting stabbed is not like getting married or buying a new car, darling. It's just not something that sticks in your mind. Shit happens.

What I do remember is that Jerome taught me an important lesson that day.

"Hey Sour!" he'd shouted over, spying me at a loose end. "Wanna play a game?"

I shrugged.

"It's called Flick."

He cast a quick look around and huddled me into a corner where he felt sure no one was watching. Now he had got my attention.

Then he pulled out two flick knives.

"Here, take it."

I took it.

The handle fitted neatly into my palm. The chrome felt smooth and polished. It was still warm from his pocket.

"Look, do what I'm doing. Flick in, flick out."

I smiled. The mechanism was quick and light.

"Let's ramp," he said. Let's muck about.

We started making phantom jabs for each other's fists.

Imagine fencing with flick knives and you're getting close. Some kids play it with tennis racquets. Some kinds pretend they're on Star Wars. And some kids in Tulse Hill fence with knives.

He was quicker than me to start, but I soon caught up, matching every flick of the wrist and jolt of the fist.

I wasn't afraid.

"See? Good, isn't it?"

I took my eye off his blade. He jabbed towards me. As he did, I went to block.

"What the fuck are you doing, you idiot?"

He had caught my hand, piercing the fleshy pad beneath my thumb.

"You folly?" he said. "S'just a flesh wound."

"That's how you lose."

You're not playing, are you, I thought. We carried on. I was angrier this time and he knew it.

It was just me and him. I started jabbing harder, more forcefully, but he was too practised, too quick.

My pride had been hurt. I needed to make a wound for a wound. The game had now extended beyond striking the other fist. Now, the whole body was in play. We pranced back and forth, dodging contact with ragged swipes of chrome.

A warm trickle of blood was streaming down my wrist. It wasn't gushing. It was just a gash, but enough to catch Jerome's eye.

I got him. In the hand. While he was flinching I got him again, by the knee.

"Ah, you fucking bitch! You stabbed me."

"That's the point, innit? You a batty boy?"

It was just a graze.

"It's not even deep."

This was getting boring. I put down the knife, stepped back and examined my wound. It was deeper that I thought. The rest of my hand felt tender to touch.

Jerome seemed agitated, but tried not to show it. He wiped both knives on the grass and put them back into his pocket.

"Call it quits, yeah?"

"Whatever. Next time, bring a better knife."

I went home and told Mum some cock and bull story about cutting myself on the fence. I ended up having to get stitches.

I decided there and then I wouldn't be play fighting again – it was annoying and inconvenient. We had only been mucking about, but if that had been a serious situation I'd have been in trouble.

But I was grateful to Jerome for teaching an important lesson. Next time, I learned, I'd better bring a bigger knife.

Islam

Islam and I didn't get on. We were very young when Mum converted. By the time I got to primary school, Mum was no longer Eleanor Raynor. She was now Ruqqayah Anwar, Muslim convert. My brother Jermaine became Yusuf. My name became Salwa. Try saying that in a south London accent. That's how Sour was born.

It was annoying at the time, but I hadn't quite clocked, aged five, how useful two names can be when you get arrested. Later days, I'd thank my mum for it. Probably most useful thing she ever did. Get arrested, use one name; get arrested again, use the other. Keep getting arrested, just make 'em up. Boydem work it out eventually, but it buys you time.

Mum had been in one of her rare calm moods when she met the man on the bench.

She said she liked his aura. "Di man looked pious."

He was slim and well-kempt. He said he'd show her a different way of life. So she thought she would give him a try.

Do you know how easy it is to convert to Islam? All you need is a front room, two witnesses, an imam and a few sentences and that's it, you're a Muslim. Eleanor Raynor was no more.

Now she was Ruqquyah, the pious. She hadn't been the best Christian, granted. But God's loss, Allah's gain.

My brother and I watched from the hallway. He was giggling. I'd soon find out he had plenty to laugh about as a boy. I would be the one who suddenly had all the restrictions. No, as I say, me and Islam were not going to be friends.

Mum didn't like covering her hair at first either. A wash before prayer, the rules about meat, all those things threw her off at first but she got used to it. She still allowed us to be kids and watch TV and listen to music.

I liked her in her white jilbab though. Better than some of the other outfits she used to wear. I thought she looked beautiful.

I didn't even mind the mosque, at first. We went to Brixton Mosque. It was one of the oldest in South London. Got a bit of attention later days, when it was reported that that beardy lunatic, Richard Reid – remember him? The Shoe-Bomber? – had attended, but I liked it.

It had a quiet, happy vibe. It was somewhere to breathe beyond Roupell Park. Instead of being indoors, sitting all alone, Mum met all these new Muslim characters. They looked peaceful.

They would cook a lot together. I must say Mum looked at her happiest in the early days of Islam.

When they came round to the house, it had to be segregated. Men downstairs, women upstairs, no cross mixing. Even dinner would be brought separately.

That was the bit I hated the most. I didn't like being apart from Yusuf. It wasn't as much fun.

Thankfully, the Saturday madrasa was still communal.

We had to learn the Qur'an. It was lots of recitation, mainly. It sounded like a song. And so much memorising! We'd memorise whole chunks, reciting them over and over again without understanding what we were saying.

Sour

We learned the Arabic alphabet. We chanted the days of the week. Once you've got the alphabet, you see, what changes the sounds and meaning are the apostrophe and symbols.

I learned Arabic words for things like table, chair, but did I understand the meaty bits? No way.

Still, I picked it up quicker than Yusuf.

"We speak English, innit? What we having to learn this for?"

"C'mon, we've got to do what Mum said. It ain't that bad."

"But it's just squiggles and dots."

"What you complaining for? You don't have to dress like some ninja. I'm the one who's got to wear this."

He looked at the headscarf framing my miserable face.

"You look bare nice," he said, and burst out laughing.

Whatever Mum put on my bloody head for the mosque, it was horrible. I felt like a misfit on the bus. I wanted the ground to swallow me up. My friends used to tease me.

"What you got tucked under there, Sour? Is you a Rasta without the locks?"

Once I got to secondary school, Mum and I did a deal.

"Listen and listen to me good," I said. "I ain't wearing this headscarf shit no more."

She started to protest.

"I ain't playing, Mum."

If she shouted, I shouted louder.

Eventually, she agreed on a compromise.

She bought a hat. It was like something the fucking queen mum would wear. It was brown and rectangular – with a brooch. I looked like a bat-shit crazy old Jamaican lady! Those early bus journeys did little for my brand-name, tell you that much. I was so upset.

Still, somehow I felt less guilty taking off the hat and leaving in the locker, than I did with the headscarf.

But there was no escaping the rest of my new "Islam-friendly" school uniform: MC Hammer trousers, brown sandals and an atrocious top. Lord have mercy, these clothes were taking the piss.

Although I was glad to see my mum happy, something didn't sit well with me and her new obsession. There were other Jamaican families going to the mosque too. A surprising amount. But it felt oppressive. I was being forced to conform to a society that I didn't understand, being forced to memorise words whose meaning I didn't know. I hated the way Islam treated girls. I hated Mum for making me go, and eventually, for all its peaceful atmosphere, I began to hate that mosque. I knew as soon as I was old and strong enough, I would be outta there before you could say Insh'allah.

With Islam came stepdads. Yasim looked like frigging Moses, man. He walked with a big, old stick and smelled like a prophet. He was strong, strict and – like most people in our household – didn't last long.

He had a strong emaan and he was strong in his faith. He was a nice guy deep down. Had a bit of a lisp. He was ginger and freckled, but of Caribbean descent. He remains the only man I've ever known to wear leather socks.

He didn't work. Nowadays, you'd probably call him "a house husband". Or maybe just "chronically unemployed". But it was a home life, of sorts. It used to upset him that because of Mum's unstable behaviour she couldn't hold down a job. Never understood what his excuse was.

He tried to get me to go to school wearing a scarf again, but he realised pretty quick it was going to be a struggle making a family like ours stick to any rules, let alone his strict Islamic ones.

Sour

It wasn't that we set out, deliberately, to get rid of him ...
Not exactly.

He wound Mum up too. When they got in an argument, she would pick up a baseball bat or go rifling through the knife drawer, just like she did when she was in one of her manic states and she caught wind of the fact they were coming to take her away again.

During one of her psychotic episodes, that kitchen drawer was always the first thing she went for.

Oh yeah, Muslim or not, my mum was a violent cookie. All the crazy demonic behaviours, I learned from her. I learned from an early age how quickly people scatter when you're waving around a bread knife.

Poor Yasim was terrified. It must have been a relief to piss off to the mosque five times a day.

"We got to get rid of him, Sour," whinged Yusuf one day after madrasa. "He won't let me go to football no more."

I agreed.

When we got home, Yasim was at the end of his tether, shouting to be heard over Mum's music.

"Ruqqayah, these kids need discipline. They are a disgrace!"

"You're not our dad," we shouted after him. "Fuck off."

The next week my brother and I came home to find the front room empty. His shoes were gone from the hallway.

"Where is he?"

"He's been and gone," Mum replied. "Me couldn't take him nuh more. If rassclat make me choose between my pickney and him, di kids dem, dey haffi win every time."

I was proud of her that day. But she could never be alone for long.

* * *

The first time we saw Derek he was fixing one of the curtain poles in the front room. "Alright, kids?" he said, noting our bewildered expressions. "Said to your mum I'd keep an eye on the place." He seemed like a cool guy so we didn't mind him helping himself to drinks in the fridge.

I noticed the spare house keys in his hand. Mum had been in and out of hospital. She must have asked him to come and check on us.

I recognised him. He lived in the same block. I'd seen him chatting to Mum on the stairwell a few times.

When Mum left hospital, she seemed happy – better than she had been in a long time. Derek soon started coming round the house a lot. He wasn't strict like Yasim. He was like a breath of fresh air.

And yet, there was something about him I didn't like. No reason. He just felt too familiar, too tactile. I'd catch him fixating on himself in the mirror, rearranging what was left of his sandy blond hair to cover a receding hairline.

I started wondering what was wrong with his flat. I think he had kids, grown-up ones, but if he did he never mentioned them. Soon he became a regular feature on the sofa.

Said his TV was on the blink, so Mum let him use ours to watch his endless hours of Formula One. That man could watch cars race around a track for hours.

I started focusing on him a little more closely.

Mum thought he was a kindly neighbour. I thought different.

He started taking liberties.

He used to draw penis pictures on Mum's photographs. That's it, I thought. He's done it now. She's got to realise this man's an idiot soon. Instead, she walked in, saw the pictures and laughed. She found it comical.

Sour

Wasn't long before he started trying to brush my thigh as we watched telly on the sofa, and began flashing himself at me on the landing as he came out of the bathroom.

Pretended his white robe just accidently fell open, to reveal his erection. In which case, why did he stick out his tongue at me at the same time? I would act like I didn't see it and jump back to my bedroom, but my blood was boiling. How dare he come into my house and try to humiliate me!

He never physically touched me, not really, never anything more than a careful brush of the thigh, or pressing a little too close when we passed in the hallway. I didn't say a word.

Althea might have moved out, but she still visited from time to time.

One evening, I passed her old room. The door was open just wide enough to see her comforting someone I recognised. It was her best friend, Suzanne. Suzanne's cousin was the father to Althea's little girl. She was crying.

I hung behind the door, and strained to listen.

"You need to tell my mum," Althea was saying.

Suzanne was shaking her head, and wiped her nose with a tissue.

"No, I can't. What am I going to say?"

"Just tell her the truth."

She shook her head again.

"I knew I shouldn't have told you. It'll cause too many problems."

I listened closer. Suzanne had met Derek a few times. They had exchanged a few words when she came up with Althea, that sort of thing. Later, he'd seen her at the bus stop and stopped to talk. She's a chatty girl, Suzanne, thought nothing of it. It was only when he got on the bus too, she started feeling awkward. He hadn't looked like he was waiting for the bus.

There weren't many people sitting upstairs. Suzanne nodded a polite goodbye and went to sit at the back. He followed her. Sat down right beside her, even though the top deck was practically empty.

He started rubbing one hand up her leg as they approached the Elephant and Castle, feeling himself with the other.

"What you doing?"

"I see how you dress. I know what girls like you want."

"Get your hands off of me," she said, louder this time.

But he squeezed her leg tighter. Ragged fingernails laddered her tights. His other arm was hammering up and down like a piston. Hers was the next stop.

Suzanne missed her stop that night, and a few stops after that.

"I told him I'd tell your mum. He just called me a slag, and said she wouldn't believe me."

I went to my room that night, knowing I had to be prepared. I didn't want my mum to go to prison. If I told her what he had done, to me or to Suzanne, she might just kill him.

I'd seen her physically attack him once already. We'd cheered her on, as she tried to strangle him on the sofa. "Yeah Mum, kill that fucker!" before it occurred that she might just do that, and we'd end up living with some bat-shit crazy lady like Ivy again. It had been against every natural instinct to pull her off him.

But now, things were different. If he's that brazen, to do that to a family friend on the Number 133, what could he do to me? I sneaked down to the kitchen, slid open the drawer, and picked a knife. My hand hovered over the meat cleaver – nah, too big – then lingered by the bread knife. That'll do. I slipped it up my sleeve and crept back up to my room, making sure the door was locked.

Sour

Then I slipped the knife under my pillow. I needed to get mentally prepared. I needed to defend myself.

That's when I started sneaking the knives from the kitchen drawer. That's when I realised I needed protection. Forget your knife at your peril.

I'm Gonna Be a Name

I hadn't always loved Cheenie.

She was Althea's daughter. Real cute, with a button nose and curly hair, a beautiful little kid.

Real talk, I used to feel jealous when everyone was focused on this baby. There were times I used to imagine suffocating her in her cot, but I guess lots of people feel like that sometimes. Besides, I never followed up. That's the important thing, innit? It was short-lived, and after a few months of her being around, we were cool.

Yeah, I learned to love Cheenie like she was my own. I used to plead with my sister to let me take her out.

"I only want to take her to the Pen. It's only down there. Look, you can see us from the balcony."

Althea relented.

"OK."

I put her shoes on, pushed her arms through the sleeves of her jacket and took her down to the Pen.

Eventually, the council added two hoops to each end, but at that point it was just a rectangular patch of gravel. We always found things to do. Like playing imaginary hopscotch in between the cracks, where the weeds were growing through the court. Or counting the bars on the fence. The fence was hexagonal, so we used to run from one end to the other, counting the bars on all six sides as quickly as we could.

Sometimes, Mum used to make sandwiches and cut up oranges for us, so we could have a picnic. We liked that. Tennis balls or roller skates were the best things to break the boredom, but they could often end in fights. You just gotta improvise.

That day we had a good play, until my sister called us in on her way back from the shop. She'd got some ginger beer and ice poles. I didn't particularly want to go in. Neither did Cheenie.

"We have to go now," I told her, zipping up her jacket.

"No," she sulked.

"Come on, mummy's got some ice poles. Better be quick before Auntie Sour gets them first."

She took my hand and stomped reluctantly up the stairwell, tripping over her shoes as she gazed back at the Pen.

When we got up to the walkway, Althea was fumbling through the blue-and-white striped newsagent bag to find her keys.

"Hold this," she said, passing me the bag as she started searching her pockets.

I let go of my niece's hand and reached for the bag.

Cheenie made her break for freedom, and bolted back along the walkway. One of the concrete slabs had been removed, and replaced with some mesh. The council had taken it off during some work, and never got round to putting it back the way it was. I'd got used to the red plastic mesh flapping around the gap.

I chased after her, but seeing me following her just made Cheenie run quicker towards the mesh where she could see the green grass of the courtyard below.

It was a 25ft drop.

For a split second I considered jumping behind her, but realised it was too high. I would die, and probably squash her in the process.

Althea threw herself at the walkway, almost flinging herself over after her.

"Cheenie!"

I can't remember running down the staircase, but I guess I must have.

The neighbours below had seen something drop past the kitchen window but didn't think for a second it could have been a child. They rushed out of their house when they heard us screaming.

I don't know who called the ambulance.

They say you're not meant to move a casualty like that. The official advice is to put them in recovery position or some shit like that, innit? Fuck that.

I scooped Cheenie up into my arms.

Her eyes were bulging. Her whole head was swollen. She looked like a Martian.

Blood dripped from her nose.

I caused this. The words were running through my mind. I caused this. I caused this. I hated myself.

As we sat outside the double doors of the ward, waiting for news, Althea couldn't look at me. I tried to hug her, but she flinched. "Don't touch me," she spat.

Eventually, Mum stormed in, blabbering some Allah talk and giving us all her quotes from the Qur'an. She'd been praying at the mosque. I couldn't bear it. I paced up and down the wards, knowing it was all my fault.

She spent weeks in hospital, wired up to the machines and a drip. They told me when she woke up she tried to call my name.

Sour

In the end, the doctors said they were happy I'd picked her up. They said it let the blood drain, or some shit like that, so I got praised for that.

Her lightness had counted in her favour. An older, heavier person probably could never have survived the fall.

She had a broken wrist and a fractured skull. But that was it. She would survive.

But it was a dark time. For the first time, I knew what shame felt like. I knew an anger I'd never known before, an anger that made me want to go out and cause harm, against myself, against anyone. I came back from the hospital a different child. I could still see the resentment in Mum and Althea's eyes. I felt like Cheenie pulled me over the edge with her. Sometimes, I wish she had.

A week later, the music went on again. "Only love will solve your problems." Over and over again, all through the night.

Tyrone had been my friend from young. He'd moved to another estate down the way, but always came to visit and see his old friends at Roupell Park. His mum was poor, poorer than ours, and his brothers knew some serious characters, but Tyrone was a good kid. He never got into badness.

He was a light-skinned Jamaican boy – we called him red-skinned, which he didn't like – and he always dressed sharp. He didn't have lots of new stuff, but the stuff he had, he kept fresh.

His only downfall was that he loved to eat. He was the kind of kid who used to come to your house, go straight to the kitchen, look in your pots, and before you knew it your dinner's gone.

As usual, he brought his tennis ball, so we went to the Pen, but we soon got bored bouncing it off the wall.

"Alright, shitheads?"

It was Tiefing Timmy. He had two white girls with him. I vaguely recognised one of them.

"You the girl whose baby fell from the block?" she asked.

"Shut your mouf," said Tyrone. "Ain't none of your business, innit."

"Kid fell from there," she said to her friend behind a conspiratorial hand, pointing to our third floor flat.

"The social should be on to you," she said.

Was she trying to incite a fight?

"Say that again."

"C'mon, Sour," said Tyrone, hearing the alarm bells. He tugged at my sleeve. "Let's leave it. They ain't got a clue what they're talking about."

The girl with the piercing – a jewel on the left side of her cheek – stepped forward. She wanted a fight.

"I said, say that again."

She walked closer, and shouted out loud.

"I *said*, you and your family should have the social on to you."

She was a little taller than me, but skinnier. I reckoned I could have her.

I barged forward, tugging against Tyrone, who was now trying to hold me back. She laughed.

"Aw," she said, sarcastically. "Little Sour getting upset?"

She pushed me hard. I pushed her back.

"Whoohoo!" Tiefing Timmy squealed at the prospect of a bitch fight. "Go on yerself, gerls!"

I took a swing, but missed. She did the same and didn't. I lunged for her face, making a grab for her hair and jewellery. I wanted to rip that stupid piercing from her ignorant face.

But she was older, tougher. Unlike me, she had been in fights before.

Before I knew it, Tyrone and Tiefing Timmy were dragging her off of me. There was no doubt about it. She had won that fight. I wasn't angry. I was blind fury livid.

On the way home, Tyrone seemed disappointed. He was a cool kid, and clever. He never got into fights. He wanted to be an engineer. But he was no pussy. He knew how to handle himself. He knew I could have done better.

"How come you didn't have her? You can handle yourself."

He seemed genuinely puzzled. I felt I'd let him down.

"Dunno. She riled me, I guess."

"She ain't all that."

We took the long way home, through the underpass and by the Chinese takeaway. For most of it, we walked in silence.

"You know what, Tyrone?"

"What?"

"You're right. That shit ain't going to happen again. I'm going to be well known."

"Oh yeah?"

He laughed it off.

"For real. That doesn't happen when you're a name to be known."

I remembered something I'd seen on the lyrics of an album: reputation of power IS power.

"I'm going to be serious, Ty. Wait and you'll see."

Dick Shits

"Why did you go telling everyone my mum was crazy? I'm gonna fuck you up for what you done, girl!"

I didn't wait for an answer. I thought Natasha was my friend.

"You make me sick."

I barged forward and pinned her to her desk in the religious studies classroom, lifting the kitchen knife high in my hot, sweaty palm so everybody in St Martins could see it.

"Sour, stop!"

The others tugged at my uniform and begged me to stop, but I wasn't listening. What goes on at home was one thing. Broadcasting it here, around school, the only place I could escape, was another. I didn't care about the consequences or the rules no more. I was angry. And I wanted to hurt that bitch.

Fast forward half an hour and Mrs Edwards, the humourless headteacher with the Margaret Thatcher helmet hair, was telling me what was going to happen. What she was really doing, though she didn't know it then, was giving me the first big break of my criminal career.

"You are being expelled, Salwa. I'm referring you to Dick Shepherd's. From now on, you will be attending school there."

I was destined for Dick Shepherd's, the rejects' school all the rest of us knew as Dick Shits.

Sour

Phillip Lawrence had just left his post as headmaster of Dick Shits when I arrived. Three years later, he'd be dipped in the chest by some 15-year-old yout as he tried to break up a fight in another playground just eight miles away. Black boys killing their white teachers! That soon woke up the world.

But let me let you into a secret: lawlessness reigned supreme long before then. What happened to that man was a tragedy, no two ways about it. I'm only surprised it didn't happen sooner.

First off, if I wanted to be respected at Dick Shits I knew I was going to have to step up a gear to thrive and survive. St Martin's was junior league. This was the Premiership.

My uniform was angelic, my pleats were proper fresh, but I was determined to be demonic.

I wore my new knife in a belt under my blazer. It was made of rabbit skin and had a rabbit's foot dangling from the belt. I'd bought it from a gypsy boy, and wore it with the kind of pride the other girls wore their Claire's Accessories.

I wasn't at Dick Shits to learn. I was there to make money. It was time to become top dog.

I soon found that if you're loud enough and strong enough, there's always someone quieter and weaker who wants to follow you. Over time, I recruited several associates willing to take my lead. They were the Two-Tails to my Sonic. Some of them, as a joke, even started calling me "Mum".

"Y'alright, Mum?" they'd shout at me in the corridor.

"Yes datter, yes son," I'd reply, with a grin. "How are you?"

"Me alright still, y'naw?"

If any of my sons or daughters got into a little scuffle, I'd know about it.

41

It helped that a lot of the Somalian kids were tiny. Three foot nothing, some of them. It was easy to pick them up by their ankles and shake them.

Sometimes, a brave friend would try to step in.

"Put him down, what's wrong wit you? He said he ain't got no money."

Lo and behold, the coins would fall from upside-down pockets. I'd leave the two-tails to pick up the change.

The kids soon learned at lunchtime to step aside and let me through. There were plenty boys doing the same. But a girl? That caught their attention.

If a girl got a bit rude to a blood, someone I considered an ally, she'd get slapped about. Spin and turn and kick. Just like the video games. I had no interest in female friends. I liked being one of the boys.

Now, you might think a place like Dick Shits would have a problem with truancy. Perhaps. But the really bad kids, the ones who caught my attention, were the ones who weren't even meant to be there at all. Dick Shits wasn't somewhere to learn, it was somewhere to meet, somewhere to talk business.

Doing the register was hilarious, man. You could have a room full of children with only 15 of their names on the list. A teacher could walk into a classroom dotted with grinning, unfamiliar faces.

What were they going to do? Tell them to go home?

Those who did try to eject them soon learned life was easier just letting them stay where they were.

Some had been expelled elsewhere, and didn't have much else to do. Others just didn't want to attend their own schools. Ours was like a youth club. A youth club where we were in control.

Yeah, Man Dem came to Dick Shits because it was loose and relaxed.

Better to be here with the rest of your bloods in a lesson, rather than out in the street alone.

Killer P – he used to crack me up, man. Don't know which school he had ever belonged to. He was an MC. A real talent. He didn't shank no one or nuttin like that. They called him Killer because of his killer lyrics. He had that Shaggy, Sean Paul ragamuffin style going on.

He liked the class of this poor little Asian lady the best. She taught Social Science. Used to put on documentaries and films and shit, so it was her own fault really. Victim of her own success, innit. Her class was meant to have been around 30. Instead, 40 would turn up. She was slim and frail and her voice barely carried beyond the first cramped row of tables.

Just as she's got the class under control, having settled in the nerds trying to learn, and soothed the disruptive ones who couldn't care less, this black boy bursts through the door, singing a cappella.

Gyal dem ah wine anna move mek di man dem take
     notice,
Gyal look so hot, when she move but she already know
     diss.

They were his own lyrics. That boy had talent. We jumped up and cheered Killer P as he started MC-ing from the front of the classroom.

"Alright!"

Bloods who knew the lyrics started singing with him, drowning out Miss Deng who looked like she was about to cry. Classmates started to whine on the tables, like they were dutty dancehall girls. I sat back in my seat, enjoying the spectacle.

> Gyal shake up your batty let mi see, gyal come over an
>   whine pun mi,
> Gyal dem ah call me Killer wid da P, mi just waant
>   pure love and harmony …

The door slammed shut. Miss Deng had gone.

"Miss, come back!" shouted Killer P. "I just spitting out a ragga song."

For some of the teachers, that woulda been a good day.

There was a maths teacher with dreadlocks. Probably fancied himself as a bit of a Rasta, knew his music, the kind of guy who tolerated no shit, one of the few who tried to keep things in order. We liked him. Poor man. He'd tire himself out chasing bloods down whole corridors. Even he gave up eventually.

As for the unpopular teachers, well, they used to get slapped down. Simple as.

Come November, there would always be fireworks getting let off in the classrooms. When it was snowing, dirty snowballs went off everywhere.

We had a sports field. It needed a sit-down lawnmower, and that lawnmower needed petrol. More than once, I looked out the window and saw youts who'd raided the gardener's shed, pouring tins of fuel from the top of the hill towards the class-rooms, and setting the rivers alight, until the grass was streaked with lines of fire.

Oh my days, that would lead to proper chaos. We were always pleased to see the fire crews appear because it meant we could hit the road.

One time I even saw a moped ridden through the corridors. Yeah, it all used to happen. Every class at Dick Shits was like a scene from Gremlins.

Kept things colourful, that's for sure. No two days were the same. Assemblies on Friday were always a highlight. One minute you're sitting there thinking everything's cool; the next some idiot has gassed both entrances and the emergency exit, and suddenly everyone is stumbling around, choking, with their eyes streaming.

You might ask how they could they get away with it. But you're not understanding. We had control of the school. Why do you think it's knocked down now?

Police officers floated through the corridors. Their presence made little difference to me. I knew there was nothing to fear from them. I'd learned that early, from a shoplifting spree with Yusuf.

We went out licking stuff from Alders, the department store in Croydon, tiefing garmz and slipping chops – necklaces, bracelets, that kind of shit – down our sleeves.

Yusuf got us caught. The police station had beige walls and lino flooring the colour of cream soda. We didn't feel intimidated or scared. We hung around, got a nice cup of tea, grabbed a sandwich – which was more than was waiting for us at home. The officers were really nice. They showed us the custody suite. It was like another fun day out at *The Bill*.

They gave us a caution that day. I still remember the nice, white police officer who said he hoped it would be the last time he saw us. "Good luck with your life," he said, as he showed us out.

And that was it. As we left, I remember smiling. If that's all the police do to you, I thought, I'll stop worrying.

Stop and search was a problem for plenty, but not for me. There were always bare complaints from the boys. But girls? Who'd stop and search a girl? More fool the Feds.

"Have you got it today?" they'd ask. Sometimes, I'd answer them, sometimes not. They never asked to see it. The secret was to let them imagine – they'd always imagine the worst.

When you know you're carrying the power to take someone's life you don't need to exert yourself.

I never flashed it. Didn't need to. I wasn't crazy in the head, y'know. Let everyone else assume, that was my motto. Only the fools will try to test you.

I knew well the effect of a flash of chrome. When my mum picked one up, I'd seen the way people would run. You got a whole sense of respect carrying a weapon, and I liked it.

Carrying a blade was like having an "access all areas" pass for the V Festival. I jumped the queues, and got the best seats in assembly. All the backstage benefits came flooding in. The two-tails stole to impress me. Others wanted to have me on their side. Resting by my hip underneath my grey school jumper was the knife, and when the situation presented itself I had every intention of using it. Otherwise, what would be the point?

I soon got fast-tracked to top dog status without even trying.

Sometimes an angry parent would give you grief, but I had no fear of adults. I had no fear of anything.

"Just do it," I thought, watching the latest hard-faced mother stride across the playground, frothing at the mouth over her bullied child, demanding to know "where is the little bitch?"

I'd watch them, stroking the rabbit skin under my blazer.

Sour

"Go on," I would dare them, in my head. "Strike me. Slap me. Do something to make me use this."

I was eager to test it out. Was it sharp enough? Would my reflexes be quick enough? I was always disappointed when they backed down. But I knew I'd have another chance soon.

I was walking home in a boisterous mood one afternoon. I had cash in my pocket, which some of the two-tails had likked from Brixton Market over the weekend.

It took only 10 minutes to walk home, but I jumped on the bus to be with the crowd. That was always good value. Sure enough, we stormed on, out of sight of the driver, pushing past the people trying to get off, and ejected some of the smaller kids from our preferred seats at the back.

The rugrats shared my boisterous mood. In those days, buses had light bulbs you could unscrew. And no CCTV. One of the crew scampered over the seats, untwisting the bulbs, and pelting them at cars from the window.

Cars started tooting. The bus pulled over at the next stop. "Exit!"

We muscled past the big Nigerian women, carrying shopping, and the pony-tailed pramfaces clogging the way with buggies off of the bus, and bolted off in different directions.

I was still laughing to myself when I reached the estate to find someone standing outside my mum's door. It was a young black guy I didn't recognise, about my age. I stopped.

"Who you waiting for?"

He spun round. He seemed agitated.

"I want my money, innit."

"What money?"

"The money owed to me by that little shit."

He gestured inside. He must be talking about Yusuf.

"Are you crazy in your head? What are you talking about?"

"I want paying."

"Seems you lost your mind. What's going on in your head? Now get off my mum's doorstep."

"I told you have some respect, innit. I gave him an eighth. Said he'd pay up."

"Step aside. I'm sorting this out."

I left him outside, ranting and raving about his resin.

Yusuf was playing his Nintendo.

I went straight past him, into the kitchen, and picked up a very large piece of knifery.

Who the hell was this character, trying to take me for some little pussy?

"Get the fuck off this estate, right now. And take your shit-ass tush weed with you."

I chucked the bag at him, which I'd picked up from the front room table, and threw at him a sorry-looking cube of resin. It was as shrivelled as this boy's bravado.

"Mad bitch," he muttered.

"I'm sorry? Say that one more time? You dickhead!"

He bolted down the stairwell, darting right around the building towards the Pen.

I pretended to make chase down a couple of flights, but to be honest I ain't never been an athlete.

Besides, he was the fearful one, so he had an unfair advantage, innit.

"Don't ever make me catch you," I shouted after him, watching him dash across the courtyard.

Wow, I gotta get fit, I thought to myself, as I caught my breath by the bins.

When I went back up the stairs, Peggy had come out to see what the commotion was.

"Nuttin, Peggy," I told her, holding the bread knife tight by my arm. "Some kids just ain't got no manners."

She smiled, unconvincingly, and stepped back inside. I heard the chain slide against the lock.

When I went back, I took the second control, put Street Fighter on pause and shouted at Yusuf what the hell he was doing.

"You don't even bun green."

He shrugged. "Was gonna try to sell it."

Then I spotted the other bags, lined up along the coffee table, alongside an empty jar.

"Yusuf, what the hell is that?"

He brightened up, eyes twinkling.

"You think I could sell it? I worked it out. You can get at least 20 wraps out of a single jar."

The wraps looked like heroin. The powder was dark beige, the colour of sand, wrapped in scraps of cling film, which had been twisted and sealed, by burning the top off.

"Number one – what you talking about? And number two – what is in those bags?"

He smiled, looking pleased with himself. Yusuf could be a charmer when he wanted.

"It's Horlicks, innit?"

I took a deep breath. He was 12. Horlicks was an old man's drink. More importantly, how did he even know that's how they wrapped heroin?

"Yusuf, last time I looked, Roupell Park didn't have a big problem with addiction to nutritional malted milk drinks."

Lord have mercy.

He nodded.

"Exactly. Costs £2.49 for one of the big jars. Sell 20 wraps for around £20 a pop, and you're in the money. Good business, innit."

"And who the fuck is going to buy it?"

"Cats are desperate, ain't they? It's just a one-off."

"Well, it'll have to be, innit, unless they're just wanting a good night's sleep. Because ain't no one going to ask again."

I felt a stab of affection for my little brother at that moment. He wanted to become a mechanic. Just as well, 'cause I knew right there and then that he wouldn't be making it as Tony Montana.

Selling fucking Horlicks.

I went to my room and put my music up loud. That night I fell asleep wondering if maybe, just maybe, it might just work.

Steaming

I had my associates at school. But back home, at Roupell Park, my crew was made up of whoever was around. Who's coming today? Who's up for it?

There was no recruitment, no initiation. It ain't no rotary club.

The ones from good homes kept riding with you till their mums or dads shut them down. The rest of us were just along for the ride.

Most days, we were just a loose collective of bored kids from the estate. Jamal, a big-built Ethiopian guy who was only our age, but looked bloody 18; Eddie, another black boy in the same block; and Sizz, the cousin of a friend. Other two-tails would come and go, but these were the main bloods.

They were up for anything. I was the only girl, and as such I occupied a role all to myself.

The trouble with being a brand-name, as I soon learned, was that once you start you can't back down. It's like grasping for the rope of a runaway balloon, innit. Your feet leave the ground, and suddenly you're stoked by the thrill of soaring high above the rest.

By the time you look down, it's too late to let go. Part-time wasn't an option.

No, if I was going to be Sour, sour I had to stay.

I wanted to see who could prove themselves. If I was going to have their back, I needed to know who was just talking the talk and who would take a risk. I told them what they could achieve, and I wanted to see who could achieve it.

I was a very callous young woman. Really, it was just that simple.

Besides, shoplifting was getting boring. That was for rugrats. I was 15. I needed to step up. Tiefing threads and popping tags just weren't my ting. Too quiet, too sneaky. That was low-level stealing. Kids' stuff. Robbing, though – robbing was different.

I had some rules. Likking a tek, y'know a punter, on the street, or drumming the yard of private houses was not on. My focus was businesses. They had insurance. That was victimless crime, innit.

We called it steaming – rushing a shop en masse, storming the aisles and clearing out the till, likking the shelves for anything we could get our hands on. The key to success was strength in numbers. One form makes many.

My crew knew I would have their back.

Targets were never mapped out. It wasn't planned like that. Steaming is about being a chancer: you're either going to get away with it or you're not. On some level, yeah, I knew that prison could beckon, but how could I be fearful of that? I hadn't been there yet.

You do the crime, you do the time. The secret was not getting caught. That was what was at stake.

We jumped off the bus a few stops early. Me, Jamal, Eddie and Sizz. Sizz had brought a friend, a short, stocky guy with a shaved eyebrow. When he pushed back his hoodie, I could see a scar running down his temple. He knocked knuckles with the boys. When it came to me, he looked me up and down and grunted hello.

Maybe not a charmer, but I was glad Sizz had brought him along. He looked broader and stronger than the rest. We needed him.

We sauntered along the pavement, not saying much. Sizz and Eddie kicked a chicken bone between them, dribbling it along the pavement, before shooting it across the road, narrowly avoiding a granny on her shopping scooter. The front wheel underneath the basket crunched over the bone as she trundled on, oblivious.

We loitered for a moment by the sandwich board outside, advertising low-cost money transfers to Nigeria. It squeaked with rust.

The automatic doors opened and a tired-looking mum dragged a moaning child behind her.

"You're getting no more till we get home," she barked at the little girl, who eventually admitted defeat and sulked along behind her.

I felt my stomach tighten with nerves.

I reminded the boys of the task at hand.

"The focus is to get the money out of the till." They nodded. "That's the job, get it done."

My right arm hung straight and heavy by my side. I liked that feeling. It gave me confidence.

Holding the collar between my teeth, I managed to zip my hoodie up to my neck, one-handed.

I took a deep breath and walked in first, face-straight.

There were no customers. I glanced up, looking for the CCTV cameras, but could see none. It was clean.

I turned to the door, and gave them the sign. We were on. The boys steamed in behind me.

"Get down!"

Jamal was shouting at the shopkeeper. He was big, much bigger than Jamal.

The barrel-chested man behind the counter didn't look scared. He looked angry. Eddie and the stocky friend jumped over the counter, toppling over the plastic lollipop stand and the lottery ticket board. Nimble hands and trainers vaulted over the confectionary shelves, kicking Tic Tacs and Twixes all over the floor.

They were going for the till.

The shopkeeper ducked down, yelling to a young boy, a son, perhaps, who emerged from the back room.

"Call the police!" he yelped.

The gangly lad stood open-mouthed for a moment before disappearing and locking the door.

Glancing over my shoulder, I did what I was meant to do, and maintained a look-out. No one was coming in. That was good.

Eddie and the cousin had turned their backs on the cowering shopkeeper and opened the till, stuffing their pockets with notes. We would be out of here in a second. The excitement pulsed through every vein in my body.

Jamal and Sizz ransacked the rest of the shop, clearing DVDs from the shelves.

What none of us had anticipated was that, of all the shops we could have picked, we had to pick the one run by a have-a-go hero. Most of the shop-owner Asian guys did the smart thing when they saw youngsters steaming their shops. Most times they let them have the run of it. But this guy, this guy was different.

The till was empty.

"Come on, let's go."

Sour

Jamal and Sizz were still steaming the back of the shop.

With their pockets full, and hot breath searing their faces beneath their scarves, Eddie and the cousin spun round, ready to make a run for it.

I felt the cold sweat of distant sirens. Were they coming? Was I imagining it? My legs were shaking. "Come on," I muttered, willing them to leap over the counter as nimbly as they entered. "Come on …"

But the shopkeeper has risen up, shouting something in a language I didn't understand.

He was brandishing a stepladder he'd been using to stock up. Eddie and his cousin tried to jump back over the counter, but it was much deeper on the other side, with much less room. The shopkeeper had blocked them in. My crew were in trouble.

I knew I needed to do something. He was attacking them. "Shut your mouf, old man!"

I was the only one left. I had to protect them.

No one had ever tried to fight back before. I felt disrespected. He had disrespected all of us. But more than that, I felt responsible. I had these guys here to do something, and because of this have-a-go hero it's all gone crazy.

I kept on shouting, until Jamal and Sizz had legged it out the double doors, and Eddie and the cousin had clambered back over the disarray of Snickers and cigarettes and out of the shop.

I kept on throwing cans till all the rest were sprinting down the road, and the street fizzed blue and red with sirens. A bitter, metallic taste flooded my mouth. My lip had been burst in the fight-back. I tripped and fell on to the crumpled man, who was groaning as he pushed himself up off the floor.

The shop fell silent, save for the heaving man on his hands and knees. I dropped the last can and fled.

The boys had bolted. I wanted so desperately to do the same but remembered: I had one advantage they didn't. Crouching behind some bins, I discarded the baseball cap that had concealed my braids, and rearranged the scarf obscuring my face into a fashionable knot at my neck.

I freed my hands from my gloves, and the bracelets from my sleeves, before unzipping my hoodie and pushing up my bra beneath my vest top.

Then, ignoring every instinct telling me to follow the rest of the crew, I took one step after another and forced myself to walk calmly round the corner and slowly, brazenly down the street.

When the boydem arrived moments later, all they saw was a cute black girl, like any other. Checking my make-up in a hand-mirror, I caught the reflection of the angry shopkeeper waving his hands around for the benefit of two police officers, who nodded into their notepads. Nobody seemed to notice me.

Yeah, in those days I worried my own self. I thought I was invincible. Sometimes, I worried I was actually possessed by the devil.

The boydem caught up with most of the crew eventually. Only Eddie made it back to Dick Shits to tell everyone what happened.

After the glory of that afternoon, my brand-name was bigger than ever. I didn't have to go recruiting no more. Man Dem came to me. Who was I to argue with that?

Real Gangs

Now you might consider all this to be the behaviour of a gang. Truth was, I hadn't even begun gang life. That was small fry. The real gangs of south London still hovered around the shadows. As for the Man Dem who rolled inside them, I had yet to make their acquaintance.

I had heard of them, of course. Tall tales and whispers loitered round the estates. Many of the darkest rumours led back to the worst estate of them all: Angell Town, less than two miles away.

That's where Keziah and Stacey lived, and visits to the house enthralled me. They were nice girls, brought up by a single mum, who worked long shifts as a caterer. She wasn't one of those layabout mums, but she was surrounded by plenty who were.

They lived in a dark labyrinth of walkways and derelict basement garages. The architect's grand intention behind this concrete maze of high-density council blocks was to create "a community spirit".

Oh yeah? Wonder where that architect is now? Enjoying community spirit somewhere else, that's for sure. By the time I learned my way around that labyrinth, the papers were calling it Hell's Gate. The garages designed for all those aspirational families proved to be nothing more than dark, dingy backdrops for drug deals and worse. The walkways were badly lit and the police presence was heavy and unnerving. Pass by during the day, you'd think the only people living there were thugs and dogs. After dark, it became a riot of sirens and stand-offs. Trust me, there was nothing angelic about this part of town.

Yeah, Angell Town was proper scary. Yet, for all the reputation it had, and the hype it attracted, I remember being disappointed first time I went. After all, I was an aspiring community leader myself.

The Man Dem of Angell Town were untouchable. Everyone knew that. They had fast cars, drug rackets and guns. They answered to no one.

They were the big league, so I'd been expecting something bigger, better, *flasher* than tame old Roupell Park.

Anyone who was anyone wanted to hang out there. So why did it seem so … poor?

I had taken the 133 bus to Keziah and Stacey's after school to find a huge commotion raging around their house.

"Over there, innit," Kez shrugged. Someone was getting chased. She didn't show much interest.

I opened her bedroom window to get a better look.

I'd spent enough time watching Tiefing Timmy to know that a police chase was hardly rare in SW2.

No, what amazed me about this guy was that he was literally jumping from walkway to walkway.

This was better than watching EastEnders.

I followed the dark shadow race towards the stairwell. He was a black boy in dark clothing and so was difficult to see, despite the flashing lights. But there was no doubt about it. He was putting his life at risk. For a moment the lights lost him, but I could see him. He had ducked, and was now climbing on to the ledge of the stairwell, preparing to jump. I held my breath. There were three storeys between him and the concrete plane below. He swung his arms big and took off.

"Shut the window, Sour, it's freezing," complained Kez, who was sizing up her latest "purchases" in the bedroom mirror, to see which would fit, and which to sell.

"What's the problem? Just seeing wha gwarn …"

"Why you interested in dem man dere anyway?"

I wasn't listening to her. The boy had just jumped down to the stairwell below and was now hanging off a balcony. Respect.

I watched him, wide-eyed at his nerve, until eventually a pair of Alsatians brought him down at the end of his assault course, and the boydem bundled him away.

He was known. He was the first Older 28 I'd ever seen in action.

His name was Daggers, a fearless character, three or four years my senior, who wouldn't hesitate to harm police if his back was against the wall. Short and light-skinned, with a strong West Indian accent, he was also, as I'd find out later, the sort of guy who doesn't take no for an answer.

That wouldn't be the last I'd be seeing of Daggers. More's the pity.

"What?"

Kez was staring at me, waiting for an answer.

"You deaf, girl? I said, 'Which top looks best with this skirt?'"

She held the sequinned boob tube up against a tight skirt, emblazoned with fake designer logos, then, like a bullfighter taunting a bull with a flag, switched it for a coathanger featuring a transparent chiffon blouse.

59

"Don't like it either. Looks cheap, innit," said Stace.

"Wasn't asking you," snapped her sister.

"Sour?"

Keziah and Stace were happy-go-lucky girls, don't get me wrong. They liked likking stuff and wearing the best gear. And they had their fun. But, how can I put this? They delegated. They didn't do the dirty stuff. They sent the other girls out to the shops to tief all their tops and skirts and shoes for them, but, end of the day, it was still just petty theft.

"Boob tube," I muttered, unconvincingly.

I was still thinking about how that yout had managed to evade the boydem for as long as he did. Don't care what he done – what that kid achieved was almost heroic, man.

Keziah and Stace proudly laid out the rest of their gear across the bed. Kez plucked a bandanna from the pile and pulled on a silver-spangled crop top, exposing her tight, flat midriff. She pouted in the mirror, flicking back her hair to show her gold hoops.

"You look like Aaliyah, babes!"

"We're thinking of going to Bond Street tomorrow. You in?"

"Nah, stuff to do, innit," I shrugged.

I was bored of shoplifting. I knew I wanted more. It wasn't my style. I could easily go robbing the garage across the road, or into town, and come back to survey our goods with the rest of them, but it no longer held a thrill for me. If these girls wanted me to keep coming to their house, I wanted more. I needed entertainment.

I was soon to find it.

Meeting the Youngers

A new life was about to begin. The irony was that my association with the Younger 28s began nowhere near the ganglands of Angell Town or Brixton or Loughborough Junction, but the one place as close to an Eden of childhood innocence as a South London girl like me was ever going to get.

Ladies and gentlemen, I'm talking, of course, about Chessington World of Adventures.

Yeah, my first day rolling with the Man Dem was on a school trip to the distinctly non-gritty, suburban surroundings of a Surrey theme park.

Like I said, Dick Shits had many problems. One of them was its popularity with the bad boys. Despite what the papers say, despite all those *London Tonight* reporters in suits and ties, talking down the camera about feral kids beyond the reach of teachers, parents and police, the truth was that some of the city's most troublesome young gangsters liked the lawless vibe of my school so much, they muscled their way through the gates and gatecrashed the lessons.

That went for school trips too – especially school trips involving Tomb Blaster laser guns and a rollercoaster called Dragon Fury.

They met us at the tube station, pushing their way on to the carriage in the same way they filed into classes.

61

There were lots of different rugrats running around, but these youts were different.

They were all dressed decently. Their trainers were fresh, their haircuts were fresh. Hell, even the waistbands of their boxer shorts were fresh. They looked older, though they couldn't have been much older than us – they were just expelled a long time ago.

They weren't hard-out established characters. Not then. They were all still young, trying to find their way and make their mark, just like the rest of us. But back then, it felt like Vinnie Jones and all his mates had just stepped on to the tube.

The loudest ones commandeered the seats in front of us, placing shining white creps on the seats and commanding the attention of the carriage.

A boy with a broad grin came up to Tyrone and knocked knuckles before exchanging a few quiet words.

"You know him?" I whispered.

"Just one of the boys from the estate, innit. Told 'em we had a trip but didn't think they'd actually come."

I smiled.

"I like them. Think we're in for an interesting day."

The moment we stepped into the park, the two-tails scurried round.

I had my own plans. I had my own delegating to do. They were ready to steal anything they could lay their hands on. I gave them a target.

"Let's see if you're going to hit it." They nodded, solemnly.

"Meet me back here by the toilets at 3pm."

The tallest of the group caught my eye. Or rather I caught his. He walked over to me and Tyrone. While he was brash and loud, the friend by his side had a quieter confidence.

"Who's this girl telling everyone what to do?"

Tyrone answered for me.

"This's Sour, innit."

I glared at him. If he had taken a liking to me I wasn't interested.

"Check you out, gyal," he laughed.

I noticed he too had his own gang of rugrats to carry out orders. It was almost like he had a shopping list of his own. He wanted to compare.

"What you hitting today? How much you planning to make?"

"Why would I tell you that? Only just met you, man. Where do you think you're coming from?"

Tyrone laughed.

"Slow down, man," said his friend, flashing a beautiful smile. "Lady wants an introduction. Allow me," he said, stepping forward. "That's Badman. His manners ain't so good."

"Quit stepping on man's territory, Drex."

"Ain't you got business to do?" he laughed, joining the rest of the Man Dem as they jumped the queues, slipped past the ticket booths and created havoc.

"He don't like the rides," Drex explained.

"Why not?"

"Paranoid. Y'know the pictures they take when you're screaming and getting tipped over the edge? The ones they try to sell you after the ride?"

"Yeah, and?"

"Man don't trust 'em, innit. Thinks boydem will use them as evidence against him."

"Evidence of what? Looking shit scared?"

Drex laughed.

"Dunno. That's a guilty conscience for you."

"Come on," he said. "I'm feeling lucky. Let's go on the Mary Rose."

I was surprised how forward he was. He clearly wasn't used to girls hesitating.

"Just me and you?"

"Why not? Man Dem will find us later."

I looked at the swinging galleon ship. The two-tails weren't due back for ages. I had time.

"OK. So you're not scared about having your picture taken?"

"Maybe my conscience ain't so guilty."

"Alright, let's go," I said. "Just remember you don't have to scream or anything, but it may harm your defence if you don't scream something you'll later rely on in court."

He laughed. "How's a girl like you familiar with that?"

"Ain't telling you," I smiled. "Hurry up. I gotta be back here for 3pm."

When the ride was over, I was heading towards the exit, windswept and dizzy, when he grabbed my hand.

"Where you going? Ride's not finished."

And he led me round the metal platform and back to the front of the queue to do it all again.

After our fourth round, we staggered off the ship and on to dry land. Oh my days, I didn't know whether to laugh or be sick. We slumped down on a bench. I realised we must have been away for ages.

He disappeared for five minutes and came back with two burgers, handing me one as he sat down on the bench.

"Which part you from?" he asked, offering me the choice of a sachet of ketchup or mustard.

"Brixton Hill," I replied, refusing both.

"No! Me too."

We found we lived three blocks away from each other. He

Sour

spotted my bracelet, which had slipped down from underneath the sleeve of my jumper, and noted the Arabic script.

"You Muslim?"

"None of your business."

"What's your number?"

I didn't like all his questions.

"What do you want my number for?"

"Man wants your number, innit?"

Fat chance. The chances of my mum tolerating a call from a boy were negligible.

"She'd rather I get caught doing a crime than having a boy call my house."

"From what man heard, she's probably gonna get her wish," he shrugged, rearranging the fold of his jeans. "If that's what you want, that's cool," he said, jumping down off the picnic table. He had spotted Badman. I knew the two-tails would be waiting for me back at the toilets, but I was no longer interested in the crumbs they had to offer.

These new characters carried weight, and that had caught my attention.

From a distance, I watched as he and Badman greeted each other, pressing shoulders and patting each other on the back. I also saw a discreet exchange as one pressed cash into the hand of the other.

"Sour! Come, man."

The pair of them beckoned me over to the fake wooden decking, where the rest of the Man Dem were falling over each other to get in to a photo booth, decorated like an old Wild West Saloon.

Nothing had got paid for that day. Well, nothing until that moment. Suddenly they were all willing to cough up for this.

The group of them emerged from the changing rooms, giggling like children at each other's cravats and waistcoats and chaps and broad-brimmed hats. Each and everyone brandished a huge plastic musket. Drex arranged his false moustache, while Badman held his gun aloft.

"Here, put this on."

He spiked some pink ostrich feathers in my hair, and fastened a black satin choker round my neck.

"Saloon girl!"

"You gotta be taking the piss."

He found it hilarious, and swung an arm round me, pulling me into the group picture.

"Cheese."

The flash bulb went off, illuminating the chains among the rawhide fancy dress.

The picture was sepia, in a big, flimsy frame that said WANTED above our heads. The boys loved it.

Drex dug into his pocket and bought another one for me.

"Present," he said. The rest were laughing.

"That's wicked, man. Look how he had his face!"

"Look at that pose!"

"Suits you, gyal."

"That pistol suits you, man, time for an upgrade, innit."

They laughed all the way home. It was the only thing they were willing to pay for. They stumped up their £2 no questions asked, and each boy took it home as if it were as precious as a ransom fee.

I rolled mine up and slipped it into my hoodie.

I often wonder where that picture is now. Me on my first day with the Man Dem. A few young friends posing with plastic guns – before the real weapons intervened and changed everything.

Welcome to the Younger 28s

There are so many myths about gangs. People think there must be some kinda grisly initiation and a fucking Welcome Pack. They're wrong. Ain't no membership or code of honour. Ain't no leaders or matching tattoos. There ain't no *rules*.

Gangs don't really exist, as most people imagine them. This is Brixton; it ain't West Side Story.

Someone once said gangs only exist "in the way that chemical reactions exist: a mixture of dangerous elements that occasionally react and then disappear".

I like that. We're vapour. We're the noxious gas that seeps through a city's estates and poisons the minds of its children. My life was one messy chemical reaction after another. And "respect" was the accelerant. You hear a lot about that, "respect". What is it? Easy. Respect is just the flip-side of fear.

Gang life has its own justice. If you show cowardice, you're out. If you hesitate for a single second, you'll be ridiculed. But if you were a face to be known, you'd be known. Bravery bought protection. Recklessness had its own rewards.

And don't get me wrong. When I say "out" I don't mean you're free. I don't mean that rejection by these boys sets you straight on the path to college. When you're that far down the line, what do you think seems the safest choice? Being on the side of the ones with power? Or being on the side of those without? I didn't pause for a second.

That was the deal I made when I met the Younger 28s. That was the world I entered. And I loved it.

Why? Because the real temptation to rolling with those boys – and they were all boys – was this: if you felt angry, you had people feeling angry with you. If you were broke, they were broke with you. If you wanted payback because you'd been short-changed by society, they had your back.

Or so I thought.

I was 15. I needed more. I needed entertainment. The Youngers gave me all the entertainment a ghetto girl could wish for.

But first, allow me to give you a bit of background. Why 28?

28s were top rank. They were the boys. They were the market leaders.

Perhaps there were 28 people originally, I don't know. If there was a link with the South African prison gang of the same name – named after 28 black prisoners who revolted against their white guards – it was never spoken of.

All I know is that in South London there were three tiers of 28s: the originals, the Youngers, and the Younger Youngers. Like three generations.

The original 28s were British-born black boys who challenged the Jamaican Yardies' monopoly around Brixton Hill; elders like Duffers had the endz on lock down.

When prison or bullets intervened, as they always did, that's when younger ones like me came in to carry on the badness.

Duffers got shot up real bad. He was a real, real bad boy, who had a humorous side. If somebody ordered pizza, he would be the first one giving orders to rob the delivery guy.

He wouldn't just take his money. He'd take his helmet, his bike and his keys, and leave the poor guy with nothing but bare feet and panic attack. When Duffers ordered pizza, you knew some poor yout was leaving on foot without his trainers.

He got killed at a party, by people he thought were his friends. The rumours were they shot him up in a fight over a girl. Only God knows the real truth behind it.

I remember that funeral, and all the soul-searching it caused round our endz. That was probably the point that the Younger 28s came into their own.

After the mayhem at Chessington, I started to see the crew more and more. I saw them at school, around the estates and rolling round Brixton Hill.

Over the days and weeks that followed, I'd roll with Badman and Drex, Cyrus and Stimpy.

Their company was refreshing. Keziah and Stace and all that emotion and bitching – too much of a headache, man. I had enough emotion from my mum and all her baseball bat swinging. Emotion, darling, was the one thing I could do without.

These guys, they had bigger concerns. They were focused on making money, and I wanted in. They didn't have time for tears and feelings and all that shit. It's just wasn't in their DNA. Neither did I.

If we had one thing in common, it was the stuff we didn't speak about: our homes. Each of these youts had it hard in one way or another. I knew not to ask about their details and they knew not to ask about mine.

But when it came to the time to represent, everyone was on the same page.

No one was in charge. One form makes many. The news-papers spoke about street kids wearing different colours – purple for Angell Town; green for Myatt's Field – or tying their laces in certain ways. Maybe outsiders would have liked that. That way, they'd know when to cross the street. But not with us, not back then. All that mattered was fresh creps and looking sharp.

How dangerous we were, you'd have to judge for yourself.

If I saw Man Dem at Morley's, the chicken shop, I'd stop and speak. If I saw them cussing with a guy in the street, I'd jump off the bus and get involved. If a delivery boy was being relieved of his Nikes and his Moped, hell yeah, I'd go along and laugh.

Nothing was ever really pre-planned. But if I was with them, when they heard something going down, make no mistake, I'd get stuck in. I had heart.

Tyrone was bemused by the association.

"So you like these guys?" he asked one afternoon after class.

"They alright," I shrugged.

"They talk about you. You seem to have made an impression."

I tried to play it cool.

"What?" I said, after he fell silent.

"Just saying, they're serious characters, yeah?"

"And?"

"Just thought you should know."

"I know."

"They asked me if you wanted to meet up tonight."

"We're going to yours anyway, ain't we?"

"Yeah, but just wanted to let you know they'll probably be around. You in?"

"Course."

"Cool, come round later and we'll hang out."

He disappeared down the corridor into his next class. I didn't bother going into mine.

I tried to ignore the flutter of nerves in my stomach. I had to keep it cool.

I didn't often go round to Tyrone's. He usually came round to mine, but Mum had lots of people round from the mosque tonight.

The Man Dem were not exactly his friends, just the boys he lived with. They knew he didn't get involved with the serious shit, that he didn't like an altercation, but they seemed to respect him all the same.

I wasn't looking forward to going round and sitting in his flat, so it was a bit of a relief to know there would be some other activity to keep us entertained.

His flat had no furniture for starters, or not much anyway. You know you've got some mums who are house proud and some who ain't? Well, this one just didn't have no style, man. No ornaments, no cushions, no carpet. Not much. I don't even think he had a fridge.

That night, we went together to see the crew. Tyrone acted as The Introducer.

It was the end of the summer term – my last term – and the nights were warm and long. The heatwave had boiled over, and the sky glowed pink beyond the jet trails leading to Heathrow.

Hanging on Tyrone's estate meant interacting with a whole new hierarchy of characters who lived in his blocks. Cars would pull up, business would be done.

That hot evening, it had an LA vibe. Man Dem leaned on their cars, rolling down the windows, and pumping up the stereos. I'm not gonna lie. It was exciting. I felt like I was stepping into a scene from *2 Fast 2 Furious*.

Lot of conversations were going, Olders talking transactions, Youngers making deals.

And lots of them were interested in this pretty new face.

"What have you been on for the day then, blood? What you been doing today?"

I recognised Badman. I'd soon learn there was little mystery to the name. Bad influence, bad man. He was the one who had to be talked out of stuff. If ever a yout was going to get you chased unnecessarily across Clapham Common for fear of your life, it was him.

He was brash, abrasive, but I was beginning to like him.

"Ain't done much, bruv," replied Tyrone.

"You remember Sour?"

Of course he remembered me, he said, looking me up and down. "Girl got her tings going on. Alright?"

I nodded and smiled. Enough to be friendly, not too much to give him the wrong idea.

Another yout, a good few inches shorter than me, rocked up, knocking knuckles with Badman and pulling Tyrone into an enthusiastic chest hug – though their chests were barely level.

His brand-name was Stimpy.

"Man made some loot today, still," Badman told him. It felt like he was trying to wind him up. If he was, it worked.

"What? And you couldn't bring man in? Why couldn't I get part of it?"

I couldn't work out whether he was joking or challenging him. Either way, this guy had balls of steel for someone so fat. He was speaking as if, when he looked in the mirror, he saw a 6 ft 3 hunk stare back at him.

"Move, man! Get outta here."

Badman laughed and shook his head, like a lion batting away the cubs that bit at his ankles. Stimpy was having none of it.

"Nah, come on seriously, bring man in. Give me some."

Badman moved to him slowly, then, grinning broadly, fastened him in a headlock.

Stimpy fought back – he was tough for a fat motherfucker – and the rest laughed out loud, enjoying the mock scuffle.

The jeering prompted a window to be unlocked two floors above. A woman leaned out.

"What ye boys doing? Wanna keep down the noise?"

Stimpy released his head from the crook of Badman's arm and wriggled free.

"Sorry, Mum," he called up.

"That's his mum?" I whispered to Tyrone. Tyrone shook his head.

"No, Stimpy ain't got no mum."

He explained that Man Dem called all the older women on the estate "Mum". "Sign of respect."

"Ye alright?"

"I'm fine," she replied, softening. "Be better if youts were quiet, innit."

"Man be good, Mum," Stimpy winked.

She rolled her eyes and closed the window. That was why Stimpy was needed by the Man Dem. As I'd find out, he was just as capable of meanness as any of them, and sneaky with it too, but he didn't look like no hardass gangster. Better than any of them, Stimpy could win people's trust. He could go unnoticed better than all the rest. He was the best look-out they had.

Another yout came over to join us. Cyrus didn't say much, and got on with transactions, counting cash and handing it over to Badman. I recognised him from the saloon photo. He'd been standing at the back, with a cowboy hat on. He was the only one who wasn't smiling in it.

"Y'alright? What you doing here?"

"Free world, innit."

Yeah, Drex was one of the names of the Youngers, and right there and then, from the way he spoke to me, I could see he did what it said on the tin: Drex was short for Durex. He was eye candy for sure. I just knew he had the pick of many. Every girl liked this fly boy.

"What's he doing?" I asked.

Cyrus had broken off from the rest of the group, and had gone along the walkway, to knock at one of the flats. He was waiting on the doorstep. The door didn't open. Instead, he was speaking with someone through the window.

Drex laughed.

"No one knows what Cyrus is doing," he said. "Doing business of some sort. He ain't trying to tell no one what he's trying to do. No point. Before you know, he's gone with it, and be seeing you later at home. He's just off."

Cyrus was a serious character. Bit of a lone wolf. He got a lot of stuff done. Too much, at times. He would be the one, I'd learn, who would be getting chased, with no warning, because of something he's done that you're not even aware of. If you suddenly heard the Junction Boys wanted to tear your head off, the reason usually had something to do with Cyrus.

Cyrus looked over, and nodded hello to us, as he rolled up a spliff. I rarely saw him without some weed. He was high most of the time. Maybe that's why he didn't talk much.

But even without going into his background or having a conversation, you understood he came from something. That boy had demons. Of them all, he carried the greatest darkness.

Another guy who joined the group got a bigger welcome than the rest. I realised I recognised him. It was Daggers, the boy who'd scaled balconies on the run from the boydem.

"Where've you been, man? Ain't seen you for a while," said Stimpy, pleased to see him.

"Got nicked, innit. Feds had me down to station for a week, took all my clothes, spun the house …"

Cyrus passed him a spliff.

"Thanks, man. So what did I miss?"

At that moment their attention was turned to two girls, Tyrone's sister and her friend, who had come down to enjoy the vibe. They didn't stay long, passing from car to car, talking to some of the guys.

They were both in their slippers, wearing denim shorts and vest tops. One of them had her hair half-combed, with a comb still poking out her braids. The other half of her hair was wild. In her hand she carried a can of coke.

"Mum wants you to go and help," she told her little brother, before taking note of me.

"Hi Sour," she said. "Y'alright?"

"Yeah, good, Chantal. You?"

"Fine."

She clearly wasn't interested in having a chat.

Stimpy rolled up behind her and put an arm round her waist.

"Looking fine tonight, girl."

She rolled her eyes, and peeled his arm away.

"Is it not past your bedtime?" she said. Her friend giggled.

"Is that an offer?" he replied. "You offering to take man? You can tuck me up real nice."

She ignored him. He caught my eye and I supressed a smile.

"Ty, come on. Mum needs you for something."

She seemed irritated, impatient. I realised she didn't like him being out here.

He looked at me apologetically.

"Wanna come up and get some food?"

"Nah," I said. "I'm going to hang here for a while."

He looked surprised.

"Sure?"

"There's chips and …"

"Ty," I said, more forcefully this time. "Don't worry about me. I'm fine."

"OK," he shrugged. His sister spun on her heel and went back up the stairwell, with Tyrone falling behind.

I spent the rest of the evening drifting through this new crowd. By the time darkness finally fell I had taken so much in, watching different characters from different tiers exchanging cash and talking business. I watched who made the most money, who felt they were smartest, who commanded the most respect.

It was all so different from home at Roupell Park where the only diversions were ball games in the Pen and relieving the shops of stock.

All of a sudden there were all these guys, smoking weed, eating food, playing music. These goings-on felt good.

I listened a lot and just took it all in, getting the feel of this new crew. Some responded when I spoke to them, others didn't. Drex made a few introductions with the rest of them, talking over me as if I was dumb and mute.

"Is she your chick, blood? You banging her?"

His name was Gadget. He wasn't known for his charm.

I smoothed the slick of hair that hung over my eyebrow and tried to look – what's the word? – disdainful.

"Nah, she's down with it, man. Even if I wanted to, she's not going to have that," he joked.

"Damn right," I said.

"Well, then how come she's around?"

"How come you got two phones?" I asked, pointing to the one in his hand and the other brick in his pocket.

"Ringtones, innit. Stereo surround sound."

He pulled them both out.

"Listen to this," and he held one up to each ear, and started dancing to the grimey tracks together, which were beeping and bleeping in strange sychronicity. He looked ridiculous in his loud clothes and designer labels. I couldn't help but laugh.

"Did you hear about my man and that chick from Brixton?" he asked Drex.

"Man said she's proper loose, like I told you, yeah, but a good bang still. He said she …"

Gadget stopped in his tracks as soon as he saw Drex's feet.

"Fuck's sake, man! You had to go get the same trainers as me. Stop trying to follow man's trend. These ain't for your class, innit."

"You're gonna have to upgrade, man, sorry."

Gadget walked off in a huff, looking like someone had just pissed on his chips. I imagined him throwing out his beloved new Nikes as soon as he got home.

That's when I noticed they all walked the same – swaggering with such a lop-sided bounce, like they had a limp.

"So you live here too?" I asked him.

Drex explained he lived with his dad on the endz. As we chatted, more boys approached to bump fists. I noticed a quiet confidence that I hadn't seen before. Yeah, this boy had heart.

They treated him with a certain level of respect. Only Daggers looked unimpressed when he saw us talking. While the rest asked me questions and played the joker, he stood back and stared at me with hostility. He seemed annoyed about something.

Drex noticed it too.

"What you cutting your eye at her for, blood?"

The volume of his voice caught Badman's and Stimpy's attention. They stopped to listen.

Daggers snorted.

"She thinks she's too nice, innit."

I might have been the new girl – hell, the only girl – but I wasn't being disrespected in front of no blood.

"What's your problem, man? Time of the month?"

They sniggered.

"Just saying I don't want no trouble, that's all," he said, and slunk back to what he was doing.

"Ignore him," said Drex. "He gets like that sometime. He thinks girls don't speak to him on account of his skin."

Daggers' acne wasn't that bad. I'd seen worse. For a fleeting moment I felt sorry for him.

"You like all this?" he asked, nodding to the guys laughing and joking behind him.

I realised I'd been enjoying myself. No one said gang. No one needed to.

"I like to be entertained, yes."

He nodded. "You and me both."

We were interrupted by a scuffle as Badman lunged for Gadget's ridiculous phone.

Sour

"You said you wanted new trainers, yeah? Well, who's hungry?" he shouted. "Man feels like ordering a pizza!"

Stepping inside, I heard an excited squeal.

"Sour's here!"

It was my brother. He was upstairs with his friends. His loudspeaker was up full blast. I could feel the bass vibrating through my body as soon as I walked into his room.

In the mornings, we listened to Gina Thompson, R Kelly, Aaliyah, Keith Sweat. In the afternoon, it was Tupac and Biggie. And at night, the night music was my favourite – we would dance to jungle music. Now that was my kind of music. I noticed Mum had passed out on the sofa and was sleeping right through it.

A hyper Yusuf jumped off his bed and pulled me into his room, where they had turned off the light and were dancing in the dark to strobe lights.

"Robot dance!" he squealed, locking his elbows and knees, and popping like C3PO.

The neighbours from downstairs banged on their ceilings, waking Mum up.

"Turn that shit dahn!" she yelled.

But when she thundered through the door, even she burst out laughing when she saw us dancing like mannequins under the strobes. Within a few minutes she had thrown off her dressing gown and was dancing with us in her pyjamas.

There were no arguments that night. Before you knew it, me, Mum and Yusuf were robot-ing under the strobes like there was no tomorrow.

But I should have known better than to relax like that. As she used to say, "Chicken be merry, hawk deh near."

The Secret

The 28s, Junction Boys, Peckham Boys and the Ghetto Boys. They were the postcode celebrities of South London. They ruled over the estates I knew like generals commanding their own little patch. They were the ones with all the latest Versace, Iceberg, D&G and Moschino gear, the ones the girls wanted to sleep with. They had their choice of women.

But there was one big difference between me and the other girls – I didn't want to sleep with them. As I got to know them all better, I became accepted as one of the lads. They just felt like brothers to me. For a couple of them, I would become willing to put my life at risk.

Loyalty stood strong. I learned that quickly. If a situation arises, and you're seen not to have someone's back, you'd be cast aside. Yeah, loyalty was a big deal. Or so I thought.

I don't know whether it was because I was a girl, or because I was a vicious girl, but I got away with a lot. I also had another advantage the rest of the "men" of the Man Dem did not. If I didn't feel like getting in an altercation, or joining a brawl on a particular day, I could leave them to it – because no one expected me to get involved in the first place.

I saw them more and more often, with or without Tyrone. When I heard people saying I heard you're part of that crew, I just went with it. No Youngers ever corrected them. Brawling was our ting. When an altercation kicked off, I would be very much involved. I was always willing to get stuck in, and that surprised them.

How did I know I had become one of them? I knew because I was accepted. With these characters you know when you're not wanted. If you weren't trusted, you'd be denounced as a fool and a folly, a waste of space. You'd be ridiculed as "moist".

They were fearless, and willing to do their ting, if necessary. Some of it was lies, some of it was hype, but you're not going to challenge them to prove it.

As I said, gang life has its own justice. If you were a face to be known, you'd be known. Mine soon became known around Tyrone's estate. Not as a girlfriend, or a sister, or some sort of groupie – I wasn't interested in any of that – but as one of the Man Dem themselves.

I ignored Drex's calls. There was no shortage of girls hanging around the peripheries for a sniff around him. I left them to it. Their hair was gelled and styled. They wore short skirts and tight-fitting clothes. I saw them throw themselves at the brand-names, and heard the way the bloods talked about them later. I was determined that would not happen to me. No, there would be no complications like that.

Most boys were scared of me and that suited me fine. Some saw me as a challenge. She's a bad girl on the street, so she must be a bad girl in the bedroom.

No one moved to me, and that was the way I liked it. I knew that was the only way I'd get their respect. Soon there were guys I didn't even know who were bragging about sleeping with me. I took no notice. I enjoyed it as my own private joke – because little did they know they were boasting about sleeping with a virgin.

Entertainment

Badness bought things, and we were of high calibre. Nowadays it's just postcode wars for the sake of it, but we had something else motivating us in the Younger 28s: greed. We were money-orientated. We wanted money. We came from homes that had none, and we wanted more of it.

Brixton was changing. On the outskirts of our estates, young white professionals were moving in, new shops were opening up among the bookies and chicken shops. New money was coming in too, at least for those born into it. We wanted it for ourselves. It was dog eat dog.

I had my own rules. Businesses, bookmakers – all fair game. Holding a knife to some woman's throat on her way home from work, as she gets the keys out to her front door, nah, no thanks. There had to be limits.

But the reality was this: if you weren't naughty, how could you fund the lifestyle? How would you pay for the Moet? Everyone said that was the only drink worth drinking. I had a bigger, stronger crew to chill with now. With more money in my pocket, I could afford the better things in life. Or at least, some of them.

No one ever questioned why a young girl in Roupell Park had a row of empty Moet bottles lined up along her bedroom window.

Occasionally you would hear of someone going to work a day shift somewhere, but truth was you were seen as a joke if you worked. It was like clown's work. Why put yourself through it?

How did I get the money? Well, I'd wake up late every morning, asking myself what was it going to be today? Steaming the small shops was for the rugrats. Rolling with Badman, Drex and the Man Dem made me more ambitious. I thought about all sorts – in the days before hi-tech security made it impossible.

It wasn't that I had been officially accepted as one of the Man Dem; but when word went round that I was rolling with the Youngers now, no one ever corrected them. I saw Tyrone less and less. I had a new crew. Besides, he was busy studying for his exams.

Who was going to the function in Streatham? Who was in for the Clapham fair? How were we going to get there? More importantly, how were we going to get there without paying?

Usually the solution was to take buses hostage. Anyone who takes public transport regularly in London has seen this happening. It's normal practice for crews to slip through the back doors when people were getting off. The drivers with half a brain usually just ignore us, but occasionally the nuisance ones would stop and invite a stand-off.

It usually begins with "Shuddup Granddad, we ain't going nowhere," and usually ends with Granddad the driver caving under the impatient cries of all the other passengers on the bus who just want to get moving.

I looked forward to the social occasions at Myatt's Fields. The Mostyn Club did regular all-dayers for under-18s. It was a Jamaican guy who put these things on. He'd serve plastic cups with shots of brandy, and had an old Rasta soundman playing the music.

Kids from all over came to see and be seen, or at least those who were brave enough. That was where I learned the intricacies and contradictions of postcode rivalry.

There were Younger 28s, of course, the Bellefield Rd Man Dem, and the rest of the Brixton lot who weren't 28s but still thought they were Charlie Potatoes. It would still be daylight, and you'd have all these kids with attitude in their best clubbing gear, pushing through the doors, trying to get into the best positions inside.

We were standing in our usual corner. Everyone knew that this was the Youngers' corner. There was always a stream of girls trying to filter through and get the guys' attention. Gadget was in a particularly hyperactive mood. He was wearing all his new designer threads, and clearly feeling pleased with himself. He seemed to be bouncing with nervous energy.

"Did you hear what Shimmer done?" he shouted over the bass.

Badman, Drex and Stimpy weren't paying attention to them. They were all staring at Gadget, waiting to find out.

"He drummed someone's yard, then shanked the hero who tried to stop him. Shanked the dude while he still had a TV in his arms!"

Badman looked impressed. Stimpy laughed and shook his head.

"Some of that older lot," said Stimpy, "they have no morals, man."

I had met Shimmer a couple times. He used to play-punch me all the time, like a big brother would.

Sour

He said I was going off the rails and turning out to be a proper little bad girl so I needed to learn how to handle pain. I'd flex my muscles and challenge him to punch me as hard as he could. He was big and muscular. When he punched you, you knew about it. It would hurt, but I liked it. I saw it as some kind of training.

"Toughen you up, innit?" he'd say.

I would go home with a dead arm, feeling proud and thinking I was a tough cookie because I had the knuckle marks of one of the Olders imprinted on my tender, bruised flesh.

When I heard he'd stabbed someone it didn't sound real, I felt a pang of disgust. I left it for the others to dissect.

Our corner was filling up. It only took a few of the Man Dem to go somewhere, before the rest followed.

I cast my eye around the club, looking out for faces that might cause trouble.

We didn't have no grievance with the Junction Boys, they were usually cool. Ghetto Boys, yeah, they were on the map but nobody was scared of them. Not really. They had a few serious characters but if you went down to Lewisham, Deptford, those parts, there was nobody really stood out for me.

Still, that didn't mean there wasn't going to be trouble.

The scanners at the door meant I had to leave my knives at home. My hand instinctively reached for my hip, forgetting that it wasn't there. Its absence made me nervous.

Gadget was trying to say something else, but was drowned out over the bass.

"I *said* that ain't all."

"Batty Boy Day, innit?" he laughed. "A few of the Man Dem took the bus to slap down some batty man."

Of course, Gay Pride. Jamaican boys like Gadget liked gay boys like gay boys like cricket. Anyone carrying a rainbow flag was regarded as target practice and a good way to test out your right-hand hooks.

Stimpy punched Gadget's chest approvingly and Badman knocked knuckles. I caught a smile lingering on Drex's lips.

I strained to listen as he told us how he and Cyrus had seen a young man on the bus and waited till he got off at a quiet stop to kick him down. As he was reciting his story, he pulled out a can of cider and topped up his plastic cup.

"Left him crying," he said proudly, doing another celebratory fist pump with the rest.

Now, don't get me wrong. I've stabbed someone for less than being gay. I've stabbed someone for speaking to me the wrong way, but anyone that I harmed was harmed because I was in an angry state, or felt my life was being threatened.

I wasn't just clear-headed going out and stabbing people. It wasn't premeditated. Injuries were just the debris you left behind, the collateral damage – they weren't the … objective.

"I feel sorry for the batty boy."

Badman looked up at me, sharply. Stimpy seemed puzzled.

Truth was, I did have morals. They might have been warped, but they were there. What was the point in risking jail just because you didn't like batty boys?

"Live and let live, man. Fuck 'em. Or rather, don't. What did he do to you?"

Gadget's expression hardened.

"What's going on in your head?"

Drex stepped in, sensing trouble.

"She doesn't know what she's talking about," he shrugged. "Anyway," he said, steering Gadget's sightline towards the dance floor, where more girls were dancing, flicking their hair and copying the dirtiest dancehall moves. "What's man on for tonight?"

Fuck 'em. It wasn't worth an argument. I poured my own cider. The club was filling up now. Man Dem don't dance. They head nod, from a distance. Even at the best club nights, it's never more than bare nods from the edge of the dance floor. Any more, and you're seen to look weak, vulnerable.

The club was now filled with kids with attitude, with people who weren't in any kind of crew; admirers, haters, people who didn't like you but didn't have the balls to do anything about it.

But we had to stay vigilant. I could see the rest of the Man Dem were distracted. They were looking out for girls. I didn't want to be caught off guard. I knew we had strength in numbers. If a rival walked through, looking for trouble, may God help them.

I felt bolder than before – these days, I had back-up.

Some faces glared over, cutting an eye at us, from across the club.

Stimpy had seen them too. Noting our body language, the rest of the Man Dem pulled their gaze from the chicks whining on the dance floor and looked up.

"Let Stimpy handle it," said Badman.

"What?" I thought. Really?

Before I knew it, Brixton's own Sherman Klump was winding his way through the crowd towards them.

"I'm going to have his back, he's on his own."

"Leave it," ordered Cyrus, who had appeared from nowhere.

Turned out Stimpy was friends with one of the top heads of the crew. I watched them greet each other, and knew that we would have no problem with them that night. I learned that if you've got two characters from different crews who respect each other like that, you don't need to take any action unless it's absolutely necessary.

There weren't many problems when the Junction Boys came into our territory. It was only when we went to theirs that you knew the Junction Boys would come out and there would be an altercation.

As long as the Junction Boys didn't turn up tonight, it would be a quiet night.

I took a sip of cider and went back to laughing quietly at the girls on the dance floor below, performing like lapdancers. Why were they all trying so hard to get to where I was standing now? I congratulated myself. I hadn't done any of that shit. I hadn't whined for no one, and yet they were out there and I was standing here, right in the centre of things.

I was already one of the boys. I already rolled with the Man Dem they were all so desperate to impress. And I was much more comfortable in my baggy jeans and loose top.

I laughed at their desperation.

Sure, I had my eyeliner and my hair was always did nice, in a smooth golden beehive. But I didn't feel the need to go out half-naked. My face was enough, darling. Besides, it's pretty hard to hide a baseball bat or a rabbit-foot belt when you're grinding away in a spandex mini-dress.

I knew I was respected. I didn't need no Perspex stripper heels. And yet, for the first time, looking at these girls just a little older than me, in their footless tights and denim hotpants and tight tops, I had a split second of doubt. A niggling voice in the back of my head was trying to say something, something about standing there, the only girl in the club in baggy jeans and a hoodie. I ignored it, and put it to the back of my mind.

Sour

Badman and Cyrus were deep in conversation. Swelled with bravado, Gadget was chatting up two girls. I scanned the club, wondering where Drex was, until I spotted him down by the bar.

Getting involved as one of the Man Dem's chicks was the first way of getting sidelined. I wasn't falling for that shit. I would roll with them on my own terms.

Which was why I'd ignored his calls.

So why did I feel so bad when I saw him, nodding his head, hands in his pockets, with a big grin on his face as some bloody chick was bent over, whining against him?

His eyes snagged on mine, and I looked away, embarrassed that he had caught me scowling at them.

No one else dared speak to me that night. I left early. I didn't feel like waiting to see who would throw the first bottle to start a brawl. I wasn't in the mood.

When I got home, Mum was waiting in the front room. The windows were bare. She was taking down the curtains to be washed. Late night spring clean. I didn't have the energy to care.

"Where you been?"

"Out."

"Out? Till crazy hours of de morning? You been out with who? Ah what bloodclart time ah mornin yuh call dis? Yuh nah pay rent roun yah so fi walk in whenever you feel like it! You likkle slut!"

"That's rich, coming from someone with four different kids to different men! You know what they call women like you? Four by fours."

She delivered a heavy slap across the face.

I wished I could have grabbed her by the neck and thrown her down on the floor, but I knew she was heavier and stronger than me. I ran up the stairs, locked my door and put my music up as loud as it would go.

It didn't matter how long I went out, or who I went with. I always knew I had a war waiting with my mum.

Yusuf's door was open. Inside his room, I could see him doing his hair. He looked like he was getting ready to go out.

"Where you going at this time?" I asked.

"Out, innit," he said, smoothing his spongy Afro into a new sweet-boy style. Some girls had perm kits, Yusuf had started using S-Curl to texturise his hair into curls.

"Looks nice," I said, noting his new Iceberg jacket and fresh trainers that I knew cost £110 a pop. They were high-end garmz.

"When you gonna be back?"

I was suddenly annoyed – he could go out all hours and Mum wouldn't say a word. It was only me she had a problem with.

"Dunno," he said.

He flashed a smile.

"Don't wait up."

High Life

"Bloodclart!" Mum had slammed down the phone again. "Salwa, who's this boy on the phone, ringin ma house?"

I smiled to myself. Drex had met his match in the old Muslim chick formerly known as Eleanor Raynor. That had been the fifth time he'd tried to call this week.

He continued trying to pass messages to me at school, asking to meet up. Hell no. Tyrone would scurry back, shaking his head. "She's in her lesson."

Yep, he might have been able to get any other chick he wanted, but Drex always got a frosty reception from me. I never turned up at the time or place he wanted.

I wasn't interested. Or at least, not enough to jeopardise my position in the Man Dem. The minute I got with him, I would only be seen as Drex's girlfriend. No. I wanted in on my own terms. I didn't want no boyfriend to vouch for me.

Mum didn't like any boys being in my mile zone, least of all ones she didn't know from the endz.

"I'm going out," I shouted.

"Bring some cigarettes back witchoo," she called. "And tell that boy no call back ma home."

It was the day of the Lambeth Country Show, one of the highpoints of the South London summer calendar. Over the next two days 100,000 people would visit Brockwell Park for the music on the main stage, a family funfair and a whole heap of nonsense, with farmers' markets, donkey rides, flower shows and blacksmith demonstrations on the village green.

Local families loved it. Man Dem came from all over London. Everyone would be there. For youts like us, it meant serious entertainment.

I had an idea. The young family a couple of doors down had this big-arsed dog, a beautiful Great Dane called Maverick. Now I happened to know, because I noticed these things, that Maverick didn't get out much. The dad used to let him jump over the greenery and piss around the Pen, but poor Maverick spent most of his miserable life cooped up in their small front room.

He looked fierce as hell, but I knew from speaking with the kids that he was a big softie.

I went round for a chat. I was in luck. Only the kids were in.

"Can I walk him?"

The sister scowled.

"Are you strong enough?"

"Damn straight! Seen these muscles, girl?"

"OK, but don't let him off the lead."

She disappeared for a moment, then reappeared with bloody Scooby doo, on a fluorescent pink rope. Wow. Even I had forgotten how big he was. She handed over the rope.

"Wait." Her brother appeared at the door. He must have been about seven. He had sticky-out ears and a pudding-bowl haircut. "He needs his treats."

Maverick's ears pricked up. He and the boy clearly got on.

"Have you got them there?"

The boy nodded.

"Good. Now go get your shoes on. You're coming too."

The boy's face lit up.

This was going to look a bit random, but Maverick knew him and he could come in handy. I needed a wingman. The seven-year-old was going to have to do.

As we walked into the park, it felt as if the crowds were parting. We'd created quite a stir, just as I'd hoped. Suddenly, the knife underneath my hoodie seemed redundant. I had the best weapon of all. If reputation of power is power, then I was on fire.

For the Man Dem, the Lambeth Country Show wasn't about picnics and coconut shies. It was about war.

I'd arranged to meet the rest by the funfair. I wanted to take my time, taking the crowds in, and checking for potential trouble in my peripheral view, but Maverick was impatient, striding up ahead, tugging us along.

I steered away from the livestock and sheep-shearing – he'd probably eat them alive – and let him tug us through the kiddies' zone instead. The boy trotted along beside us.

The park was huge. You needed eyes in the back of your head. Trouble could come from anywhere. No guerrilla street-fighting here. It was an open battlefield. Anybody could move to you at any time. You're vulnerable – unless of course, your companion is 10 stone of slobbering dogmeat. I had the kind of protection none of the rest of the Man Dem could boast – a dog no one would fuck with, a child no one would hurt and breasts no one would suspect of belonging to a troublemaker.

Maverick dragged us past the entertainers on the village green, behind the main stage.

Of course, the first people you're usually on the lookout for – local rivals who've got a beef with you for some reason, other youts with old grievances – they're not the ones posing the greatest danger. Not this time.

No, big events like Lambeth leave it wide open. The show was a magnet for unfamiliars who didn't know the territory but wanted to make their mark, and create some trouble. Youts from Tottenham, Hackney and beyond. This was their away day.

It's ironic, innit, but on days like this usual rivals like the Peckham Boys, the Ghetto Boys and the rest are the ones you can count on to keep their distance. Familiars didn't bother each other. We all knew our own role. We respected each other's space. There would be no trouble from them today.

Gadget spotted me first.

"What the fuck is that?!"

"Calm down," I laughed. "He's got one too," pointing over to one of the rugrat's dogs, tugging on its lead, growling angrily at Maverick.

"That's a Staffie," spluttered Gadget. "You've brought a fucking horse!"

"And who's the kid? Its fucking jockey?"

"Aidan here is helping me keep Maverick happy, ain'tcha Aidan?"

The boy smiled absently, distracted by all the fun of the fair.

"Anything kicked off?" I asked.

"Not yet," said Gadget, sucking on a strawberry lace, surveying the park. "There's talk some London Boys are on the rampage. Ain't seen none yet."

I spotted a burger van. "Here, watch him, OK?" I tied Maverick's lead around some fencing, outta sight of any stewards, and ordered Aidan to stand guard. He did as he was told.

"Want anything?"

He whispered something shyly.

"What?"

He pointed behind me.

He whispered it again.

"I want to go on the donkeys."

"You're shitting me? But you're just going around in circles. Looks bloody boring."

Aidan's little face looked embarrassed. He cast his eyes to the ground and fell quiet.

I assessed the situation. Cyrus, Badman and the rest had now arrived, and were deep in conversation over by the rides. They looked serious.

The sun was shining. Couples were lying back on tartan rugs, eating ice cream. Families were eating by the barbeque. There didn't seem no sign of trouble. Not yet. But it wouldn't be far away. I noticed the arrival of more familiar faces among the crowd. The ranks were swelling.

I looked at Aidan. It wasn't just Maverick who was cooped up all day. I never saw those kids outside.

"OK, but make it quick. Gadget, come here. Do us a favour, man, and look after him for a second?"

"You're taking the piss, man! I ain't …"

"Ain't nothing to worry about. He's tied up. He's not going anywhere. All you got to do is stand by so, y'know, he doesn't get boisterous, innit."

"Boisterous how?"

He stepped gingerly towards the dog.

"Just do it. I'll be back in a second."

I took Aidan over to the donkey rides, and gave him a couple of coins as he joined the queue. "That's my payment for hiring your dog. I'm gonna get a burger, and I'll meet you back here once you're finished, OK?"

He looked delighted. As I waited on my burger, I caught sight of his blond bob as he was lifted onto the saddle and led around the ring.

I'd nearly finished the burger when I got back to Maverick. He was looking anxious, whimpering and tugging at the post. Gadget was nowhere to be seen.

"Man's useless."

Maverick was getting really unsettled now. I poured him some of my coke, and a greedy tongue sponged it up from the grass. He was pulling towards the open park. "What's wrong, boy?"

Out of the corner of my eye, I saw someone sprinting. Youts were running left and right. Stimpy saw me.

"Sour!" he shouted. "It's on!"

Man Dem were being rushed. Somebody screamed. A steward in a fluorescent jacket started jabbering into his walkie-talkie.

The coke can fell from my hand, leaving Maverick to lick up the rest from the hot earth. I grabbed my knife from my belt, and bolted into the fray. One form makes many. I jumped into the scrum.

Sharp-edged trainers thrashed at my shins. Random fists punched into my kidneys. It was a brawl. Twenty, thirty, possibly more kids were locked in combat. A hand reached for my throat. Another arm wrapped itself round my neck. I tried jabbing the knife behind me, but it sliced through thin air. I couldn't breathe. I wanted to stab the arm that was holding me in a headlock or the fingers pressing on my throat, but there was too much movement. I couldn't get a clear cut. I would have stabbed my own self. The knife fell from my grasp, into the grass.

Sour

My eyes were watering. The grip refused to loosen. I squirmed and wriggled and gnashed my teeth, but I couldn't hold it for much longer.

Pssssszzzt!

I heard a canister explode. It sounded like a firework. Gadget must have brought his CS gas. The spray stung my eyes, till I could see nothing, and burned all the way down to my lungs. The arm slipped away, the fingers faded from my throat. I collapsed on to my hands and knees, coughing and spluttering like all the rest.

Blindly, I fumbled around for my knife in the grass, fumbling till I felt the familiar touch of the bone handle. The gas would buy us some time, but not a lot.

Eyes streaming, chest on fire, I staggered back towards the rides. Amid the chaos I heard whooping. Gadget had come up trumps.

Maverick was pacing back and forth, having bent the fence post, which was almost uprooted completely. Beside him was Aidan, looking lost.

"Untie him," I shouted, scrambling from the smoking carnage.

I grabbed his hand, and the three of us bolted out of Brockwell Park faster than you can say chlorobenzylidene malonitrile.

And my dog-walking days were over.

Boydem had made bare arrests but none of us. Lambeth had been a big success for the Man Dem and we were all feeling confident.

There was another breakthrough. My mum didn't hang up the next time Drex called. I'd managed to persuade her we were friends, nothing more.

That was the deal. I'd go to his dad's house to pick him up or he'd meet me outside the police station with the rest of the Man Dem. That was it. But despite all my efforts to convince myself otherwise, something was happening.

I started recognising the same feeling whenever I turned up by the tree by the station on Brixton Road and couldn't see that beautiful smile in the crowd. I think it's called disappointment.

The rugrats had been doing well. They worked together as a team. The more they did, the quicker, smoother their operations became. I liked having money in my pocket. And I loved going out and spending it.

The Friday night jungle raves in the West End were our favourite haunt. They always started the same way: with some shopping in Bond Street.

The £200 from their latest steam was burning a hole in my pocket, and I couldn't wait to spend it.

The thrill began just buying that Travelcard. Even hopping on that Friday afternoon train felt exciting. It felt like something new. As soon as I stepped off the train on to that platform, I felt like I had joined the corporate world of London, swept up and away in an army of soulless soldiers. It was fast-paced, everyone walking in different directions, bumping into you, into each other. No smiling, no speaking, no nothing.

Emerging from Oxford Circus tube, I felt like a tourist entering a whole different city. The illuminated streets looked beautiful and daunting. I threw away my McDonalds, keeping the large coke, and made my way to Bond Street. Today, darling, I was going legitimate.

I went to the same shop we all went to: Proibito. When I say they had a selection, I mean they had a selection. Iceberg,

Moschino, Dolce & Gabbana, Versace – or Versase, as I called it back then.

I was a big D&G fan. The shop was always full of youngsters, attracted by the loud garage music and the excess of designer labels. Only groups of three were allowed in at a time. That was how they controlled the door. Mean-looking security guards floated the floor, every now and again chucking out kids caught swapping the labels and trying to stuff Moschino's finest into their bags. I could feel them watching me, judging me, as I browsed the rails.

The staff were helpful to others, cold and stand-offish to me. I couldn't blame them. I was used to it. I liked the smugness, this time, of proving them wrong.

My hand brushed over all the neatly folded clothes until I saw what I was looking for: that Versace logo. I fell in love with this devil head, with snakes for hair. Medusa. Now there was a chick with heart. It was repeated along a whole row of beautiful trousers.

It was a novelty picking an item on account of its size. I was used to lifting the ones that were easiest to steal. If you lifted something that fit, it was a bonus.

I picked up the beautiful trousers. I had to try these on.

It was a novelty, picking them up, draping them over my arm and walking face-straight to the changing rooms. I had never done this before. Usually, by this time, I was heading for the door.

That night at the Mostyn Club had got me thinking. I couldn't just dress exactly like the Man Dem no more. If I was to be Queen Bee, I needed to dress like one.

The trousers were tight, with stripes down them. They would go nice with my tight-fitting crew-neck vest top with a bit of pink, a bit of lime green. Every outfit needed new train-ers. Reebok Classics, obviously.

I wriggled out of them, satisfied I looked the part, and walked proudly to the counter. I knew I was going to be judged, but I didn't care. I had money! Money talks. I was buying legitimacy. I joined the queue. I felt like I belonged.

Then I had a thought. I wanted to buy Drex a gift. But what? He didn't like the loud stuff. No Gadget garmz. I spot-ted a mannequin wearing a silk bomber jacket. It was multi-coloured. I counted my money. I had enough. I grabbed one and took it to the counter.

That day, I walked out of Proibitos wearing my bags of pride.

It was time to go home, get ready and do my hair.

"Wow, you look super-nice."

Kez had come over to pick me up. I realised I hadn't seen her in so long. I was glad to see her.

"How does it stay up?"

"Hairspray, innit."

She was admiring my new beehive. I'd dyed the front honey blonde, and smoothed the rest of my thick, black hair up on top of my head. I'd used about an entire can of Silvikrin to keep it in place and now it felt storm-proof.

The beehive served a second purpose. My hair had got so long, but I could never go out to a function with it left down. Left me vulnerable, innit. Anybody could pull it, or set it alight in an altercation. I was probably the only girl going out that night wearing a beehive for safety reasons.

I'd lashed on heavy flicks of liquid eyeliner and matted out my fresh skin with Iman powder. My skin was still clear back then – I didn't go imaging up my face with tattoos till later. The finishing touch was my new gold lipstick. Yeah, I was fly.

Sour

I checked my nose piercing in the mirror and squirted on Jean Paul Gaultier. Mmm. I loved that bottle. So feminine and beautiful.

I was ready.

"Hold on," said Kez, "how are we getting to this place? Cab?"

"Nah, let's walk to Brixton. Trust me, there will be a carriage awaiting."

I was liking my new lifestyle. Telling you, man, I used to walk down Brixton High Street like there was a red carpet before me. I got my swagger on. I drank champagne and wore designer threads. Every night was a different club night: the Astoria, Vegas, Telepathy. I knew I could walk in alone to any one of them, and always know someone. Being one of the Man Dem might have given you rivals you'd never met, but it also gave you connections.

Sure enough, we were walking on the hill for just a few minutes when someone started to beep. We ignored them at first, obviously, as all teenage girls bored of being beeped at on the street are prone to do.

"Sour?" came a voice I recognised. "Stop blanking, man."

It was Badman. He was too young to be driving, but that didn't stop him cruising around in a shitty jalopy thing. It looked like a shed on wheels, which was his pride and joy.

He had stopped the traffic, face-straight, to shout across to us. Angry motorists swerved around him, beeping their frustration. He ignored them.

"Where you going?"

"Astoria."

"Come on. I'm going to roll in there later. Jump in."

We hopped in – Keziah in the back, me in the front – and he put his foot down.

Now I had heart, but I had no stomach for Badman's driving. He weaved through the traffic, swerving around buses and jumping red lights like Pac Man on crack. Kez fumbled for her seatbelt. Badman seemed oblivious.

His windows were down, blowing up our hair. I checked in the wing mirror. My beehive was holding up pretty well. Like I said, storm-proof.

"Astoria's gonna be a jump-off tonight," he said. "How's man getting in?"

We had checked that.

"We got tickets, innit?"

Badman checked his phone, letting the car drift across the lanes. Kez yelped and he corrected the wheel just in time. This was a high-speed flipping drive.

"Are we going to be on time?" asked Kez, realising how late it was.

I prayed that we'd get to the venue at all.

"If man ain't got a ticket, how you going to get in later?" I asked.

"Don't worry, man. Deal with that when we get there, innit. Gonna boar through."

Using bodily force to get past security was a tried-and-tested method. One form makes many. As long as there was enough of you, it was much easier than you think.

I suddenly noticed what he was wearing. His jeans were dirty and stained. He looked like he hadn't changed his top in days. If you didn't look sharp at the Astoria, you wouldn't last long.

"Bruv, what you wearing?"

"Don't watch ma garm, Sour!" he said, suddenly self-conscious. "Feds nicked me overnight, innit. Gotta go home and change."

"And you wonder why you don't get no girls …"

He let go of the steering wheel to play-punch me.

"Watch the road, man!" I shouted.

He laughed and threw his phone on to my lap.

"Phone, man, see if man's going."

It was already ringing. Drex picked up.

"You rolling out tonight?"

"Yeah, whole crew's rolling tonight," he said. We arranged to meet inside, and I threw the phone back at Badman, who had pulled up near the Astoria across double yellow lines.

He had reminded me. I was going to give it to him inside, but this was better. I pulled the multicoloured silk bomber jacket out of my bag.

"Here. Give this to Drex for me, yeah? A delivery he requested. Thanks for the lift."

Badman nodded, and chucked it in the back seat.

The whole world had come out tonight. Kez groaned when she saw the queue. I didn't. I was heading straight to the VIP where I knew one of the characters on the door.

Security guards hauled boys out of the queue, patting them down. No one was paying attention to the girls.

We slipped underneath the velvet rope and stepped into the flickering lights of the dark nightclub, where the bass line pulsed through our bodies.

We headed to the bar. Guys were tagging us from left and right, all wanting to have a chat, buy us a drink. It was annoying. Kez got cornered for a second by some poor guy who looked like something from the zoo. He grabbed her by the shoulders.

"Come here," he smiled. "You ain't going nowhere."

I stepped in. I was tempted to switch on him, but it was too early in the night. Outgoing fire attracts incoming fire. I didn't want no one here knowing I had a heart, unless they really had to.

"I advise you back off, right now, blood."

Without saying a word, I made it clear there was no point arguing. He shrank, and melted back into the crowd.

Apart from thugs like him, the vibe was nice. Everything was cool. I wondered if there would be trouble. I scanned the room looking for faces to be known.

Peckham Boys didn't really bring no drama to nights like these. It was the crews from further afield you had to worry about in the West End – the Turks and Chinese crews, mostly.

"What's gawn on?"

"Ty! Ain't seen man in ages."

I gave Tyrone a big hug. He loved his clubnights, Ty. Had more music than anyone I knew.

He introduced himself to Kez and she smiled back. Of course. Why hadn't I thought about this before? He bought a round of double rum and coke, and we laughed and joked around, talking shit. I was happy to let the pair of them go dancing, while I maintained a lookout from the bar. I liked to see them getting on so well.

I caught the multicoloured jacket out of the corner of my eye. Drex was threading his way round the dancefloor, scanning the club. He was looking for me. My stomach tightened, and I remembered the vows I'd made to myself.

On the other side of the dancefloor, I could see Tyrone and Kez. They were holding hands, moving away to a quieter corner to sit down at one of the tables.

"What do you think?" Drex looked pleased with his gift.

"Man looks sharp," I said.

He took my hand. I flinched.

"Relax," he said, softly. "I just want to say thank you. Come on, follow me."

I put down my rum and followed him.

"But we gotta keep vigilant. Stimpy said he reckoned some of the Enfield boys might move to Cyrus. They've been making threats …"

"They can handle themselves," he said.

Drex lead me downstairs to a chill-out room, cloaked in dark, velvet curtains.

"We can't be down here. I said I'd have their backs –"

"That's what I like about you, girl. You got heart," he said.

He leaned closer. "Can I tell you something?"

He smelled good.

"I feel safer with you than I feel with the rest of the Man Dem."

I had his back. Now I knew he had mine.

He put his arm around my waist, pulled me close, and kissed me.

My mind erased all thoughts of the Man Dem and those who might move to them. The only boy I cared about was the one I was with at right that moment.

Drex's hand was warm, yet it made me shiver as he gently brushed my waist and the exposed skin of my midriff. When his fingers reached the Medusa head, he hesitated. He looked down at the floor and back up at me, eyes twinkling. I noticed for the first time he had great teeth.

"You're dangerous," he whispered, feeling for my bum and sliding around the chains that pressed between us. He pulled me closer.

Beyond the curtains, the bass vibrated deeper. I don't know how long we'd been there when Stimpy raised the alarm.

"Where you been? Man been looking everywhere," he squealed. "It's a brawl!"

We ran upstairs. Crowds were running in each and every direction. Bouncers were rushing in. Stimpy slipped in and out of the gaps. We followed him to the exit.

"One of the Enfield crew tried to move to Cyrus. Bust a bottle over his head and stabbed him with the neck."

I didn't know which one it was who did the damage. It didn't matter. We knew what we had to do.

"Where are the others?"

"Don't know," said Stimpy.

"We said we'd regroup at the far exit."

I never wanted to be too far from the drama. For a moment, I was angry I'd missed it.

In altercations like these, we knew we would have to find each other like magnets. Strength in numbers. Stimpy must have passed the word round the club quickly. As we regrouped at the exit, I saw more and more faces that I recognised. Badman had been right. The whole crew was here tonight. Some I didn't even know their names. I just knew them from the estate. Others were faces to be known. I tried to get a feeling for what was going on.

No one asked how Cyrus was. That was not the primary concern. The objective was to find the Enfield yout.

Gadget staggered out into the street. Usually when your friends are taken to A&E, you've got to wait till they're released to hear what happened. But this time we had witnesses. Gadget had been with Cyrus at the time.

"See what he's done? I'm not having it."

He paced back and forth, ticking like a timebomb.

"What did he look like?"

Sour

"Man was Turkish. Vicious little shit. Small, skinny. Yellow Stone Island jacket."

Badman stumbled out after him, his new trainers covered with blood. He had a wild look in his eye I knew only too well. "Gotta get this yout, innit. Man can't be coming, thinking they're brave enough to bust man's head."

The rest of us said nothing. There was no talking. We were getting ready for action. We were saving our energy to perform.

Someone needed to take control. I pulled Gadget and Badman to one side.

"Did you see which exit they were heading for?"

"Could only see two. This one and the other one on the far side. Must be that one."

The club had been evacuated. Police cars started to pull up at the front. An ambulance must be on its way. We spread out like hunting dogs in a pack – far enough to minimise suspicion but close enough to keep tabs on each other – and weaved our way through the crowd, trying not to be too bait.

Girls were crying. Officers were taking statements from witnesses. We were not deterred.

Drex gestured over, pointing to his eye. He was asking if I'd seen any of them yet. I shook my head. Some of the Man Dem were buzzing off the alcohol. This was a club environment. Man had to sober up fast. Others who joined us outside had their own agenda.

I scanned the crowd for Turkish-looking faces. My heart was thumping. I felt a twinge of excitement. A yout snagged my eye. He looked Turkish. Could it be him? An exit spilled out on to a side road. He was standing at the bottom, next to a friend. I was about to yell, but remembered the Stone Island jacket. Not bright enough. Hold on. Not yet.

Hang on. The yout he was speaking to turned round and caught my eye. Small, skinny. Yeah, he looked like a guilty little motherfucker. As I turned round I saw the yellow Stone Island jacket.

Badman had spotted him too.

"That's the guy!"

"Jump him!"

We charged.

Some characters just cower, and take the beating. Others think they're Muhammad Ali. You can get some serious kung-fu fighting shit going on. This was one of those times. We got him quick, just as well, as he was a nimble little fucker. He was skinny and sinewy. Looked like the boy could run. Luckily for us, he never got the chance.

His boys leapt in, punching to the left, kicking to the right.

I didn't just do things for the sake of it. If my boys are fighting, I needed to get involved.

I ran with a flying kick, and jumped straight in. I could fight. I knew how to take care of myself. Whenever an arm or leg made contact, I firmed the pain and tightened my fists.

I'd lost sight of the yellow jacket. All I could see was a scrum of designer labels and scuffed trainers.

Someone yelled.

"The Feds!"

That was the sign to split. Man Dem began to disperse. I ran too, not caring which direction I was heading for. I didn't look back. Once we'd split, we'd split. There was no regrouping. That just makes it too easy for the Feds. It was known: you make the journey home on your own.

I kept running until it was safe enough to walk. I stopped to catch my breath. At this point I didn't care if someone had followed me.

Sour

I walked through quiet back streets, past offices and restaurants shut for the night, until I was back on Bond Street. It was almost light by the time I got on the night bus.

I slumped down in the back seat of the top deck. It wasn't too busy. I just wanted to get home, and thought about having a bath. I wondered whether Tyrone and Kez had seen any of the action, or whether they made it home early. They were both sensible. I knew they would be safe.

Did I think about that yout in the yellow jacket? Hell no. If he has come up to my mates, starting trouble, why should I worry about him? He was the least of my worries. No one had mentioned Cyrus's injuries. Guns and knives weren't involved. It was only a fist fight. How bad could it be?

You only need to worry if it comes back to you. And it wouldn't. The Turkish boy had only seen me for a moment.

As long as the Feds haven't come for you at seven in the morning and kicked down your door, you're fine. Even if you do get nicked, what they gonna do? We were young. It was all fun. No one had been killed. All we did was give someone who deserved it a good fucking hiding.

I rested my head against the window, trying to take in what had happened. I inhaled deeply and imagined I could still smell Drex. I closed my eyes and smiled. Yeah, that blood had ruined the whole night. We had a whole vibe going on.

I thought about the open bottle of Moet in my bedroom, and decided I'd finish it when I got in. I realised I was hungry. I wondered if any mum had left any chicken and rice for me in the fridge …

The next night, we met in our usual spot by Brixton Police Station. You would see very quickly who was missing, but that evening everyone was present and correct. No one had heard from Cyrus.

"Police come to your house?" asked Badman. "Anyone been nicked?"

Everyone shook their heads.

"Who was them guys anyway?" I asked.

Stimpy knew. Stimpy always knew. "Jags. He's connected to the Enfield crew. Some bruv said he was the cousin of one of the youngers."

Stimpy started laughing. "Did you see the way Sour come with that running fly kick from behind?"

Gadget grinned. "And you, bruv. You did an uppercut to blood's face. Jags and his boys were trying to fight y'all off like ninjas. They had no chance. Crazy night, man."

"So what's the deal for tonight? Who's hungry?" We traipsed across the road to Morley's chicken shop.

Cyrus's name was barely mentioned.

Kitchen Drawer

I sat cross-legged on my bed, watching Drex clown around. He was telling a story about the time Stimpy stole a police car. I didn't believe a word.

"You're lying."

"Man did! Cross my heart and swear to die."

"So, why's he not in jail?"

"Too young, innit?"

I laughed. "Keep telling bare lies, your nose gonna reach Brixton Hill."

He rolled his eyes and shook his head.

The engine roar caught our attention. It sounded much closer than the car park. I leaned over to the window and pulled back the curtains. Outside, on the walkway, we watched a grinning Yusuf pop out from underneath a motorbike helmet.

He was riding a moped. Or rather, he had just ridden a moped up the ramp at the end of the block and had parked it outside the front door. His feet could barely touch the ground when he sat on it.

He looked up and saw our puzzled faces at the window, and waved.

"Man gotta be kidding!" exclaimed Drex, sounding impressed.

Yusuf wiped the sweat off his face, jumped off and bounded into the house and up the stairs.

"Well? What do you think?"

"What do I think?" I said. "I'm thinking how the fuck did you get the money for one of those? That's got to be about £2,000? If you stole that, Yusuf, someone is gonna be marking you name."

"Chill, sis," he said. "I ain't been tiefing no mopeds. That beauty is all mine."

"But how?"

He gave me a frown.

"You tink you're the only one in this house who can make money?"

Yeah, sometimes I was too caught up in my own shit to remember that Yusuf was showing himself to be a bit of an entrepreneur too. Shit, he was becoming a serious little rugrat, man.

I'd been so shocked by Yusuf's new purchase I wasn't paying attention to the angry footsteps thumping up the stairs.

The door flung open. I saw Drex's eyes widen, but before I could look round I felt an agonising whack. It sucked the breath from my lungs and made my vision a blur. It took me some seconds to recognise the screaming voice. It was Althea. She was wielding a baseball bat and she had fury on her face.

I had meant to be babysitting Cheenie but sacked it off when Drex asked if I was free. I'd told her to fuck off over the phone – I had company, that's all she needed to know. She wasn't happy.

Stars flashed before my eyes.

She had hit me with a baseball bat. As far as I'm concerned, that was attempted murder.

Sour

I threw myself at her like a girl possessed. We rolled around the floor, kicking, biting and scratching each other's face.

Drex didn't have a hope in hell of prising us apart.

Yusuf tried to block the doorway.

"Mum!"

Mum cussed something from her bedroom, and put her music up louder. Her door stayed closed.

I wriggled from her grasp and bolted out the door and down the stairs.

"Don't let her get to the drawer," shouted Yusuf, belting down the stairs after me. "She's knife happy."

Why was no one helping me? I was the one getting beaten up here! Just because I was naughty, everyone always assumed the arguments were my fault. Bitch cried wolf once too often, I guess.

Yusuf spread-eagled himself across the kitchen door.

"Whatever you're about to do, Sour, don't do it," he begged. "Ain't worth it."

I heard Althea storm out the house, banging the front door behind her. Her silhouette passed by the frosted glass of the kitchen window, towards the stairwell.

"Lemme past, Yusuf," I growled. I'd never raised my voice to my little brother before. He was wasting precious seconds.

"Alf's just a bully," he pleaded. "Please Sour, don't do it."

I pushed him out of the way, and yanked open the drawer. I ran out of the front door, the kitchen door still swinging behind me, the drawer open with one knife missing.

Drex yelled at me to come back. I paid no attention.

I knew the route she was going to take to catch the Number 2 bus home. I spotted her purple parka on the street and sprinted after her.

She was waiting at the bus stop when she saw me running towards her.

"Fuck off. Didn't you get enough back at the house?"

"I ain't no coward. You did that in a coward's way, Alf, sneaking up behind someone like that. You coulda killed me!"

She said something under her breath and smirked.

"What did you say?"

I was goading her, so I could justify what I was about to do.

"Shut your mouth, you little bitch. Think you're some gangster now? Learning tricks from your new friends?"

I knew if I killed her there would a whole lot of disruption. But Lord have Mercy, I wanted to teach that bitch a lesson.

She didn't expect me to stab her.

I jabbed for her twice, missing the first time, puncturing her thigh the second.

She clutched her leg.

"What the fuck?"

She only needed a few stitches in the end. Drama queen.

Yusuf and Drex were still at home when I walked back into the kitchen, ran the bread knife under the tap, dried it with a towel, and calmly placed it back into the drawer.

Althea never attacked me with a baseball bat again. Nor, for that matter, did anyone else.

Mysteries

The code was that getting caught ain't cool. And yet, something was bothering me. The Feds didn't turn up at my door at seven the morning after the club brawl, or any other morning for that matter. And it niggled. There were things I was getting curious about.

Drex and I were a couple. The Posh and Becks of our postcode. The Peckhams, if you will.

I pretended his constant calling was irritating, but secretly I had grown to like it. The phone rang just as Mum was wandering past in her dressing gown. She passed it over. She didn't need to ask who it was.

"When you coming to see man?"

"Seriously? No hello Sour, how you doing?"

I could hear him sighing. "Hold on, give man a chance! Wha gwarn? You cool?"

"Good, thanks for asking."

He paused. "Gonna come and see me now?"

For someone nicknamed Drex, he didn't exactly have a silver tongue. As it happened, I was planning to go and see him; I just liked hearing him beg.

Drex was one of the luckier ones. His parents weren't around, but he had a nice home in Stockwell Park. His dad treated him like the little prince of the household – he was real spoiled, with his own quarters and a badass stereo system – the kind people had in their front room, he had in the bedroom. The house always smelled of nice cooking.

I'd go over to his and we'd listen to music in his room.

His dad was strict, and when it was dark he'd start to cuss. "Come on, young lady," he'd say, "time for you to be going home."

Until then, we'd laugh and joke and kiss. Nothing more. He never moved too far. I liked that. "My Heart Belongs to U" by Jodeci: that was our song. He'd sit on the bed and mime the words to me, acting the clown.

He looked ridiculous.

"Why you singing to me for?"

"Coz that's how I feel, innit. Don't you like my singing?"

"No!"

"Fine, won't give you your present."

"Oh yeah?"

He retrieved a plastic bag from underneath his bed. It was a Nike Air jacket – top trend, real cute. It suited my hair and make-up and looked good with my Reeboks. I wore the hell out. I wore it with pride.

Yeah, for the calibre of girl I was, he was on my level.

And I loved him. He loved me. When he said he felt safer with me than with the Man Dem, that was the biggest compliment anyone could ever give me. He knew I'd always have his back. I would have moved to anyone for him.

I felt comfortable with him in a way I'd never felt comfortable with anyone.

Yet, no matter how much I loved him, and how many times he asked, I had no interest in taking our relationship to the next level. I'd heard too many conversations outside the police station about the chicks they'd banged.

Sour

I'd been one of the boys too long. I knew what they talked about.

It seemed a girl's power went up in smoke the minute they heard she had slept with someone, even the chicks they really liked. When I think about it, *especially* the chicks they really liked. I wanted more than that. I wasn't going to make the same mistake.

Yeah, I was curious about something, but truth was, I was curious about something *else*. Something everyone was doing and boasting about afterwards. Everyone but me.

This was my other secret: I had never been arrested. Not properly, that is. Sure I'd been picked up, that time with my brother, but as I said, that was more a kiddies' tour of the station.

Things had changed. I'd grown up.

I was one of the Man Dem now. I was meant to be a brand-name. So how could I not know what the inside of a police station was like? I'd see friends, guys from the estate getting arrested, then they'd be back the next day, bragging about their experiences. I listened to their stories, but I knew that, deep down, I had no idea about the reality of what had happened in between.

There was no shortage of boydem stopping and searching all the young black men I knew. What about the cute black girls? That's discrimination, innit.

I wanted to know what the justice process was actually like. I needed to know. For me, the mysteries of the police station and the courtroom were much more interesting than any of the mysteries of sex.

Careful what you wish for.

Right Girl, Wrong Crime

The irony was that, when I did finally get nicked, it was for something I didn't even do. But that's karma, innit? Right girl, wrong crime.

I knocked on Tyrone's door.

"Come on, I'm bored. Let's hit the road."

He started moaning about studying, but I just laughed at him, and shouted through to his mum that I'd have him home soon.

We jumped on the bus and headed to Brixton Market. I found it funny – I couldn't remember the last time I'd been with someone who paid his fare, but Tyrone didn't seem to see the joke. When we got to the market, he was talking – boring stuff about school, his college application – but I wasn't really listening. I was thinking of what kind of naughtiness I could get up to. Let's call it my episode of expressing myself.

"… so yeah, application's got to be in next week. Do you know how much an engineer makes?"

Poor Tyrone. Always talking, talking, talking.

The market was particularly busy.

"See that butcher chopping up meat over there?"

The stallholders were Eastern European. The couple had been round the market for years. Didn't smile much. Probably coz they were always stuck behind this stall. He had his cleaver in hand, chopping fillets on request, while his wife was taking orders and operating the till.

I noticed when a lot of customers came at once she started chopping and bagging things up too, leaving the till unattended behind her.

"Watch."

I walked round the back of the stall, waited for my moment, and when they were both distracted I leaned over and pressed the bottom right button on the till. Ping. The drawer came open. There were so many notes. I didn't even think stallholders could make that sort of money.

I likked a £20 note for me and a £10 note for Tyrone.

By the time the wife spun round, the till was exactly how she left it. The butcher made a swing for me with the cleaver.

I ducked through the tarpaulin, into the street.

When Tyrone came out to join me, his eyes were open like a barn owl.

"I can't believe you just did that. By yourself? Face straight?"

I gave him his tenner. He looked puzzled.

"All that? Just for a tenner? You've already got money."

"I wanted to show you."

"Show me what?"

I beamed. "How easy it is, obviously."

But his expression was not the one I had expected.

"I've got to get home."

We were walking back to the bus stop, in silence, when we stopped to speak to the group of youts on the corner. I knew Styles from Roupell Park. The rest of his crew were cool.

"What you on?"

We chatted for a bit, until I turned round and realised Tyrone had gone. Fuck him. More than that, Styles and his crew seemed a bit wired. He had one eye on me and another on the glass doors of Woolworths.

An excited whisper buzzed round the crew.

"This one."

"Yeah. Let's do it."

"Catch you later, yeah?" said Styles. He was acting strange.

The white woman was carrying a flat-screen TV, fresh from the shop. She was struggling. From the other side of the road, I watched Styles and his crew surround her. Seconds later she had been relieved of her new purchase, in broad daylight. The rest of them were sprinting down the street, before she even got a chance to scream.

Respect. Now, that took heart.

Suddenly, my tiefing from the butchers felt pretty amateur.

I didn't think to run too. After all, this didn't have nothing to do with me. Trouble was, I'd been seen by witnesses, hadn't I? Boydem arrived a few minutes later and scooped us all up.

This time there was no nice day out at the old bill. This time round they treated me like a criminal. I recognised the police officer at the station, and he recognised me.

"You and your friends have had a busy day," he said, not looking up as he filled out his paperwork.

I'm innocent, I wanted to shout. Sort of. It was only thirty quid! That ain't even my crew.

Instead, I just huffed and puffed.

All I had on my mind was ... how am I going to explain this one to Mum? Being thugged on the streets was one thing, having to explain why I've been arrested is another, and getting clapped down in public is just dread.

I knew due to my age I would need an appropriate adult. I knew Mum was on her way. I knew I had to brace myself.

In the interview room all was calm. Mum had a face like thunder. The officers clocked that she wasn't happy. I just gave

Sour

"No comment" answers throughout my interview. It wrapped up quite quickly as I wasn't saying much.

"Oi! Watch the nails," I spat, when they took my prints, putting their dirty ink on my nicely done manicure, pressing each finger into separate boxes on the paper.

"Look left, look right."

They didn't warn me I was going to have a mug shot taken. I started frantically trying to smooth my hair. I wanted it to be a good one.

"Hang on, I ain't ready."

The flash went off anyway.

My hair wasn't even done right.

"Your details will be kept on file …"

He droned on about the youth court and some nonsense about a date for the hearing being sent to me in due course, but I wasn't really listening.

I was just taking in the interior of a building I'd sat outside so many times. I had to admit, I felt disappointed. It was much more boring than I'd imagined. There were lots of leaflets and notice boards at reception. It felt like entering the world's worst leisure centre.

The officer seemed in no mood for banter. In fact, hardly anyone spoke to me at all. They kept me in the cells overnight. No more nice cups of tea, or wishes of good luck. At least, on the plus side, I'd finally been served an injustice by the state. Boydem could finally become the enemy for me too.

"OK, so this is how the game goes," I thought, as we left. "Now I've got a story to tell."

Mum lectured me all the way home. I didn't pay her much attention.

I was getting to grips with the system. And really, if that was it, what was there to be fearful of?

Getting in Deeper

"Sour, come on. Get a move on!"

Stimpy and his friend were shouting up to the window.

I leaned out of the bath and reached across for my mobile, careful not to get it wet with bubbles.

"DOWN IN 15" I texted, and lay back in the tub.

I always made a point of having a nice long bath before going on the road. I might never have seen the inside of a prison cell, but I was pretty sure spa treatments weren't part of the package.

If ever there was a chance I could spend a night inside one, I wanted to be clean. No girl likes that less than fresh feeling. Stimpy would have to wait.

The Youngers were getting younger. There had been some changes since Cyrus's death.

And the Olders? Well, they were getting fewer. Cyrus was dead. No one ever mentioned his name, and had Stimpy not told me I wondered how long I would have waited to find out he died the day after the altercation.

A new generation of rugrats were chasing at our heels, only too eager to take up the empty places.

They kept us on our toes too. They were hungry. They had that fire in the belly. They were willing to learn, adapt easily and willing to take risks. As a result, we were willing to teach them. Stimpy and I had agreed to go out rolling with this new crew. They respected us as elders of the group.

I heard they had been doing well. Grabbing not just hundreds but thousands of pounds at a time.

They were never violent. They didn't want to hurt anyone. Just run into the place and disappear, that was their plan. That's what I liked about it. I wanted to see how these guys moved.

If they've got a quicker, easier way of earning money than I have, I wanted to know about it.

I told Drex I'd see him and the rest of the Man Dem later.

In the meantime, I had business to attend to. Little did I know when I agreed to it that it meant leaving the house at flipping seven in the morning. Stimpy threw a pebble up at the window. "Come on!"

His friend held his finger down on the doorbell.

"OK, OK, I'm coming."

I got out of the bath, wrapped myself in a towel and padded across the hallway, still dripping wet.

Man, these guys were worse than my mum.

Still, every new day brought a new buzz. New Man Dem brought a new vibe. I knew an adrenalin rush was going to be had.

I dressed in my usual gear: hoodie, tracksuit bottoms, vest top, and shoved some jewellery in my pocket.

As soon as I pulled on that tight vest to flatten my boobies, my posture changed, my voice became deeper. I was ready to roll like a boy.

They wanted to go way out, far out of town. Out of London in fact. It was a serious day trip, with train tickets and shit.

There were five of us in total. They seemed like switched-on kids, but the risk of rolling with strangers was niggling at me. This made me uneasy. I made a promise to myself that from now on I'd only take risks with Man Dem I know.

They were laughing and joking, and betting each other who would be first to set the pace. Their lack of an exit plan worried me. They hadn't seemed to have considered beyond getting their hands on the cash.

I started regretting getting out of my bed so early for such an amateur operation. I shared my concerns with Stimpy.

"I've seen the cash these kids make, Sour," he said. "Trust me, they know what they're doing."

Half an hour later we were approaching a small car showroom in a shitty High Street.

The lively one pulled up his scarf and yanked down his baseball cap.

"Ready?" he rasped.

"Go!"

He ran in first. In the flash of a few seconds they had all run in, Stimpy included.

Shall I even bother? For a moment I thought about leaving them to it and carrying on up the road, but I knew that was unforgivable. Even if I didn't know the rest, Stimpy was my blood. I had to have his back.

The tallest one had already jumped over a car towards the back. I yanked the bandanna up over my mouth and raced inside.

There were more customers than I'd expected. I could see immediately the mistake they had made. All three had darted into the office, leaving the least intimidating one of them all – Stimpy – to control the floor.

I knew the police would have been called. They were on their way.

Sour

The staff were compliant. That was one thing. They were listening to orders. No have-a-go heroes here. Not at the moment.

What was taking them so long?

My heart thumped. My pulse throbbed. I puffed out my chest, spread my weight, and stood as wide as I could. The customers were getting restless.

I sensed that one of them, a bookish guy wearing glasses and dad jeans, was thinking about doing something. Stimpy had his back turned to him and didn't see him get to his knees.

I had to make a decision.

"Leave it, let's go!" I shouted.

My hands were trembling.

We needed to get the fuck out. Just get the money and then get out. What was taking them so long behind there?

I could hear the police sirens. I looked at the double doors on to the street, and back again over the counter. Still no sign of the Youngers. Stimpy was looking at the street too. The sirens were getting louder.

One boy appeared. Where was the cash? Where were the others?

"They're locked in," he shouted, sprinting for the door.

Stimpy and I both looked at each other and bolted towards the sunlight.

The boy went one way. We went the other.

I grabbed Stimpy's arm and dragged him into a side street.

"What you doing? We gotta get –"

"Take off your hoodie and link into my arm."

"What? Let go of me!"

We'd pulled the bandannas from our faces and stuffed them into our pockets. I whipped off my hoodie and tied it round my waist, and loosened up my hair.

"Trust me. Just link in, and walk slowly. Like me and you are rolling on a date."

The penny dropped.

Stimpy put an arm around my waist and sauntered down the street as if I was his girl – to the police officers arriving on the scene we were just an innocent young couple in love.

Stimpy went to visit the rugrats in prison not long after. He couldn't wait to tell me what he'd heard.

"They said the police kept on asking them back at the station, 'What did you expect to find in an old car showroom?' They said they had to stop themself from laughing. The police were right. What a waste of time."

I got lucky. I knew my luck was going to run out some time. I didn't know that it would happen that very same day.

Betrayal

Stimpy and I got back to Brixton early that afternoon. He decided he would stay in and lie low, but I couldn't wait to tell Drex, Badman and the rest what had gone down. I walked to Myatt's Field but they weren't there. Tyrone said he hadn't seen them around. I remembered Drex mentioned something about a rendezvous in Angell Town, so I headed that way.

By the time I approached the concrete maze it was getting dark. The vampires would soon be coming out to play.

I swung alone on the swings and considered going back home. That's when I remembered. He said he was going to Daggers' flat. It was nearby. Daggers was one of the few of the Man Dem to have his own place.

He had grown on me. The Man Dem liked him. He was a main character – he fought when he needed to fight, he robbed when he needed to rob. He was someone to be respected.

Everyone used to go and hang out at his a lot.

By now it was around 11-ish. A perfect time to go see who was jamming at his house.

I knocked at the door.

He seemed surprised to see me. A bit sleepy. I thought for a second I might have woken him up.

"Alright," he said, with a sluggish smile. "What's gawn?"

"Where's dem lot?"

"Dunno. Haven't seen them all day. They said they'd come back here when they're finished doing what they're doing. Come on in."

For a young person, his flat was neat. Decently done up too. He had nice equipment: leather chairs, the latest console …

He offered me a drink.

"Coke's fine."

He chucked me a can and opened himself a beer.

We sat down and made ourselves comfy.

"Where you been, Sour? How come man ain't seen you?"

"I've been around."

"Yeah?"

"What you been up to?"

I thought about telling him about our lucky escape but hesitated. I didn't quite trust him enough for that.

"Ah, nutting, man. Roads are quiet, y'nah. I'm keeping my head low."

I asked after his mum and sister, who I knew from Brixton Hill.

He put on some music on the stereo. Snoop Dogg. He noticed me eyeing up his console.

"Wanna game of Street Fighter?"

"If you think you're hard enough."

He laughed, pulled out a second player remote from the box under the TV and threw it on my lap on the settee. "You got brass balls, gyal."

"I'm being Chun-Li."

He went for Zangief, the wrestler.

Sour

We played for the rest of the evening, laughing and shrieking as we pounded each other with spinning piledrivers and lightning kicks.

When I started listening to Snoop Dogg tracks for the fourth time, I realised it was probably time to be leaving. I glanced at the clock. It was after 1.30am.

"I thought you said Man Dem were coming here?"

"Yeah, they knock on my door anytime. They'll be here soon."

"Thanks for the game, but I'm going to go, innit."

"Why?"

He leaned forward, too close for my liking, and put his arm on my shoulder. I leaned back. His breath stank.

"Stay."

As I tried to get up, he pinned me down to the settee. It stank of cat piss. At first I thought he was joking. I thought we were play-fighting.

"No, really, I need to go."

"Go where?"

I squirmed, but he was too strong. He had thick arms, from going to the gym.

He threw me back.

"Get off of me!"

I tried to shout some more, but he applied his body weight to my chest, pinning me down on the settee.

The Streetfighter game flashed on the screen, paused for the next game. The tinny soundtrack went on and on, on a maddening loop.

I felt suffocated. I couldn't breathe. It dawned that no one was coming. Panic rose in my chest. He yanked at my trousers. Why hadn't I kept my knife belt on? I could see my knife lying in my drawer at home, of no use to anyone.

Why didn't I have it with me?

I fought to keep my jeans on, but I was no match for him. Daggers pressed down on top of me. I felt like I was in the sea and drowning. He was wrapped round me, inside me, pulling me under.

Resistance was futile. I couldn't believe what was happening. Let him do what he's going to do, I told myself, as he groaned, and squeezed my breast till the skin drew blood. I stared at Chun Li repeating the same kicks over and over again, waiting for the game to resume, and had never felt so powerless. You can't beat him, Sour. Just let him do what he's got to do.

As he pulled up his trousers, he had the cheek to be normal, asking me how I was getting home, and what I was on tomorrow, and chatting about the Man Dem. I fastened up my buttons with trembling fingers, grunted a few monosyllabic responses, and gathered up my stuff.

I didn't look up. He showed me to the door.

"See you tomorrow," he said. The door fell softly behind me.

The streets were quiet.

That walk home that night was real serious. I felt dirty and cheap. Worse, I felt like an idiot.

How could I have been so stupid? Did I bring it on? Did I say something to give him the wrong idea? I shouldn't have been there at that time. I was the one who went knocking on his door, after all, not the other way round. I replayed the events in my head, over and over again. Did I say something that could have been taken in the wrong way? My mind hurt, trying to process it all.

I tried to shake out the voice that kept saying it must have been my fault.

Sour

I couldn't think straight. Everything was clouded in thoughts and tears.

But I was one of the boys ... No one would dare do that. Maybe I wasn't as invincible as I thought.

I was tormented. I should have done more to protect myself. Yeah, the walk home that night was real serious. The same thoughts rattled round my brain on repeat.

By the time I got home I had made a plan. I knew exactly what I was going to do. I decided not to take action immediately. I would wait.

In the meantime, all I wanted to do was have a bath. I lay in it till the water ran cold. It gave me no pleasure. An ugly thought rose up in my mind: if I killed him, I would be committing a crime against my own. I didn't sleep that night. Quietly, with my knife under my pillow, I cried for the first time since I was a child.

For the next few days I didn't go out. I didn't answer the phone. I didn't talk to no one.

"Salwa!" Mum yelled. "That bloodclart's on de phone again. Speak to him, or tell him to stop disturbing dis house."

"What's going on?"

Drex sounded annoyed. There was no warmth or mischief in his voice.

"What you talking about?"

"Man Dem saying you're cheating on me. S'true? Say you sleeping around?"

"You for real?"

If only he knew. I didn't have the energy to go into it.

Turned out Daggers was bragging about banging the Queen Bee. Of course he was. Word had got around.

"Man Dem's round at his house now. Come round. Man wants to know what went on, innit."

The prospect of being in that house again made me feel sick. But at the same time, if everybody was there, I could feel safe. If I didn't go, there would be no one to defend me. He would poison their minds against me and say what he liked. They'd think I was a sket like all the rest.

But there was another advantage of paying that flat a visit. It would give me another look at the property as well. Certain details could come in handy. Were there other exit routes? Where did he keep his weaponry? Those things needed to be accounted for, before I put my plan into action. I pulled on jeans and a hoodie, and whipped on my belt.

The door opened before I could knock. Inside, around a dozen of the Man Dem were waiting for me.

Drex was sitting on the very same settee. He had pain in his eyes. I resisted the temptation to look for Daggers' guilty face. I wasn't ready to look him in the eye. Not yet.

I was surprised to see so many guys in that small room. All the brothers were coming together to find out what was going on.

Badman was the first to speak.

"Daggers been telling some stories, innit. Why was you coming to man's house late at night?"

"Said you came knocking near midnight."

"See, we're a bit confused. Thought you was with Drex? You're his ting! Not inna da sket behaviour, blood! Tryna take man for ediot? Allow dat man!"

So this was gang justice. They were asking me to wage war against my own crew. This could break up a brotherhood. So be it. I told them the truth.

Once I'd finished, the room went silent. Stimpy, Gadget, Badman and Drex said not a word.

"She's a bitch," protested Daggers. "Man can't trust her."

I looked around at this band of brothers, the boys I was prepared to put my life on the line for, and wished for one of them, just one of them, to speak up for me. What about all those promises of having each other's back? What about loyalty and standing strong?

"Anyone gonna stand up for me? Anyone gonna *do* anything?"

Everywhere I looked, I was met with a blank face.

Stimpy caught my eye, then looked away, embarrassed. The rest shuffled their feet and said nutting.

Gadget moved to the sofa, and took up the remote. Badman moved to the fridge.

"Well?" I asked the room. "Is that it?"

The room went completely quiet. Silent.

It was a guy I barely recognised who spoke up. He was one of Daggers' friends.

"Well, man. Is it true?"

Daggers laughed in his face. "Fuck that shit. She's lying, man, I'm telling you. Gyal comes over, says she wants it. Any man would bang dat, innit?"

He laughed again, more nervously this time.

"I know you, man. I know when you're lying."

The room remained silent. I was so angry I could barely speak.

"Well, unless you want anything else," I declared, trying to keep my cool, "I've got things to do."

With that, I left, but not before remembering to pay attention to the kind of locks Daggers had on his front door. I would be returning – next time there would be no witnesses.

Drex followed me outside. He caught me by the wrist.

"How could you do that?" I cried.

"Do what?"

"Not have my back?"

He looked upset. He had trusted Daggers, I knew that. I knew he felt betrayed too.

"What do you want man to do?"

That was the moment I realised. I shouldn't *have* to tell him what to do. He should have just done it.

He was a boyfriend, a colleague, a teammate. If anyone was going to hold my corner, it should have been him.

Instead of defending me, he chose to do nothing.

"Leave it," I said, shrugging him off. "Fuck people, allow it, I'll deal with it myself. If something is going to be done to him, it's going to be done by me. I'm going home."

But Daggers got lucky. Turned out the Feds had already paid a visit. He was safely in prison and wasn't expected out for a long time. Jail saved that coward. And he doesn't even know it.

A lot of things changed after that. Respect was meant to be what it was all about. Where was my respect? I had been served an injustice, and I didn't see no one stepping in to respect me.

These were the boys I'd run into a violent, tooled-up scrum to defend. I wasn't asking them to kill or even maim him. A good beating would have done. Hell, a word in my favour woulda been something.

Maybe we weren't so cool after all. How could I ever defend them again?

Some time later, I would hear another horror story involving two younger girls, who were taking the bus not far from Daggers' flat. Some of the younger Youngers – boys who I'd seen growing up around the estates and recognised as some of the rugrats – pressganged them off the bus and into the piss-stinking stairwells of Angell Town.

Sour

There must have been ten, twelve of them. The schoolgirls were a few years younger than me.

One girl was locked in a derelict basement flat with nothing but a stained mattress and excrement smeared across the floor. The other was kept at knifepoint in the stairwell outside. There, the cheeky lads I had known, the kids who had grown up aspiring to be like the Man Dem, lined up and took it in turns to rape them. The High Court judge called it one of the worst cases he'd ever seen.

I couldn't believe it. Word on road was that the youts said they were innocent. I didn't think they were capable. But then again, you can't vouch for no one again. I learned that the hard way!

I tried to imagine what those girls went through, and what those boys were thinking when the ringleaders urged them on. I imagined the weaker ones following the strong ones, all the good inside them wilting when urged on by the bad.

I'd had a taste of what it was like to feel powerless. I realised that pussy ain't got no face. Whether you're a hot gyal, ugly gyal, posh gyal or hood rat – once a yout has that intention for you, there's not really much you can do.

I realised if it could happen to a brand-name like me, then it can easily happen to anyone.

Devils roamed round Brix City. It was getting harder to ignore that little voice, growing louder and louder inside my head, telling me that I roamed with them.

There was no turning back.

I became a loner, a female soldier. It had been a mistake to go to his house that night. I knew that now. It taught me one important lesson: no matter how streetwise you think you are, no matter how many knives you have or things you have done, you'll always be powerless when you're horizontal.

The Art of Stabbing

People don't keep still. They don't tell you that. They wriggle and squirm. There are occasions when you really want to get someone but it's not happening until you hold them down.

Yeah, trust me, shanking takes skill. Sometimes, all it takes is quick reflexes. Sometimes, it takes strength. But it always takes heart. Above all, you gotta be quick.

What's it like, stabbing someone? It's like this.

There are times you don't even know it's happened till you get home and see the blood on your blade. But there are other times that stay with you, times that you replay over and over again in your head.

You can feel yourself breaking the skin. That's the moment. That's the moment that matters. Until then, it's just like prodding a piece of meat. When you poke it you can't feel anything back. It takes some force to get beyond that – you'd be surprised. That's the hardest part. After that, it's up to you. The possibilities are as long as your blade. What I do know for sure is that knives always slide out much easier than they slide in.

They slide out quick, man. That's it. A split second, and it's all over.

Thick, soft, surprising. That's what it's like when metal meets meat. Never wet. Blood comes later. And for the person holding it?

There was no mistaking that feeling. It was like sending a Bat signal straight up to the sky. I was sending a message. It said: I'm letting you know I have control. I have control over you. *This* shows what kind of character I am. I have the power to do something.

Instilling that fear was what I thrived on. It made me feel ten feet tall, a force to be reckoned with. It screamed my name loud without saying a word. The right jab at the right moment could beam my brand-name across Brixton.

There's a saying: "Duppy know who fe frighten when night dark, dogs know who fe bite." Ghosts know where to go haunting, dogs know who to bite. The strong will prey on the weak, but a ghost's real strength is recognising the ones who will spook the most. I was that kind of ghost.

Outgoing fire attracts incoming fire, and it was the same in gangland. Ain't clever to go round stabbing just anyone. If you've got your own repertoire going on, and another blood has his repertoire going on over there, you stick to your own side. *Duppy know who fe frighten.*

But if a no-name starts making trouble, that's when you have to act. And that's what I did.

The no-name was known to certain men but didn't belong to no one. Who his connections were, I don't know. All I'd been told was that he was spreading rumours, and talking about all the things he'd do to me next time he saw me, how I'd better sleep with one eye open. All that shit.

"She thinks she's bad," he'd bragged. "When I see her I'm going to move to her."

People think because you're on the road and you're wayward, there's no code. They're wrong.

When someone sends you a death threat, see, you're in a

situation. You're going to do one of two things. You're going to hide or you're going to confront the problem. I ain't never been a hider. Daggers knew it, the Man Dem knew it and now this skinny little runt knew it too.

I always had threats coming from somewhere. Often, it was rude girls relaying a message from one of their bloods, Chinese whispers that were never quite right when you finally caught up with the source.

"Never heard of him," said Tyrone, shaking his head, when I asked him who this joker was. No one else seemed to know either.

But he certainly seemed to have heard of me. I wondered what he'd heard, and whether it had come from Daggers. I figured he wanted to make a name for himself taking on one of the Man Dem and reckoned the girl would be the easiest target. Fool.

We arranged to meet.

I'd hesitated over the kitchen drawer, wondering which knife to take. I went for an old, medium-sized one that Mum used to pierce packets before putting them in the microwave – no serrated edges, nothing big, nothing flash. No point taking one of my designer ones. I was only going to have to throw it away later. I might as well throw away one of hers. I left my favourite blade in my bedroom drawer and squeezed the kitchen knife into the rabbit foot holder. My lucky charm came with me no matter what.

It nearly fit. Near enough. I smoothed down my hoodie, checking my clothes were baggy enough so that it couldn't be seen. I leaned closer into the mirror. One of my eyes had started to water, due to it being so cold. I laughed to myself. I looked like I was being attacked by a spider. I dapped my little finger on my tongue, and wiped away straying tears to neaten up my eyeliner. Better.

Nobody knew what I was planning. I liked that. The Man Dem didn't need to know shit. All that mattered was they heard about it later. I knew I wasn't trying to kill. No need to be so dramatic. I just needed to teach this fucking idiot a lesson.

We'd arranged to meet outside the barber shop around 8pm. I surveyed the shop from across the street. A pack of guys passed by, fists punched deep in their pockets, striding lazily down the road. Nah, it couldn't be one of them. Too old, too relaxed. Besides, we'd arranged to meet alone. An Asian boy crossed the road, but he seemed to be waiting for someone else. Yeah, it wasn't him. He stared straight past me.

As a few more minutes ticked by, I wondered if I'd missed him. At that moment, I saw a skinny frame, skulking up the street with that same swaggering limp of all the bloods his age. There was no mistaking this was my date for the night. He looked a little older than me, no more than 17, and stood a good few inches taller. His expression was cast in a permanent frown.

I stubbed out my cigarette. I'd been smoking a lot more of late – always menthol, always slim – and crossed the road, making a beeline straight for his direction.

Postcode celebrities were one thing. But beyond the brand-names, there were always the ran-on's, the ones whose names would float about for a while if they were lucky, but soon disappeared. They were the ones who wanted to make their mark. When they missed their chance, they would fade out very quickly.

I called them hurry-come-ups. From his unconvincing

swagger and the uncertain flicker around his eyes, I could tell this boy was one of them. *Duppy know who fe frighten.*

I walked up behind him.

"Come with me, I want to talk to you about something."

If he was startled, he tried not to show it. He said nothing and followed me round the corner.

It was on.

"What's your problem?"

I wanted to know.

"Don't have no problem. Only Man Dem been talking, innit?"

"Oh yeah? Saying what?"

"Saying you banged your way to being a brand-name."

"Is that so?"

As I thought. Daggers.

"Why do you think it's OK to be sending messages my way? Did you not think I would find you? Do you not think I'd come and fuck you up?"

He bragged some more, hurling insults, but I wasn't listening no more. I didn't care what he had to say. There was no good reason behind his threats. That's what got me angry.

He was just playing at being the big boy. My hand was warm around the knife handle. I felt a twinge of excitement. That familiar thrill began to pulse through my body. I waited for my moment.

"I ain't taking no threats from no idiot chick, you're not bad blood, you're not on dis ting," he laughed. He took a step forward; all I saw was a black bandanna wrapped around his wrist with a small blade pointing out. He punched me in the face, then tried to stab me.

I moved to him quick and plunged the blade into his leg. I felt the skin tear and muscle pucker before the knife slid free.

Sour

"Oh yeah? *Now* you've got something to do me for."

He fell back, disbelief in his eyes. Run? Darling, I walked off, face straight. No sweat off my back. I know it sounds warped but I had to stab him for his threat to be valid. Remove the knives and what were we left with?

It would have all just been a waste of time. Without the blades, it was just playground insults.

It was the knowledge that knives were involved, that one of us was going to have to attack, that made it bigger. It made us serious. It made us adult.

As for remorse, all I felt was injustice. I had been picked upon for no reason, by someone I didn't even know. That wasn't fair. He had caused this. Anyways, I wasn't aiming to kill. That's why I stabbed him in the leg. Femoral artery wasn't exactly in my vocabulary.

I crossed back over the road, leaving him to stagger back the way he came, with a real limp this time. I looked back to watch him.

He had stopped by a bench, holding himself up with one hand, and pressing the other down hard on his thigh. He was no longer paying attention to me. When I got on the bus and looked back down the street, the bench was empty. I felt satisfied.

I leaned my face against the bus window, and enjoyed the feeling of the cold drips of condensation against my skin. The streets of London blurred below me, with parade after parade of grubby shops, with their Fake Fried Chickens, betting shops, all-night grocers and Turkish off-licences, each one almost indistinguishable from the next.

I thought about his reaction. What had he been so shocked for? What was he expecting? Knives never quite had the same shock for me. Suppose that's what happens when you've got a mum that brandishes a meat cleaver whenever she imagines the boydem are coming to lift her. You get used to being on edge, or at least the risk of encountering one.

I never heard anything from that little fucker again. No news meant good news. First, it meant I needn't be worrying about any more threats. And, second, you only hear about the people who die.

I slept soundly that night. For the next few days, I heard from no one.

Playing Hardball

"Mrs Raynor. Could you please open up? It's the police."

It was late in the afternoon.

I pressed my back against my bedroom door. My chest was still heaving from the sprint up the street. I felt faint. As I said, I ain't never been no athlete.

"Who's dere? What's all dis noise?"

I could hear my mum on the warpath.

"Get off my doorstep, we ain't done nutting to no one. Yuh tink me barn yesiday?"

I hurriedly whipped off my belt and shoved the stained knife under some dirty clothes. It wasn't exactly the hiding place of a criminal mastermind but it was all I got. My heart drummed hard against my chest.

Mum was going down the stairs. I peeked through the door and saw a flash of her dressing gown. If she'd put on her dressing gown, it meant she was going to open the front door.

I opened my door quietly, slowly, to avoid it creaking. My niece was home, sitting on the bed, alone, watching cartoons.

"Sowa!" she called, throwing her arms up for a cuddle.

I shook my head gently. "Not now, Cheenie," and pressed my fingers to my lips.

Then I slipped into the airing cupboard.

I slid the door closed and waited for Mum to open the door. I couldn't hear exactly what the officers were saying but I had a good idea.

I tried to count the footsteps as they came up the stairs – two, maybe three of them? No, two.

Mum was still shouting.

"Dis is a disgrace. She not here, I'm telling you. Not seen her since she went out dis morning."

There was a huge bang. They'd broken down the doors. Why did they always do that? It's very bad manners.

They'd just made life very hard for themselves. Mum was going to go apeshit now.

I tried to quieten my breathing, but the more I tried, the louder it became. The feet stopped on the landing.

It was a woman's voice.

"What are you saying, sweetheart?"

No, Cheenie. No.

The airing cupboard door slid open. Cheenie was pointing straight at me, with chocolate-covered fingers. I had been given up by a four-year-old, sucking her thumb, twirling a blanket.

In hindsight, I probably shouldn't have stabbed him in front of everyone. But I was having a bad day.

"Yuh remind me of your puppa. You ah get pun me nerves. Cyant wait till yuh get up and move outta me house. Come outta me house."

"Bloodclart! Don't come back!" she shouted after me as I'd stormed into the street.

Boiling with anger, I pushed past the neighbours coming up the stairs – "fucking rude bitch", they shouted after me – and headed for Brixton Hill. It was a Saturday. Dick Shits was shut and Roupell Park was quiet.

Sour

Then I remembered about the dance classes. It was some summer school project run by the council. There was a dance studio where they taught street dance and hip hop and all sorts of shit. I used to like going there, dancing with the groups, before I became serious. I stormed up the street, rage thrashing around inside me. Yes, I'd go burn up some energy there.

As I pounded the pavement, the same questions bubbled to the surface. I hated that family who lived below us, the ones I'd pushed past. They seemed normal, with their normal mum and normal dad and normal pram. Why couldn't I have a mum like that? And a normal dad?

Why was I the one who had to put up with all this shit?

I felt the threat of tears. I would not let myself cry in the streets. That's what girls like Keziah and Stace did when they got dumped or wanted sympathy. I didn't need sympathy from no one. What I needed was a new life. I asked Allah, God, Jah Rastafari, whoever, why things weren't different. As usual, I got no answer.

The dance studio was open. I could see youts hanging by the revolving doors. They had gym bags slung over their shoulders and were laughing and joking. They must have just finished the earlier class. There was no one I recognised.

I walked into reception. It smelled of swimming pools, and had a sticky floor that made your trainers squeak. I heard the music booming from a distant hall, and could see the class had started beyond the glass door.

The woman behind the counter was calling me, but I ignored her and pushed on towards the turnstile barriers. The metal arm jarred against my stomach.

"– I said, you need a ticket."

"Well, gimme a ticket then. For that class."

"It's already half-way through."

"S'fine. I'm warmed up already."

She glowered at me.

"It's full."

I could see her looking at my earrings and beehive. I realised I hadn't brought any of my dancing stuff.

"I see space right there. Look."

"I. Said. It's. Full."

The hard-assed bitch was in no mood to argue.

Forget it, I'd go elsewhere.

I powered through the corridor towards the social room. Maybe I'd see some of the Man Dem there.

A group of guys were standing in the corridor, by the vending machine, blocking my way.

"Move."

Most were smart and shuffled out of the way. But the loud one. Let's just say I didn't like his tone. He squared up to me. Mistake.

"I didn't hear you say 'excuse me'."

The truth was, if it hadn't been him it would have been someone else.

One of his friends tried to grab me, but I fought him off. Another sprinted down the corridor, to grass me up to that battleaxe on reception. The loud boy wasn't so loud now. He was no longer squaring up. The smirk had been wiped off his face.

He was crouched down at the side of the vending machine, staring at the blood seeping from above his knee.

I belted down the hallway and spun out of the revolving doors. I could barely remember the walk home. Why hadn't I binned the knife? Next thing I knew, I was inside my bedroom, chest thumping, shoulders slumped against the door, wondering where the hell to put the bloodied blade.

The two policewomen bundled me into the car.

OK, I thought.

"Let's go to the station and get on with it."

"I suggest you admit it," said the policewoman once we arrived.

"I hope you know this is serious."

They were treating me like I'd killed someone! They labelled up my clothing, bagging up my stuff into evidence bags with numbers on them. Sample one, sample two …

What's wrong with these people? I wondered. It ain't that serious.

I toyed with telling them the trainers belonged to my brother, that if they did checks they'd find it was someone else's blood, and that if they must know the knife I actually used was still upstairs, but thought better of it. No point now, innit.

The holding cells were no place for a woman. The toilet had no bin for sanitary products. There was no place to put the "bloodclart" that inspired the insults. You couldn't even wash your hands.

Still, I know it sounds warped, but I liked cell time. Some bloods hated it. But I didn't feel bored or suffocated. Outside, I felt trapped – by Mum's illness, by sleazy stepdads, by pressure to stay Sour. But here in the cells, I felt free. It was timeout from the rest of my life.

When the cell door closed, I felt oddly relieved. Finally, I had a space that was mine. I think they deliberately stick you in there to freak you out. That made me laugh – boydem had no idea I actually liked this! It wasn't home. It wasn't the same claustrophobic place where Mum slapped me down and I tried to slap her back.

I made myself as comfortable as I could and took the opportunity to catch up on some sleep.

I was rudely awoken by the duty officer and led into the interview room.

I knew the drill. I would need an appropriate adult.

I really couldn't be bothered with getting done over in the station in front of Feds by my mum.

Don't get it twisted, Mum wasn't afraid of getting physical with me, face straight. I wasn't scared of her.

But my day had been bad enough. I was in no mood to have her in the corner, creating a scene. Besides, let's face it, far as adults went, my mum had never been appropriate. So I asked the duty solicitor to stand in instead. She agreed.

I was still sleepy when the senior policewoman came in and introduced herself. She had short, mousy grey hair and her face was red and ruddy. The glare of the artificial lights was unkind to the spider veins that cobwebbed her cheeks.

She was bloody meticulous, though. You could see she was in charge. Pretty much like every woman cop you've seen on TV. Tough, humourless. Her tone was serious. Very Scott and Bailey. Insisted on a lot of eye contact.

This woman was a grumpy old bitch, no doubt about it, but she impressed me. She was treating me like an adult. But if she wanted to scare or intimidate me, it wasn't working.

"You're looking at GBH section 18, wounding with intent … minimum seven years."

I shrugged.

"Yeah, so what? I did it."

I wasn't getting any thrills from being here this time. There was no trauma, no fear. I just felt like … an inconvenience.

If she wanted remorse, she wasn't going to get it.

I'd already put my hands up straight away. What else did she want from me?

Had I tried playing hardball, I could tell she would have ripped chunks out of me. She was the type who wouldn't think twice about keeping you up until 3am, asking the same questions over and over again. Yeah, she looked that type. This one goes the extra mile.

She didn't like me. That was fine. Why should she?

As she droned on, I wondered who'd identified me. No one had dared mentioned my name before – they were too scared. Not this time, and that niggled.

Fair enough, the gold beehive was pretty distinctive. I was never going to be hiding long. Once that description got to police, it was always going to be difficult, but I didn't alter my hair for no one.

I realised my mistake. I'd crossed the barrier, innit. People inside gangs don't call the Feds when they get hurt. I'd hurt someone outside the circle. Fool.

She looked down at her notes. "I see you're soon to be 16. You can say goodbye to the Youth Courts. Inner London Crown Court, more than likely. I hope you know the Crown Court has great sentencing powers."

"Whatever."

Did she think I was some sort of idiot?

Still, her words struck a nerve though I tried not to show it. Age had always been our friend. That had been the mantra among the Man Dem. If you're not 16, they can't put you in prison. Everyone knew that. If you're younger than 16, you're alright. It was the golden rule that kept everything innocent.

No one ever talked about what happened after.

A panicked thought flashed across my mind. I thought about my mum. How would she cope if I went down? Who would look after her?

"… you were lucky he wasn't more seriously injured."

Bail or no bail, what difference did it make? I stepped back out into daylight.

I took my time walking back to Roupell Park. I needed quiet. I needed calm. I knew it wouldn't be waiting for me back home.

Speaking to no one, I stepped through the broken door frame, went up the stairs and collapsed on my bed.

When I woke, I thought I was still dreaming. I heard a voice I recognised in the other room. I rolled over. The door had creaked open. The figure of a man was standing in the doorway. His face was still silhouetted as my eyes adjusted to the dark.

"Hello, Salwa."

He was standing over me now. In shock, I could barely breathe. I leapt to the edge of the bed.

"What the fuck? Get the fuck out of my room or I swear to god, man, I'll hurt you."

It was Derek.

He was taken aback. He left behind a little girl. What he failed to understand was that I was a big fucking person now.

He didn't move. He'd put on weight, though he was still wearing a T-shirt I recognised. It was stained yellow at the armpits. He stood there and smiled.

Which part of fuck off did he not understand?

"I said … get the fuck out of my room or I'll kill you."

I reached for my knife, and let him see it glint.

"If my bedroom door is shut, why do you think you can walk in? Think you can stand over me, like a fucking pervert?"

Sour

I was proper angry.

"Calm down," he laughed, nervously. "Just saying hello."

He stepped closer.

"Face straight, if you take one more step towards me you're gonna get hurt, and I'm packing a bag right now to stay on Her Majesty Service."

Mum ran in, waving a chicken leg.

"What's wrong wit choo? Being disrecpectful to the big man? Ain't seen him for years. He's fixing the door, innit. Have some manners."

As soon as I heard her stick up for him, I wanted to bad her up too. I switched on her.

My mum saw Sour for the first time. All that fear as a kid, all the nights I went to bed locking my door, sleeping with a knife under my pillow, suddenly rose back up to the surface.

"Take your friend out my space. Don't make me turn over this whole yard."

"Ah who da bloodclart yuh ah chat to? Don't make mi haffi strike yuh."

Derek stood there, with his stupid, vacant face. I noticed the greasy hair poking from the collar of the T-shirt, stretched too tight over his man boobs.

"Leave her, Ruqqayah. Girl's probably drunk or on drugs …"

Had Mum not walked in, I would have easily got up and stabbed him in the neck or the heart right there and then. No arms or legs this time. No messing.

"Althea! You sister gaarn mad, lost her mind. Come down and speak to her. She got my illness!"

Derek took Mum's arm and pulled her back to the kitchen.

Althea had come to pick up Cheenie. We'd been getting on better, me and her. She walked in.

"What's wrong?"

"Something I've never told you, but I'm telling you now coz I'm old enough and angry enough."

"What?" She looked panicked. "Tell me."

"See that fucker?"

She didn't need clarification. She rolled her eyes.

"Yeah?"

"He used to try to move to me. I don't care if you don't believe me. He used to –"

I stopped in my tracks. Althea was nodding.

"I believe you."

I was surprised.

"You do?"

"He used to try it with me too."

I didn't feel reassured. All I felt was pure rage. I pushed myself off the bed, towards the door.

"I'm going to kill him."

Althea pulled me down again.

"No, no, that's not the way to do it. Think about it."

She was right. I sat back down, and pulled my knees to my chest, while I was thinking of the next move.

"I know about Suzanne too."

Now it was Althea's turn to look startled.

"I heard her telling you one night."

She said nothing.

"You know," I said, "I used to be scared to tell Mum. Thought she'd kill him, no questions asked, then we'd have no mum, but it's different now. She needs to know."

"Nah, I'm not sure. You know what she's been like recently."

Her cowardice suddenly made me angry.

"Allow being dumb! What about Cheenie? You want that man in the same house as your daughter? What if he tries the same with her?"

Sour

We both looked out the door, towards the sounds of him and Mum in the kitchen.

"Is he with her now?"

Althea stood up, anxiously.

She knew I was right.

"Let's go and tell her. Now. As soon as he's gone."

"OK."

Althea went to check on Cheenie, who was watching cartoons in Yusuf's room. By the time she emerged, Derek had left.

"Come on," I said. "We shoulda done this a long time ago."

Mum was sitting on the sofa in her dressing gown, sucking on a menthol Superking. Her hand was trembling. I turned down the stereo and told her to sit down.

"Ain't seen the man in years," she mumbled. "Allah brought man back to me and you freak him out, like a little banshee."

After a while, her tone softened. We waited for her to calm down.

She shouted through to Althea in the kitchen.

"Babes, gonna fetch me some peanut punch from the fridge?"

Althea handed her the drink and she stubbed out the cigarette, mumbling about a gift from Allah.

"Mum, we got something to tell you."

"I'm sorry," she said. "I know you ain't done nuttin wrong, I know. I told boydem I'm gonna sue them for that door."

"No, no, Mum, it's got nothing to do with that."

She looked confused.

"What's it to do wit?"

"Derek can't come back here."

Althea nodded.

"Man's a good man. I don't want no disrespecting, hear? He's a good man."

"No, Mum, you're not understanding."

I was getting impatient.

"… he used to try and move to me when we was younger." I looked at Althea. "Both of us. Man's a pervert. We can't let him near Cheenie."

Mum's face dropped. "What you talking bout?"

She started shaking her head, and lit up another Superking. "Why didn't you tell me?"

"Was worried how you'd take it, innit."

She sucked on her cigarette, still shaking, then pressed the stub into the ashtray.

"Yuh want chicken? Me ago make some soup. Yuh want some soup?"

"Do you hear me? He can't come back here again, understand? Derek IS NOT ALLOWED IN THIS HOUSE. OK?"

She looked confused, frightened almost, wrapping her headscarf securely. She straightened up her gown and applied Vaseline to her lips.

"Not allowed in," she repeated, reaching for her prayer beads. "He's not coming back …"

That night she fell fast asleep on the sofa. Her scarf had loosened and had fallen open and she was shivering in nothing but a Muslim gown.

As I stood over her, ready to help her to bed, I paused. I glanced at the young woman in the black and white picture on top of the TV. The smooth beehive was gone, so too had the smooth, straight line of her nose, and that bright, eager smile. But her skin was still fresh. The girls in our family, we all had good skin. Yeah, my mum had had it tough, you know, but she could still look beautiful.

I shook her shoulder gently, and levered her up off the sofa by the elbow, as she muttered and grunted to herself, half asleep. I slipped her feet into her sheepskin slippers and guided her up the stairs.

"You're a good girl," she muttered, as I lowered her into bed. "You know I love you, don't you?"

She stroked my hair.

"My family is all I care about. I love you all …"

I wanted to reply. I wanted to say lots of things, but the words got stuck. Within minutes she was fast asleep. I tucked the covers round her shoulders, switched off the light and softly closed the door behind me.

A few weeks later, after I finished breakfast, I saw Derek laid back on the sofa in the lounge drinking a cup of tea.

From that day on, I swore to myself I ain't got no mum no more.

Yout Club

Considering the crazy life that I had, you had to laugh that my first court hearing would be for the one crime I didn't actually commit. But that's karma, innit?

That afternoon at Balham Youth Court was like a social occasion. I'd got lucky – Crown Court could wait another day. This was like a community centre for kids. I clocked a few familiar faces milling around, waiting for their cases to be called. There were some Junction Boys, and a few of the Youngers. The benches were crammed with youts, laughing and joking. I cast my eye across the crowd, looking for the Man Dem.

Stimpy saw me before I saw him. I was surprised how happy I was to see him. Daggers seemed a long time ago.

"What's gwarning, girl? Man ain't seen you around."

"Been busy, innit."

A few months had passed since the Daggers incident. I'd been on the road, doing my ting. They'd been doing theirs – some, it turned out, with considerably less success. I hadn't heard from Drex, and he hadn't heard from me. Which was fine by me.

"Badman's gone down. Boydem hauled man outta his bed in a dawn raid. Man got bare years."

"What did he do?"

"Man ain't heard yet. They lifted Drex too."

He saw me flinch.

"Sorry, Sour. I thought all the Man Dem knew …"

"Course I knew," I snapped.

"His chick's not taking it good."

This time I made no effort to conceal my shock.

"What chick?"

"The one he's been dating. She's pregnant too. Gonna pop soon. Real shame."

"Stop talking rubbish, man."

Stimpy liked his gossip, and I knew not to trust a word of it. We'd only broken up a few months ago. I laughed it off.

"It's true. Man seen her belly!"

I knew Stimpy when he was joking. This didn't feel like one of those times.

"You serious?"

"For real."

I bit my lip and tried to calm my thoughts. So much for feeling safe with me. You really can't trust no one in this world. So be it.

"'S alright. It's cool. So who is she?"

I was curious.

He frowned. "What you asking me for? You're the one who threatened her … She said you were going to kick the kid outta her."

Now this kind of fake drama angered me. Idiots trying to bring my name down was one thing; Stimpy believing it was another.

"Stimpy, man, gimme a bit of credit."

He looked embarrassed.

"When Man Dem said you were rolling on your own …" he mumbled.

"Forget it."

The court was busy. The clerks hurried back and forth, looking like harassed witches in their little black cloaks, carrying files and ducking in and out of courtrooms as the tannoy called out a roll call of cases.

I looked across the public waiting area, and noticed a guy looking over to us. He seemed pretty confident, leaning back, one foot up on the wall, arms folded low across his front.

"Who's that character?"

"Cruz. He's from Junction."

I'd never heard the name. There had been no trouble between Junction Boys and 28s for some time – we were cool with each other – but it meant I hadn't had much to do with their serious characters.

Beside him was this larger-than-life character who reminded me of Jaws from that James Bond. Quite intimidating to say the least. If you was a guy on the road, let's just say, you would have been intimidated. He smiled a big, stupid smile. His front teeth were missing.

"That's Gumbo," chirruped Stimpy. "Come on. Let's say hello."

Now, as I've explained, Man Dem don't just do that with anyone.

If he got that level of respect from Stimpy, he was probably worth knowing.

I went over with him.

Cruz knocked knuckles with Stimpy and said hello.

"Alright? What you doing with this blood, girl?"

Stimpy introduced us.

"Sour? What kind of name is that?"

"She's proper, blood. Serious chick."

He shared a mischievous grin with Gumbo.

"How can she be serious? She looks cute."

"I am standing here, you know. You can speak to me straight."

He whistled loudly.

"That right? Then, furthermore, why you even here?"

"Got my own case going on, innit."

"Oh yeah? What you in for?"

"Two counts of robbery."

"Two?" Gumbo burst out laughing and clapped his hands. "No way! I wouldn't let no girl rob me."

He clearly thought he was a bit of a joker.

"On a serious note," I said, turning to the brick shithouse, "how the fuck you so big, man? You're massive."

Cruz chipped in: "Big friendly giant, innit." I couldn't help smiling.

"Anyway, what you in for?"

"I'm here for my bredren, innit." He gestured to the BFG, who didn't look the least little bit worried he was the one in the docks.

"So you're a bit of a bad girl?"

I shook my head.

"Got it wrong, man. I'm in here for something I didn't even do."

"That's how it goes, eh?"

I laughed. I liked this guy.

"Seems so."

At that moment my name was called on the tannoy. My solicitor, an awkward Bangladeshi guy who didn't look much older than the rest of us, picked up his briefcase and beckoned me over.

"That's me."

"Thought you said your name was Sour?" asked Cruz.

"Gyal gotta have a few."

"Go and do what you're doing, gyal," he said. "When you come out, we'll finish chatting."

Yeah, I thought. I'd like that.

The courtroom was new to me.

The clerk showed us to our seats. Sitting straight ahead of us, higher up than everyone else, was the judge. Everyone was in suits. What is it with 9–5s, man? Why ain't none of them got no style?

I'd worn my favourite trainers and my normal clothes. No one told me you had to dress smart.

I sat down, behind the wooden panel. My co-defendant was none other than Styles, one of the crew who'd been on the road that day. He was good value, Styles, a bit of a joker. I was glad he was there to keep me entertained. I didn't blame him for me being here. That was boydem's fault, not his.

The charge sheet was read out.

I had been charged with two counts of robbery.

The first alleged that that Saturday morning, just before I met Tyrone to go to the market, I was among the teenagers who surrounded a young brother and sister and robbed them of their cash, trainers and jewellery, just a few minutes' walk from Roupell Park.

The second charge alleged that, later on that afternoon, I was part of the same group who went on to relieve a young woman of her newly purchased television outside Brixton Market.

While I happened to be merely a witness, in the wrong place at the wrong time for the second charge, it just so happened that I was present at the first robbery. The kids lived on the same estate. They were a few years younger – maybe 12, 13.

I knew them and they knew me. That morning there were pure youts on the road, all bored, all looking for entertainment. They weren't my usual crowd, but they were eager and willing, and what else was I gonna do? Stay at home?

It was a big entourage that day. And yes, I'm not gonna lie, that afternoon those kids got swarmed like a big bunch of bees, relieved of their cash and the gold chains around their necks, not to mention the chicken and chips they'd been sent to buy from the shop.

Now, I'm not saying I wasn't aware they was getting robbed. All I'm saying is that they wasn't my hands doing the robbing.

Bloody hell, all the inconvenience they were causing me now made me wish I had tiefed their stuff off them after all. Bloody rugrats.

As the lawyers droned on, I found myself getting drowsy. The suits talked and talked and talked. I struggled to stay awake.

Lord have mercy, court was dull. Until, that was, Styles took the stand. Big mistake.

The judge was a dour white lady.

Styles stood up to confirm his name and address. Then he started to speak. I snorted with laughter, prompting a dirty look from the clerk. The judge's face started to wrinkle up with confusion. I could see her straining to hear. She didn't understand a word he was saying.

"'Mon man, how can man be robbing kids of their tings while man's on mobile phone? Man's not an octopus, innit."

The judge pushed her spectacles up her nose, and addressed the clerk.

"Should we have an interpreter here?"

I snorted again.

"No, Ma'am," came the whisper.

Styles was affronted.

"Man speaking English, innit!"

"Well, Mr Belmont, could you please speak more clearly so the court can understand you? Thank you."

"These trampy kids have got it wrong, Mrs Judge, swear to God. They're confused, man. They're looking for someone to blame. Man didn't want none of their cheap shit."

It wasn't the strongest legal argument.

My mind started wandering. It occurred to me I hadn't asked what Stimpy was in for. I looked at the clock, and wondered whether Cruz and his crew were still hanging around.

The suits talked some more, and I struggled to stay awake, until eventually a clerk stood up.

"Court adjourned."

What?

But they hadn't even heard my story yet.

"Don't worry," the lawyer explained as he shuffled out with his suitcase. "There were delays today, so they'll hear the rest tomorrow. You've got nothing to worry about."

He nodded goodbye.

"See you tomorrow."

Happy days. It wasn't even 4pm.

"Sour!"

It was Cruz. He had been waiting.

"We're going to bounce now. Let me drop you home now, innit."

Perfect. I even get a lift.

"Gotta do a few things first."

Fine by me. I had nothing to do. Furthermore, I was intrigued. I could tell this boy had this level of respect. I wanted to know this guy. I forgot to wait on Stimpy.

We jumped in his car. Ford Escort Convertible. Low suspension. Tinted windows. Clean interior. No souped-up boy-racer shit. This was the car of a serious player. He drove fast. But you didn't fear for your life – he was a better driver than Badman. Which wasn't hard.

"Shame about Stimpy."

"He'll get the bus. Or he's probably still there, socialising."

"You're funny, girl."

"What do you mean?"

"Stimpy ain't going nowhere. But he'll have bare time for socialising. They say Feltham's a friendly place."

"What?"

"He went down, man. Likking one tek? No way he was getting away with any of that shit."

Oh.

"Like I say," covering my tracks, "Man Dem do their ting, I do mine."

He smiled.

I felt comfortable in Cruz's presence. He wasn't flirting. He just treated me like one of the boys. The way I liked it.

I didn't recognise the route he was taking. We seemed to be going nowhere near Brixton Hill.

"Want to come round my endz? Can introduce you to some people."

"Yeah, sure. I ain't in no rush."

He swung right across the bus lane, no indicator, towards Clapham.

"Hungry?"

Now that he mentioned it, I was. The Golden Arches glowed up ahead, like a big, yellow smile.

We pulled into the drive-thru and ordered two extra-value meal deals – Big Mac, fries and Coke. All I used to eat. He paid.

As we unwrapped our burgers, he told me about Gumbo's performance in court, and chatted about bloods we knew in common. Turned out we were better connected than we realised.

He let me polish off the rest of his chips, which I did happily, and said he wanted to take me to the Badric Court estate, where he grew up. The kids he rolled with would later gain fame as the So Solid Crew, but even back then I could see he was a guy with connections.

I'd heard about this estate, but never gone down there. That was the frying pan. Go there and expect trouble. You'd be a Younger blatantly raving on their endz. That was asking for it.

As we cruised up Battersea Park Road, heading deeper into SW11, he chatted about the pirate radio stations he was involved with, and how he was friends with some of the DJs.

In my head, I quickly calculated up the risks. I was crossing enemy lines. Did he know I was a Younger? Stimpy introduced us, but it was never spelled out I was actually one of the Man Dem. What if someone recognised me? I was fresh meat. It was too late now. Any excuse I gave now would raise more suspicions.

"Alright?"

He'd noticed I'd gone quiet.

"Yeah, why shouldn't I be?"

Number one, it was still daytime. That was in my favour. Number two, I wasn't on foot, I was rolling in a vehicle. And not just any vehicle; one being driven by a serious character.

Nah, I told myself. This was going to be fine. I was getting a sneak peak behind enemy lines. Smart thing to do was just relax, and take it all in. It wasn't yet dark. Seeing this place in the daytime would be a whole different vibe.

"Yeah, you shoulda tuned in last Sunday. Man was spitting some bars."

He seemed smart, switched on. I imagined he would be quite a good rapper.

Postcode rivalry was a funny thing. The personal didn't really come into it. It's your crew and their crew. Dem and us. Simple as that.

Sometimes I'd forget they were individuals with their own names and faces. Now here I was meeting bloods just like me. No aggro, no reputations, just banter with someone else's friends.

Rolling with the Man Dem, often you don't even get to hear what triggered the argument. No one cares how it begins, only that an injustice has been served. It's a matter of honour, of respect. You just get drawn in on this wave, as everyone else joins in for the ride.

Don't get me wrong, that's the point. That ride is really what it's all about. That's the naughtiness that draws us all in like a magnet.

At the same time, you're doing something noble. You've got your peer's back. If your peer is in trouble, you know you're defending him. No one ever stops to ask whether your peer is right or wrong. No, that would threaten your ride. So you just jump in. And before you know it, your face has been blacklisted and there's a mob of knife-happy youts after your skin.

God forbid if one of your friends stabs one of their friends. Then your name is getting called up too. If someone asks what started it all, you have no idea.

But what do you do? You can't go to police. What would you say? That's a whole can of worms that best stays shut. Boydem like to get to the bottom of stuff, Man Dem like to glide across the top. Feds like evidence and allegations. That's a risky strategy. People in glass houses, know what I'm saying?

Bottom line is if your name has been called up, you just got to know you've got to protect yourself. Knowing who started it and why doesn't help no one.

We parked up. I took a deep breath, checked out my hair in the wing mirror and stepped outside.

Junction isn't a big place. If Roupell Park was claustrophobic, this estate was even smaller.

Their estate looked glum and grey, lots of buildings made of concrete slabs, all crowded together. I noticed immediately how all the blocks faced each other. They didn't have no Pen or big green space like we did. Roupell Park felt more like a garden. This felt like a proper project.

As Cruz walked through the estate, young guys came up, squeezing him on the shoulder and knocking knuckles. He seemed to know everyone.

Yeah, he had decent jewellery, fresh skin, a flash car. I didn't fancy him, but I imagined there would be many a girl who did.

He was warm and friendly, but made sure to talk business out of earshot. Had one of the Man Dem done this, I'd have been offended. But this was our first day of being in each other's company, and he didn't know how much to trust me. Even if he's got big deals going on, he doesn't know who I am. I respected him for that.

Instead, we kept conversation on the straight and narrow. Surface level. It was refreshing.

People were friendly. There was no deep conversation. They were just hanging. They didn't ask too many questions.

Almost, for a moment, I didn't have to be Sour. I could have been Ama, the shop assistant, or Eva, the beauty therapist. I could have been anyone. Everyone I spoke to was taking me for face value. I liked it.

And yet, I felt something I hadn't expected to feel. I felt sorry for some of them. I mean, it was all a bit shabby down here. How did these guys do it? In my crew, not everyone was attractive, but they were cute. These characters, Cruz excepted, just seemed so ordinary …

Junction Boys, I thought. What was all the fuss about?

Gumbo arrived to join us. He clearly had his fans too. Youts were coming up and slamming shoulders with him. Girls shouted over congratulations. He'd been cleared. They seemed pleased he would be hanging around a little longer.

He started rapping, showing off his MC-ing skills, spitting rhymes and acting the clown. Soon everyone was having a go, the next guy trying to beat the one before.

I laughed at their antics until it started to get dark.

I hadn't even noticed the time, until Cruz came over and said he was going to take me home.

"OK, cool." I'd had a fun day but it was getting late. I needed a ride outta here, or else I'd be stranded, South London Cinderella, with my pumpkin in the wrong postcode, and a coachman who could switch from friend to foe at any moment.

"Where do you live?"

"Brixton Hill."

"Good," he smiled. "I've got some business to do in Brixton. Then I'll drop you off."

That suited me fine.

"You know the Bellefield Man Dem?"

We had pulled up on Bellefield Rd, a few minutes' walk from Brixton Tube. I'd known the guys from Bellefield Man Dem from the early days at Roupell Park. Hadn't seen them for a while. It would be nice to hang with some familiar faces.

We'd parked but he showed no sign of getting out. Cruz, it appeared, had other ideas.

Instead, he was staring at the house where we had pulled up.

I recognised the yout who opened the door. He'd join us on occasion hanging at Morley's or outside the police station. He had a few kids to different girls.

Cruz sat behind the driver's wheel, staring this character down. He made no attempt to get out the car. The boy shouted to people inside, and more youts came to the window. They looked as if they had seen a ghost.

Still, Cruz sat there, giving them this grimacing look. I suddenly clocked what was going on. I knew exactly what that look said.

It said: "I know where you live. And when I'm in the mood, I'm going to catch you."

They had seen me in the passenger seat.

"I think it's time to go," I said, clocking the seriousness of the situation. It was getting uncomfortable. No, it was more than uncomfortable. This was dangerous.

"I said, move!"

Cruz said nothing, put the car into gear and pulled away. My days, he was a character of his own. I started to panic. This was serious. They'd seen me, alongside an enemy. I was now marked too. My name was going to get called up. I was in mix-up.

I walked back into my estate in a state of flux, listening to the roar of his engine as he sped off.

"Idiot," I said to myself. I wanted to be angry with him, but he was just going about his business. I was no hurry-come-up. I could pick my own company. But rolling into Brixton with a Junction Boy? I'd taken a risk, and things had backfired.

Shit. By the time I'd reached the Pen I could see Tyrone. He was already speaking with a yout I recognised from the

Bellefield crew. Word travels fast. Tyrone must have come to see me. He was not only The Introducer. He was the Peacemaker too.

"Sour, what's gwarning?"

OK. Might as well face this down now, before it gets any bigger.

"That girl's mix up," said the boy. "She brought Cruz to man's house. She's setting man up to get nyam."

This was one of the worst crimes you could commit on the road. And, specifically, it was one of the worst crimes a girl could commit: disloyalty. I'd seen it happen. Honeytraps, distractions, whatever. It usually involved girls betraying youts, giving information from one side to another, or simply swapping sides. And usually, it got boys stabbed.

"Stop lying on people," I protested.

"Telling you, bruv, the gyal brought Junction man to man's yard."

Tyrone told him to calm down for a second, and pulled me to one side.

He understood the charge. I belonged to Brixton. Stimpy saying hello was one thing. Now, thanks to my little adventure with my new Junction friend, all they saw was a Younger rolling with the enemy.

"Sour, what the fuck?" said Tyrone in a quiet voice, making sure the angry guy couldn't hear us. "Is he for real?"

I tried to tell them they were making a fuss over nothing, but I knew how bad it looked. I tried a different tack.

"What the hell would I want to set him up for anyway? He ain't got no money. I don't need anyone to do my dirty work."

Tyrone seemed disappointed in me. Man Dem's anger I could take, but when Tyrone gave me that look, something stung. He was the only one left I trusted.

"You know what," he said. "I didn't expect that from you. Now it looks like you're some set-up chick, innit?"

Now I was getting angry. I felt like I was a serious enough character to decide who I rolled with, and who I didn't.

"Tyrone, please, listen to me, yeah? That boy had nothing to fear from me."

"I know that," he said. "You're not the problem. You're mixing with devils."

"Cruz?" I laughed. As I said, crews were made up of two types – the characters who were prepared to do physical harm, and the hurry-come-ups who followed them. This Cruz yout was a serious character, for sure. But he was hardly Satan.

"Don't worry, blood. This man's cool. We're friends."

Tyrone shook his head. "You're not understanding," he said, correcting his voice back to a whisper. "He's got beef with that boy, Tremor. Feud's been running for months now, since he slapped Tremor's cousin on the cheek."

Ah. Awkward. Now that I did not know.

"Still, that's his business, innit."

Tremor wasn't one of my boys.

"Telling you, man!" shouted the yout, pacing up and down. "She's dissing it."

I walked back to confront him.

"Look you, you little dickhead, shut up. If I hear anything more outta you, me and you gonna have war, OK? I don't like you spinning out my name like that."

I knew that once you've got certain labels, like slag or set-up girl, that shit sticks.

Who knew what caused the altercation between Cruz and Tremor? The way they were making it out, it was as if he just went out and victimised an innocent. Maybe Tremor deserved it. At least, there's two sides to every story. I was getting bored of the Man Dem always being on the right side, and everyone else's always being on the wrong one.

"Quit rolling with those guys," he said, half-threatening, half-sympathetic. "They're serious guys."

"Let me cut this conversation here, OK?"

It was getting late, and I had another early start tomorrow. I hated early starts. Bloody courts. Nine to five – clown's work, man.

I turned my back on both of them, and headed for the stairwell.

Tyrone ran after me. This time his tone was softer.

"Listen, he ain't that cool, that's all I'm saying. If Man Dem find out, there's going to be trouble."

It would be another year before that feud came to a head, at Lambeth Country Show. All the crews were out. The park was crawling with Man Dem, all fired up and ready for trouble.

The whole park ended up chasing Cruz down the street. Someone ended up brandishing a chopper on him. When people are pulling blades on you at a funfair, you know you're in deep.

Yeah, Tyrone was proved right, as usual. That man was a devil. I just was taken in by his good side.

But that was one thing about Cruz, he always got away. Man, that boy could run. The whole park was running him down. So what did he do? Ran straight into a police station to save his life. Smart guy.

That's when I started thinking; sitting in his passenger seat that day was probably the most dangerous thing I'd ever done. That car could have got shot up there and then, for all I knew.

They say reputation of power *is* power, and it's true. But the moment that illusion slips, you're a sitting duck, just like all the rest.

In For a Shock

They kept adjourning and longing out the case, until my 16th birthday came and went.

"See you later."

Yusuf grunted goodbye from his bedroom. He was still half asleep. He was staying at home less and less, so it was unusual to see him lying there with all his shit scattered over the floor.

There was only a day left of the hearing.

As soon as I got this boring shit out the way, I was going to buy a pair of new trainers, then meet him outside the cinema.

"Don't be late, yeah?"

That morning, Styles and I were back sitting in the same uncomfortable seats, losing the will to live. I was watching the clock. 11.45am. The solicitor said we'd probably be done before lunch.

The judge seemed even grumpier than yesterday. She had already reprimanded us for not taking the whole circus seriously, when the rugrats gave their evidence. How could you not laugh? They didn't seem to know what the hell was going on.

And what was going on with the heating in this room? It was sweltering.

When the suits got up, that's when my brain switched off. A few minutes later – maybe longer – Styles kicked me in the shins.

"Sour, wake up," he hissed.

I'd nodded off.

She was telling us to rise. I wondered why. She ain't the Queen. I stood next to Styles. He took my hand. Suddenly, things started feeling serious.

"You have both been accused of robbery," she said, "a crime for which you appear to have shown little or no remorse."

I wondered whether I would have time to get to Oxford Circus and back for the trainers.

"Mr Belmont, I'll deal with you first. This is clearly not your first offence …"

If I got the Tube straight there and back, I could meet Yusuf in time for the 6.50pm showing.

"You have been found guilty of the charge. In conclusion, I have no choice but to sentence you to 90 days' detention at Feltham Young Offenders Institute, where on account of your young age you will be held in A wing …"

Styles's hand slipped from mine as he put his hands up to his head. He exhaled and shook his head in much the same way as if he had just seen Crystal Palace lose at home. He was going to Feltham. That meant I was going to Feltham too, to join the rest of the Man Dem.

An overweight male prison guard waddled over and led Styles away. For all his bravado, he seemed a bit tearful.

"Stay in touch," he said, as he followed the guard out. "Don't break the chain."

As he left the courtroom I suddenly felt exposed. The judge was now giving me the same long speech, but my mind was already distracted, trying to remember everything I'd heard about Feltham. It was near Heathrow, I knew that, because Man Dem were always talking about the noise of the planes when you're trying to get to sleep at night.

On the plus side, there were connections to be made inside Feltham. Man came out harder, better prepared for all sorts of shit. There was no messing with someone with a spell at Feltham under their belts.

The judge went on. It had been a long time since I'd been addressed by my real name.

"... You too have been found guilty of one count of robbery, despite a number of reprimands and a final warning. I appreciate your young age, but as the Youth Justice Board can offer no suitable alternative it is with reluctance I am obliged to send you to Her Majesty's Prison Holloway ..."

At that point the rest of the courtroom melted away, prison guards and lawyers disappeared. Even the judge faded into nothing more than white noise. There was only word which had connected with my brain: Holloway.

Holloway? She had got it wrong. That was a hard-assed women's prison.

I was one of the Man Dem! I was one of the boys! I should be going where they were going. I felt like I'd been punched.

An overweight female prison guard appeared, keys hanging off her badly-fitting trousers. I began to panic. What was going on?

I looked over to the lawyer, the same dickhead who said I had nothing to worry about.

"What's she talking about? Why did she say Holloway?"

He fastened the clips on his briefcase, and leaned over.

"You can phone me," he said.

What the hell would I want to phone you for?

Sour

Yeah, I thought, if I ever fancy going to prison again you'll be the first person I call.

Four months. Was that what she said? I was angry at feeling sympathy for Styles. What was he worried about? He'd be spending the next three months socialising with Stimpy and Badman and, hell, even Drex. At least he'd be with the rest.

I was out on my own, with all the hard-ass old women. And I hadn't brought anything with me. I had brought no clean clothes. I didn't even have my eyeliner.

I heard more footsteps coming up for me, and before I knew it I was leaving behind the hot, brightly lit courtroom and descending the stairs into a labyrinth of dark corridors and awkward silence. It felt like an underground police station.

Just take it all in, Sour, I told myself. It's not like I'm being sent to the death chamber. Just take it all in.

There was a long wait in a low-ceilinged room that felt like a custody suite.

Another fat woman – was being plus size compulsory when applying to the prison service? – escorted me out of the back door into a Securicor van.

From the outside, I'd always just thought they were big communal vans, with seats. She swung open the door.

"Nah, sorry, I ain't going in there."

The bus had cells!

Now I ain't a big fan of enclosed spaces. I'd always prefer walking to the top of a tower block than taking a pissy lift. Sure, a night in the cells at Brixton police station to get away from home was fine, but these portaloos on wheels? They had to be kidding.

The prison guard bundled me in, and locked the door.

There was enough room to sit down, and that was it. I could touch the walls, elbow to elbow.

There were no cushions and nowhere to stretch your legs. The only option was to sit ramrod straight.

There were air vents above me, and the radio was on. They were playing songs. I took a deep breath and told myself to keep calm. No good hyperventilating here.

OK, maybe this ain't so bad. Jimmy Nail came on the radio. 'Crocodile Shoes'. I tapped my feet along, on the metal floor. The engine started and slowly the van drove up the ramp, and out into the afternoon gridlock of South London traffic.

I sat strapped into my sweatbox, trying to listen out somehow for the moment we crossed the river, imagining the slight rise and dip of a bridge as we crossed from south to north, but the rumble of the road gave away no clues, leaving me just to guess blindly at taxis and tourists, bike couriers and cars that criss-crossed our path through Central London. It felt like the longest drive of my life.

I worried about Yusuf waiting alone outside the cinema. I needn't have. Turns out he'd forgotten to meet me anyway.

Holloway

I recognised those big brick walls from the news bulletins. Some part of me was still expecting our destination to look like just another big police station. But these walls felt military. They felt serious.

"Concealments?"

The belongings I tipped out into the tray were pitiful. Oyster card. Chewing gum. Lip gloss. That was it.

There was none of the softly-softly approach that had cushioned every other "official" experience up until now. No, I realised. These guys mean business.

I wanted a bath. I needed a bath.

I joined a queue of other women at reception. They were all much older. They looked like they had done this thing before. Some acknowledged my presence with a nod; most ignored me. No one was talking. Everyone looked tired and bored. Nothing felt real.

An unsmiling guard fingerprinted me, and handed me a checking-in pack, with a bar of soap, toothbrush, deodorant and other such luxuries.

I filed through to the next room.

I was told to strip.

I ain't doing that!

Strip.

It wasn't optional.

Nobody had ever seen me naked. Even I didn't like to see myself naked. They're were even wanting to look up my ass! I thought, I'm not crouching over no mirror, or bending over for no one.

"I said I ain't doing that," panic rising in my voice.

This place was run by flipping perverts! I didn't want to take off my clothes. I screamed and shouted until I could shout and scream no more.

But the guards were deaf to my protests. My shouts barely seemed to register. The orders kept coming. Strip. Bend over. Wear this. Take off that. Resistance is futile in these situations, innit.

They left me ranting and raving, till I had no more energy to argue. Guess I wasn't the first to protest.

I unzipped my hoodie, pulled off my vest top, kicked off my trainers and peeled off my jeans. Then handed them over.

I was offered a shower. I took it.

I put on my standard-issue prison gown, and stood, shivering, clutching my checking-in bag and the crumpled tangle of my clothes. They led me out of reception and down deeper through the rest of the checkpoints.

It felt like being in a hospital. But oddly quiet. Almost silent. All I heard was footsteps, as wardens walked and their keys jangled. Nobody made noise. This world had its own order. This building had its own code. And screws were the boss. That was obvious. They have last say, and what they say, you actually do. I learned that quick. These were the only rules I'd ever known that could not be broken.

From that moment on, I was no longer a name, I was a number.

Sour

We seemed to walk for miles, one unending corridor after another.

My wet hair dripped lukewarm drops down the back of my neck, and I could feel other eyes looking at me. Gripping my bag, bed-linen and towel close to my chest, I took my time, shuffling along in the hope that deliberately small steps would prevent my gown from flapping open.

I braced myself to hear cat-calls, and see arms waving through bars, Hollywood-style, and was kinda disappointed when there were none. I was all ready to hold my head up high.

I wondered why it felt familiar, and then I realised. This was like going into care. Or at least a grown-up version.

I knew what it felt to be the new girl in an institution, to stick out like a sore thumb, when you're dumped in a group where other friendships are already made, other secrets already shared, old rivalries are already live and kicking. I'd survived and thrived in places like that. Ain't no reason to be scared now, I tried to tell myself.

For the first time in a long time, I felt young. Too young. This was an adult place, I was out of my depth. My feet were kicking frantically but I couldn't touch the bottom.

I knew the golden rule in those situations and I was going to stick to it: keep your head down. Coping mechanisms were kicking in, innit. Take it in, block it out, that was my motto.

This was going to be a new experience. All I had to do was take it in and block it out.

But even as I promised myself I would do everything I could to keep afloat, all I could think of was the dark water below, fading into black. I was in deep now. I had to try not to sink.

We'd reached my wing: D3.

The cell door opened. The guards stopped. I hesitated. I stepped forward, and the door shut behind me. Suddenly I got these three pairs of eyes staring at me. It hadn't even occurred to me I wouldn't have my own cell. I could feel myself shrinking, like Alice in Wonderland, after seeing the bottle marked "Drink Me". Three women were staring down at me. I felt like I was two foot tall.

In care, you see, I was used to having my own little room. You barely pay attention as you're being introduced to new people and new staff coz kids who are there one day are gone the next. Ain't no point making friends. Waste of time, waste of energy. Same deal with staff on their shifts. They ain't in the market for getting too attached. It was a quick turnover. If you're smart, you don't attach yourself to no one. Right at that moment I realised a friend was what I wanted. This was not the place to find them.

Suddenly, I found myself standing in a cell in the largest women's prison in Europe. There was nowhere to hide.

There was a strong smell of cigarette smoke. And perfume.

"Oi, we've got a new one!"

"Y'alright, luv."

The voices came at once, everyone asking me the same question. None moved from where she was. They all stayed in their beds.

"How old are you?"

"Just turned 16."

"She's a bleeding baby!"

"She shouldn't even be here, fucking animals."

"Oh my god, ain't she cute?"

I noticed they were all wearing their own tracksuits and pyjamas.

"Babes, why are you in a fucking gown?"

"Asked for a shower, innit."

"At reception?" asked the loudest of the group. "And you walked all the way here in that?"

I nodded.

They burst out laughing.

"Aw, bless."

Klaire was in her 40s. She had a short fringe, with long, lank, brown hair down to her chest, and deep cigarette lines around thin lips. Yeah, she had a smoker's voice, but there was something about her that gave her a hint of glamour. She'd probably been stunning when she was young.

I wasn't surprised that her bed was the one with all the products and perfumes around it. She had pots of Oil of Ulay and all the good stuff that white women use, as well as tweezers, emery boards and nail varnish. She even had an Imperial Leather soap. That was top soap.

She was wearing a nice camisole, with trousers to match. Only people of decent calibre dress nice to go to bed. I reckoned she was a brand-name in her world, and I wasn't wrong.

The dorm had four beds. Mine was the empty one by the door.

A Somalian woman was sitting cross-legged on the furthest one. She looked up and nodded at me, but didn't say much.

She wore her hair in cane rows and was super-slim. Looked like a bloody marathon runner in her white vest. She didn't speak English too well, but she understood.

She was the first to sleep and first awake. Liked her smokes. Yeah, Yasmin was cool. Didn't trouble no one.

Then there was Heather. Or Hevah, as she pronounced it. She was the oldest. In her 50s. She was like someone's grandma, like some bloody granny activist. I never did find out what the hell she was doing in there. More than all the others, you always got the feeling she was the one you shouldn't ask.

"Who's gonna make a cuppa tea?" she asked.

Tea and fags, I would soon learn, were that woman's world.

Klaire gestured to the single bed.

"Sit down, luv."

She looked at my checking-in bag and the collection of clothes I'd worn to court.

"Is that all you've got?"

I didn't have deodorant. I didn't even have a razor. I glanced at her Oil of Ulay, coveting the cosmetics, as I thought of my eyeliner sitting in my make-up bag at home.

She chucked me a small bottle of Nivea moisturiser.

"There, you can borrow that. Pay me back later."

"Thank you."

The cell had one sink, with a sponge and washing-up liquid, and one toilet with a door.

Underneath the sink was a beige bucket. Excellent. Me and that bucket were going to be friends. I realised I'd be relying on the old Jamaican way of keeping clean, darling.

This wasn't somewhere to be shy. If I wanted to be clean, and damn right I did, then I knew I'd be spending a lot of time crouched over that bucket, dabbing my armpits and crotch with a flannel. It's funny how quickly you get used to losing all inhibitions, in the name of personal hygiene.

I was so tired, dog tired, but as I got under the thin covers it was clear that Klaire and Heather were in no mood for being quiet. They had fresh meat to mother.

"Bloody disgrace, shouldn't even be here in the first place," tutted Heather.

There was a warmth between the two of them. They were

a unit. You could see they'd served a lot of time together, and they had information to impart.

They spent the rest of the night telling me what I needed to know. First and most important was which screws were good and which were bad.

"Be good with that one," they warned me. "He sometimes brings things in if you're nice to him. Chocolate, wine, y'know, minor contraband.

"If you're going out to exercise, you got to wait to be called," she added. "It gets bloody cold out, but it's the only hour you get to stretch your legs, so use it."

"You smoke baccy?"

I shook my head, but she paid no attention.

"You gotta plug it up."

"What?"

"You just got to shove it up there, babe. Plug it up."

Slowly, it dawned on me what she was saying.

"But be careful, yeah, coz if they suspect for a single second you've got something, they'll de-crutch you."

Yasmin snorted.

"Don't like."

"Fat Sandra," Heather nodded, solemnly. "Look what happened to her."

"Yeah, just a couple days ago."

I was curious.

"So, what exactly do they do?"

Klaire laughed.

"What do you think they do, babes?"

I looked at her blankly.

Heather stepped in.

"They hold you down, spread your legs and take it down. Bastards are rough too."

Klaire nodded.

"Gotta plug it up hard."

Number one, I don't smoke. Number two, even if I did, I ain't got no intention of plugging anything anywhere. I thanked them for the advice anyway.

After a while, Heather's advice turned to snores, leaving only Klaire to natter away. She talked and talked till I was wide awake once more.

Turned out she wasn't too bothered about being in prison. She and her husband had a big house in Essex with cars and double garages, and she knew she was going back to it soon. Her husband was in prison too. Dodgy business deals. He'd be out soon too. The nest egg they'd both built up was safe somewhere else, she hinted. Worth doing the time for, I guessed. Within a year she'd be back enjoying her comfortable life.

She talked about her son, who was going to take over the family business, and her Alsatians.

Yeah, Klaire would teach me a lot over those few months. She taught me how the words "no comment" are my friend, and to always think about DNA. She taught me that drugs meant money, and that it's always better to get mules to swallow than to carry. Above all, her chat about her swimming pool and her home gym and her three holidays a year taught me that crime pays far more richly and more frequently than I had ever imagined.

I fell asleep that night listening to the snores and steady breathing of the drug dealer, the drug mule and the grandma whose crime was never discussed. The prison was completely quiet. There were no sirens, no screaming, no pressure. I closed my eyes and drifted off, numbed by a strange sense of calm.

* * *

It felt natural to walk out into the landing to the shower rooms, but those doors weren't opening till the screws felt like it.

Yasmin was already sitting up in bed. She looked like she had been awake for hours. Heather yawned and stretched as Klaire brushed her teeth in the sink, washed her face, and dabbed her various lotions on Costa-leathered skin.

I was glad I'd remembered to wash my underwear in the bucket before going to sleep. It was still slightly damp, but at least it was clean.

The heavy door lurched open, allowing in a flood of light and the clatter of morning activity. Night-time had been so quiet. But with daylight came noise and chaos. I could hear cackles and laughter and cheerful shouts as the women greeted each other on the way to the showers.

A whole new world awaited, outside on the landing.

"Morning!"

A stream of tired, puffy, smiling, growling, thin and fat faces filed past. It was supervised chaos.

I wondered if Holloway did baths. I moved to follow the loud, lairy exodus, but Klaire shook her head.

"Uh-huh, babes. Them first, then us."

It felt as if I was surrounded by caged animals and I was the cub.

Unlocking times, I learned, was 8.15 to 12.30 and 13.45 to 19.30; less on Fridays, Saturdays and Sundays. Or at least it was meant to be. "Sometimes you just get an hour, depending on how many screws are around."

Prison robs you of lots of things, but worst of all it robs you of long-lies.

Breakfast began at 8.15.

I followed the exodus to the canteen, bleary-eyed and wishing I'd worn better clothes to court. None of the women seemed to be wearing a prison uniform, which was a bonus until I realised how rubbish my own wardrobe options were.

Whatever was being cooked, it smelled hideous. I knew before I'd even reached it that there was nothing there I'd want to eat.

"I ain't even hungry," I whispered.

"You will be," said Klaire. "Take what you can get."

Inmates stood behind vats of gunk, wielding their serving ladles. I did what Klaire did, and picked up my plate at the beginning of the line.

They said it was porridge, but it looked and smelled more like glue. I didn't touch a drop and went for some toast instead.

Heather and Klaire talked between themselves. They could probably tell I wasn't in the mood for chatting.

I glanced around the canteen, but couldn't see no one the same age. They all seemed so much older. It was as if I'd got the wrong room and wandered into some hard-as-nails coffee morning. I wasn't meant to be here. It felt like there had been some mistake.

"Remember your VOs, yeah?"

Klaire was speaking to me.

"What?"

"Your Visiting Orders. Make sure you get them. You're allowed three or four a month, depending."

I realised Mum wouldn't know where the hell I was. Who was going to tell her? Didn't trust that bloody lawyer to sort out shit.

Maybe she hadn't even noticed yet?

Still, I was in no hurry to see Mum cussing and howling inside here.

"Thanks, but think I'll leave it a while. Gonna get used to things myself, innit."

Klaire looked impressed.

"Smart gel."

I left the rest of my toast and got up with the others, leaving my plate on the trolley.

Heather stayed in the canteen, while Klaire and I walked back across the landing. You couldn't see up nor down. It was just one straight corridor after another, like a hospital ward. The place smelled like a hospital too, of chemicals and mopped floors. There were at least 30 doors on our landing. Grim and grey. The walls were magnolia with green lino floors.

We passed a straggle of women, lined up along the corridor.

"What are they queuing for?"

"Education block."

Lord have mercy, people were so bored they were queuing for school. Probably ain't as much fun as Dick Shits, I thought. I'd already decided I wouldn't be going back after the summer holidays. I'd passed my mock exams – and done well too – and only my history teacher seemed sad I wouldn't be coming back.

I'd liked Mr Wilson. He used to write nice things in some of my essays, not that I paid much attention.

That headmistress, though. She could fuck off and keep her school. Little did I know that by the time the next term came around I wouldn't have much choice.

Klaire talked me through the different areas of the prison. There was a wing for pregnant women, and a mother and baby unit, as well as special units for lifers and women on remand. I told her I still ain't seeing no wing for cute little black girls.

Her laughter spiralled into a smoker's cough.

"Word of advice, babes. If one of these dirty bitches asks you to go to the library, they ain't wanting to read you poetry, yeah."

The library, she explained, was a bit of a lovers' lane.

I vowed there and then never to set eyes on a single book.

"Don't be doing anything stupid, either," she said, as we passed another cell door. "Silly bitch in there, covered herself in toilet paper and set herself alight. Ran down the landing like a screaming banshee."

"What happened to her?"

Klaire shrugged.

"Stupid cow died, innit."

"No way, man. Is that a gym?"

I peered inside. It looked good. But my excitement soon evaporated. My heart sank. I knew a claimed territory when I saw one. Ain't no space for no newcomers in there. Each machine was taken. Pumped-up women sweated at every station, pressing and pushing and punching away like they owned the place.

I had heart, but I ain't stupid. Oh well. Judging from the vats of glue, I wasn't expecting to be eating much in here anyways.

It was a long-arsed walk to the exercise yard. It looked a bit like the Pen in Roupell Park – like a basketball court without the nets.

There wasn't much exercising going on. A couple were power-walking back and forth, but the rest leaned against the walls, smoking and chatting.

I surveyed the crowd. Something was odd. Then I realised – there were men in here too.

Maybe some of the Man Dem were about as well? I started scouting the crowd for faces I recognised.

"I thought this was a women's prison?"

Klaire's frown softened.

"How come there's a dude over there?"

He was wearing a string vest that showed muscular arms, and his baggy trousers were deliberately pulled down to reveal the tops of his boxer shorts.

Klaire raised her over-plucked eyebrows and smiled.

"Ssh," she said. "You'll hurt Marcia's feelings."

"What? That's a Marcia?!" I looked over again, my eyes not believing what my ears were telling me. "You're shitting me? She looks more like a Marlon." Turns out the Holloway Woman Dem were deceptive.

I'd been exempt from all that lesbian shit. I'd grown up in an Islamic household. I knew robbers and dealers and much, much worse. But I'd never met anyone I knew was gay.

Klaire chuckled.

"Yeah, she's cool. She's got girlfriends in here. They all fight over her. Loves the attention, that gel. Better hope she doesn't take a liking to you, or you'll make them all jealous."

The screws did a head count. I breathed in the air, and looked up at the overcast sky as dull and grey as old knickers that got stuck in the wash.

You'll be alright, I told myself. All you gotta do is keep your head low and keep to yourself.

After half an hour, we were herded back inside and sent back to our cells for lock-up. Dinner, if that's what you call the rubbery reheated chicken in a fluorescent sauce masquerading as "curry", was over by 5.30pm. My God, the food! I wouldn't have fed that shit to a cat.

I'd never seen chicken and rice look like that. Also, something else troubled me. The inmates did everything. That was plain to see. Screws were there to open and close doors but the inmates did all the donkey work – the washing, the cleaning and the thing that troubled me the most, the food. I remembered the faces of the women wielding those ladles, preparing the food that evening, and made a mental note not to piss any of them off.

What if they didn't like you? What if they did something to your food? I vowed to eat as little as possible. It wasn't going to be hard.

The screws supervised the loud, jeering mass of women back across the landing. "Evening association" was over. The cell door thudded shut.

I lay back on my narrow bed and stared at the ceiling, trying to process my first disorientating day. For the first time in a long time, I felt … safe. No threats, no stress, no Mum. Prison ain't so bad, y'know. I smiled inside. Who knows, I thought, I might even like it here.

Safe Haven

Over the weeks that followed, I found myself settling into life at Her Majesty's Pleasure with considerable ease.

Don't get me wrong. Fights erupted. Junkies wailed and gnashed as they went cold turkey. Every now and then you'd see or hear of an inmate being rushed to the medical wing in another failed suicide attempt.

It was tedious having to tell your story 100 times, and it was hard to tell which was more disgusting – the buckets or the food. On the bad days, mental cases would throw tampons and clumps of hair around until they were sedated. On good days, you'd manage to clean your crotch, crouched over a bucket with a rag and soap, while somehow keeping your dignity with the strategic placement of towels.

It wasn't easy, but for the most part the girls looked out for me. I was the baby after all. Something about me seemed to bring out the mothering instinct in them all.

Klaire and Heather kept me right. Even Yasmin was a calming presence. They knew when I felt like being sociable. They accepted the days when all they got was a nod and grunt.

One night, lying in bed while the rest were sleeping, I told Klaire about life on the road. I told her about all the crazy stuff and how I was tired of it all.

"That ain't the way, love," she agreed. "You should move forward. You need to try something new when you get outta here, get a steady income.

"If you were my daughter, that's what I'd be telling you. Ever thought about drugs?

"Girls like that," she whispered, gesturing over to the sleeping Somalian, "that ain't the way to do it. I don't mean none of that mule shit. I'm talking about business, making *real* money …"

I listened with interest.

I didn't fill out a Visiting Order that week, or the week after. In fact, I didn't want to see anyone and I didn't want them to see me. Each night I listened to Klaire's advice.

Truth was, I was enjoying the time-out. Inside that cramped dormitory that smelled of fags and hand cream, I'd found space. In prison I could be myself. I didn't have to survive on the streets. I didn't have to act top dog no more. There were no boys to betray me, no liars to lock their doors and pin me down. The Man Dem were a distant memory.

I never did find the courage to venture into the library. Or the gym. Most days I was happy just lying on my bed. The days began to blur into each other.

Until one day I came back from lunch to find a white form waiting for me on my bed.

I checked the other beds to see if everyone had one, but they did not.

"What's this?"

"Read it," said Heather, with a smile.

The sheet said my name and prison number.

"It says 'early release'."

The others nodded.

"I think I'm being moved."

"What else does it say?"

There were initials I didn't understand: "HMP ESP."

Klaire whooped.

"East Sutton Park! You've fallen on your feet there, girl."

I was being transferred to East Sutton Park open prison in Kent. Immediately.

They seemed genuinely happy for me. Even Yasmin cracked a smile. And yet somehow I couldn't share their elation. I didn't want to leave. The prospect of leaving was much more terrifying than entering.

Within a few hours I was saying goodbye. I didn't really know how. Klaire gave me a big hug, and pressed some cash into my hand. Though I'd never seen her do anything that broke the rules she always managed to have extra privileges tucked away here and there. She was subtle, I had to give her that. I was surprised the boydem ever caught up with her.

I didn't know what to say, so I said nothing. She told me to take care of myself and remember what she had told me. I promised her I would. I waved bye to the others.

Numb and slightly shell-shocked, I followed the guards through the corridors to a window, where another warden passed me my lipgloss and Oyster card, sealed in a see-through bag, emblazoned with Her Majesty's prison logo.

Within an hour I'd been whisked beyond those red brick walls in another Serco sweatbox, and was on my way down the M20 to my new home. The only time I'd ever left London was to visit my dad in various prisons around the country. I thought of those long bus journeys with Mum and Yusuf and remembered how exciting they had felt. Now, here I was on a prison excursion of my own. One of these days, I thought to myself, I'd leave the city and go on a nice old jaunt that didn't end up at a jail.

This journey seemed to take even longer than the last.

It felt like we were driving to the end of the world. At 40mph.

It was dark when we arrived. I had been expecting just another Holloway. Boy, was I wrong.

The van pulled up and the doors were unlocked. I stepped out of the portaloo-on-wheels and stretched.

"What the fuck?"

Had I just arrived on Emmerdale Farm?

First up, there were no brick walls. Reception was a big old mansion house. Everything seemed antique, with lots of dark wood that creaked and smelled of history.

I was half expecting the staff to appear in hotel uniforms with a tray of complementary drinks, and ask when I wanted to book in for the horse-riding and spa sessions, so it was quite disappointing to see them in their boring old screws gear, with keys on their belts. But that was where the similarity with Holloway ended.

I liked the old guy who checked me in, immediately. He looked like Dr Chris from Richard and Judy. He had a kind face, and a Northern accent I couldn't quite place. He came from somewhere in the countryside I'd never heard of.

"You've come light?" he said, noting my distinct lack of belongings.

"Yeah, cash and clothes are over-rated," I sighed.

"We'll see what we can sort you out with," he smiled. Then he showed me some keys.

"These are for the back door."

"You're shitting me? Next, you're gonna tell me I can just nip out to the shops whenever I want ..."

He laughed. "Not quite."

He gave me a brief tour. "This is the main house. There are 32 dormitories, and we have around 100 adult and young offenders here. At the moment you're the youngest."

Yeah, story of my life, innit.

"We've got lots of classes, so I suggest you try out as many as you can. Give them a go and see which ones you like. There's art, cookery, computer studies, creative writing …"

As he went on, I craned my neck and gawped at the wood panelling and pictures. If Kate Middleton ever went off the rails, I thought, this is probably where she would end up.

"And don't forget this number." He handed me a card to go with the rest of the booklet and welcoming pack. "This is the number your family can call you on."

"No way?!"

I could speak to Yusuf!

I had missed no one while I was in prison, no one, that is, except my little brother.

Dr Chris talked me through the timetable – you could only phone at certain times – and explained the wage system, for those who worked in the house throughout the week. The more you worked, the more privileges you could buy at the weekend.

Once he'd booked me in, we went up the creaking staircase and he showed me to my room. It felt like a haunted house, albeit one where the ghosts had to do a bit of housework now and again and were probably too comfortable to go spooking anyone.

There were no lock-ups, Dr Chris explained. Hallelujah! You could go to the bathroom when you wanted and you could move around freely. I checked out the bathroom. It looked nice and clean. I couldn't see but I bet there was Imperial Leather soap lurking somewhere.

The dormitory had a lino flooring, and the beds – simple, steel-framed affairs – looked comfortable enough.

There were no locks on the bedroom doors. Yeah, I smiled to myself, I can work with this.

Dr Chris explained that there was a curfew and we were expected to be in bed by a certain time.

"In ESP," he said, "we trust our residents to be responsible for their own actions."

Keys, lino, and now they trust you?

That blew me away.

"So, that's you. I'll let you get settled in and introduce yourself. See you tomorrow."

I kinda wanted to keep him, but imagined he probably had a lovely wife and rosy-cheeked children to get home to.

"Thanks."

My new roommates must still have been socialising because there was only one girl in the dormitory when I arrived.

"Hi," she said, getting up off her bed and shaking my hand.

Her name was Jenny but she looked like a little Arabella to me. She was a dancer, and she was beautiful. As delicate as a doll. Looked like butter wouldn't melt.

We got chatting. When she spoke, I had to try hard to stifle my laughter. She was proper posh! Like proper Home Counties, probably-had-a-pony posh. You could tell she came from a good family.

She was in her mid-twenties but even then you could see she was the kinda kid who'd gone to tap-dancing and ballet, and had teddies in her room. She had one with her now. She talked about her parents, dance classes and the exotic places she'd travelled. She didn't like to go into detail about the drugs, and I didn't ask.

We got on well, Jenny and I, but out of all the women I'd meet she made me the angriest. Or was it the saddest? She hadn't wanted for nothing, that girl. And she'd gone and got a criminal record. What a waste. I had my excuses, but what were hers? For me, well, it was expected. For her, it had been completely avoidable. She'd had all the chances I would have loved, and she still blew it.

Sometimes I used to wish that I was born with a silver spoon too. I assumed that, once you started life that way, all would end OK. You'd be set for life. So it was disheartening to see a girl that had it all being incarcerated.

I stayed awake wondering about the differences between me and her. Was my excuse really much better than hers? Did I have less responsibility for my actions than she did? Which estate girl should be more ashamed – the one from the country estate or the one from the sink?

Jenny showed me that money can't buy happiness, love and, more importantly, peace within. But who was I to judge? If being financially stable isn't enough for some, then so be it. We all took our chances, and we got caught.

I fell asleep that night with something niggling at me. I had my period, maybe that was it. On a ladies level, it's not fun having your time of the month in prison. I could hold my head up high, I could hold my own among the inmates, and tell myself I was doing OK, but nothing reminded you of your loss of freedom like counting out your tampons.

Keeping yourself clean suddenly required effort. I was 16. I was still getting used to my monthly cycle, and I won't lie, I was embarrassed. I didn't want nobody knowing things like that, but in those close quarters there ain't no hiding it. Your own body becomes public property. Your dignity's taken away from you, innit.

Still, the rest of my new roommates were warm and friendly. Nice, sweet girls. That made me laugh. I was in the goody-goody room.

Tess was a gym fanatic. Bloody Mr Motivator. Always trying to get me to go work out, every five seconds. She didn't have anything left to burn off. She was equally enthusiastic when it came to cleaning and housework, doing everything twice as quick and taking particular pride in polishing the banisters. The others were just nice white girls who didn't bother no one.

Getting ready for bed, I walked out of the dorm, across the landing to the bathroom. No supervision. No lock-up. No mopping my armpits over a bucket.

I don't know why they called it a prison. East Sutton Park was more like a mid-market hotel. The vibe was relaxed.

If I wanted to punish someone, I sure as hell wouldn't send them here. I hoped tomorrow wouldn't get much better because I had a feeling already I wouldn't be wanting to go home.

I floated down that staircase like a ghetto princess. In the communal breakfast area there was proper choice of food – after Holloway, I'd have appreciated anything – but those scrambled eggs, man. Don't think I've ever enjoyed food as much in my life.

This, I thought, must be what boarding school feels like. Only with a lot less twats.

We were going out to work in the garden. ESP, you see, had a farm and a shop that sold its produce.

If I wanted to earn money to pay for phone cards and the tuck shop and treats for our room, I had to earn wages.

Sour

It was fucking cold, man. Jenny chucked me a woolly hat and some gloves. Bearing in mind I ain't never been to the countryside, I followed her and the rest of the girls as they overalled up, pulled on their Wellington boots and those PVC jackets that workmen wear at roadworks, and stepped out into the unknown.

It was a long-arsed walk to the polytunnels, trudging through autumn leaves, failing to appreciate the views over the Weald.

"Why are we here?" I asked Jenny.

"This is our job for the day," she explained.

"What is?"

"Emptying those polytunnels, and filling those ones."

"You mean to tell me we're going to be out here, planting cabbage?"

"Yep."

Now, do you think that sat well with me? If there had been some … purpose … that wouldn't have been so bad. But as far as I could see, we were simply having to dig up the roots on one side and replant them on the other.

I was flipping annoyed. It felt like slave labour. I'm a Brixton girl, I thought. Ain't much use for green fingers in the ghetto.

Needless to say, I found myself having a lot of toilet breaks, as I counted down the hours till 4pm.

After that, it was happy days. You could do what you wanted. There was a communal lounge with sofas, even a games room where they had bingo on a Saturday night. If you were bored, there was a hair salon, with a proper wash sink with mirrors and shit. Now that I was happy about.

This gold beehive didn't maintain itself, darling. It was time to give my hair a bit of TLC. Yeah, I was a dab hand with the wash and blow dry – I could give Vidal Sassoon a run for his money, damn straight – and I soon found myself a niche.

The other girls started coming in to get their hair done too, and I soon got to know everyone.

Got our own little congregation going, around that sink. If Holloway gave me time to keep myself to myself, ESP brought me back out of my shell. Before long, I was hopping from room to room, enjoying the different vibe in each one. Hell, I even liked the women in the God room.

They were all church-goers in the dorm down the hallway. If they were all on this born-again Christian vibe, I wondered, why were they even there? Turned out the nice older lady had found God through fraud, and was always trying to preach me out of my wicked ways. I enjoyed winding her up. I'm sure she thought she'd have me converted by the time I was outta there.

Every now and then, I'd pop in to see Ginger. I'm not kidding: think of one of the characters from *Prisoner: Cell Block H* – denim jacket, low haircut, shirt collar turned up – and you're not far off. She was the top dog, no mistake. She had all her little followers.

She was Scottish. She called me "the bairn" and I could barely understand a word she said.

But she liked to banter, and looked so bloody comfortable, I wouldn't have been surprised if her release date had come and gone and she had just decided to stay.

"If ye get yersel intae trouble, kid, just come and see uz, awright?"

Ginger just dominated. The shelves around her bed were better stocked, and she had a proper quilt and comfier cushions than the rest of us. Like Klaire, I was never quite sure how she managed it, but she managed it alright. She must have had arrangements with the screws, but I never saw anything to give it away.

She liked to ask me about my life on the road. When I told her about the robbery that sent me to jail, she chuckled for ages.

"Robbing bits from two wee kids? What kind of shite robbing is that?"

"I didn't even do it. Trust me, ain't my style."

She chuckled some more.

"What kind of piece did you use?"

"Guns? Ain't no guns involved in this scenario."

"You're taking the fucking piss? Polis must have been right pissed off with you then …"

She caught the twinkle in my eye.

"Like I sayed, if you ever need anything, doll, just let uz know."

Yeah, ESP was just a whole bag of fun, a whole new world. It felt like I'd gone away for a treat. I'd been there a while before I gave Roupell Park a second thought.

"What's up?"

"You got a phone call."

I raced to the phone.

"You alright?"

"Yusuf?"

Hearing my little brother's voice was like having someone snap their fingers in front of my eyes. It broke the spell. I wasn't sure how to feel about that. But it was good to hear from him.

"Yeah, I'm cool, man. No need to worry about me, I'm alright y'know. What you up to?"

"Usual. Some serious shit going down, but money's rolling in. People keep asking for you. Man can't believe you're in jail."

It was as if he was bringing me news from a different continent. I realised I'd barely thought of any of the names or faces I'd left behind. I also realised that, Yusuf excepted, I hadn't missed a soul.

His voice had properly broken. He was growing up alright.

"How's Mum?"

"Not good. She went off last week. Kept on saying you'd been kidnapped and taken back to Jamaica. But then she went to the shops and made the biggest load of punch you've ever seen so ain't all bad."

I thought of Yusuf having to deal with her on his own, and felt a pang of guilt. He had only just turned 14. He shouldn't be having to deal with that shit.

"Do you miss me?"

"Yeah! You kidding?" he said. "Gonna come up and see you next visit, innit."

"Yeah? Sweet."

I hadn't had any visitors yet. I'd watched the other girls get excited on a Sunday morning, putting on their make-up and best clothes, and asking me to do their hair, but I'd yet to feel the need to do it myself.

The phone started beeping.

"Think that's my time up."

"OK, cool. See you on Sunday then, yeah? Want man to bring something?"

I was being rushed by the beeps. I couldn't think of anything.

"Magazines, maybe?"

"Which ones?"

"Don't matter, whatever."

"OK. Later, sis. Keep the faith."

The phone went dead.

"Bye."

I stood holding the receiver for a moment, then quietly headed back to my room.

That Sunday I joined the ritual enjoyed by the rest of them, putting on my freshest hoodie, and using the tongs to curl ringlets in my hair, before walking across the grounds to the Visitor Centre.

Though I was excited to see Yusuf, part of me was apprehensive, anxious that the reminders of home would burst the safe little bubble I'd managed to maintain in prison.

The door opened and the crowd of eager faces poured through. Some threw open their arms and exclaimed their greetings; kids squealed, "Mummy!"; others just quietly held their wives and girlfriends tight for as long as possible before the screws reminded them of the rules, and encouraged them to face each other at either side of the table.

Yusuf bounded over and gave me a hug.

He had shot up in the past couple of months, and had cultivated the fuzz on the top of his lip into an unconvincing 'tache. Before I'd gone to court, it didn't seem so long ago I'd catch him sucking his thumb. He had done a lot of growing up over the past couple of months.

He looked like a serious character. His hair was smoothed into curls, and he was wearing a whole new outfit of designer threads.

His eyes were as wide as saucers.

"This ain't prison, man, it's a hotel! Does it have a swimming pool?"

"It's a disgrace, innit?" I joked. "Thinking of writing a strongly worded letter to my MP."

The Visitor Centre was also particularly nice, with big mahogany tables, a play area for kids, and nice views of the grounds. I could see why guests wouldn't be worried about you when they came to see you here.

"Lord ha' mercy!"

There was a whoop from the door.

"Where is she? Mi waan to see me daughter."

Yusuf looked sheepish and shrank in his seat.

"I had to bring her, sorry. Or she wouldn't let me come alone."

It felt like a long time since I'd seen Mum. I didn't know how to feel or what to say.

She too craned her neck, and made a long whistle as she took in all the mahogany panelling. She looked like she'd lost weight. Her hair was done and she was wearing a new top I hadn't seen before. On the front, it had a leopard made out of sequins.

She gave me a big hug, and held me away at arm's length to inspect me up and down.

"You're thin, how yuh look so marga. Knew dem nah feed you properly."

I had missed her chicken and rice.

She just kept staring at me.

"You OK? You never phoned, gyal just disappeared. You OK? How you just gaarn a court pun yuh own? Nah seh nuttin to me? Just gaarn like ghost. You shouldn't do dat. You never tell me nuttin. I'm your mum, Sal!"

"Yeah, I'm OK."

"Ah wah dis?" she said, admiring my new lodgings. "It nah look like weh me goh fi see yuh puppa."

No shit.

I know when she's going off because she talks fast. I didn't want her embarrassing me in front of the other inmates, whose families were all behaving nice and quiet. But her pace was normal, not too quick.

Sour

Her eyes were the other giveaway. They'd go glossy and watered over, as if she was forgetting to blink. Again, she seemed fine. She carried on chatting, about the long journey here and the letters from the power companies threatening to cut us off. Best of all, she wasn't quoting from the Koran. When the Koranic quotations come out, that's when you know.

Nah, Mum was OK. I was proud of her for keeping it all together.

I had put her out of sight, out of mind. I'd wanted to forget about the road. If you keep thinking about the road you're going back to, that's when you're going to get depressed.

Yusuf wanted to know everything. What was it like? What did I do? Where did I eat?

I told him about Dr Chris, how he was like a friend who was really caring and helped me any time.

"We have our lunchtime chats now. He's from the country. Said he ain't never heard of Brixton."

"No way?"

"Yeah. Says he's only been to London a couple times."

Yusuf found that even weirder than I did.

"Yeah, but he's cool. I really like him."

"So, is prison hard?"

I thought about this before answering. Harder than being on the road? Harder than watching over your shoulder, or facing down threats?

"Nah. It's fine once you get used to it."

Yusuf nodded, taking it all in.

"So how long you got left?"

"Dunno. Got four months and that's nearly two gone already. Can't be long."

"Sweet."

I noticed he seemed jumpier than usual. Excitable. As if he had things he wanted to tell me but couldn't.

"So how's tings? You doing OK?"

He looked over his shoulder to check how closely the screws were listening.

"Some serious shit going down," he said. "Man's making serious queen's head." He made a whistling sound. "Honest, sis, squillah like you wouldn't believe!"

As another screw walked past, Yusuf smiled and leaned back on his chair, looking pleased with himself.

I scowled at him to shut up.

He saw my expression and clocked that this was not the best place to be discussing his latest business ventures.

We spent the rest of the visit chatting about home and food, and what I was missing at Roupell Park. Not much, it seemed.

Maybe I was putting on a brave face. I ain't gonna tell them the dark thoughts that keep you lying awake at night, wondering what the point of it all was, wishing you'd go to sleep and just never wake up.

So I smiled and joked and made sure Yusuf knew he didn't need to worry. They both left on a happy vibe that day, and that's what I wanted.

It wasn't my fear of being inside that I wanted to shield her from. It was my fear of going back on the outside. The longer I stayed in prison, the more I worried about my release.

Maybe Mum knew it too. Was that why she went away so happy?

Maybe she thought I was safer in here, too. She could finally keep tabs on me.

She and Yusuf had brought a reminder of home, a reminder of the life I had to go back to, and it had unsettled me.

Sour

Sure, I felt guilty for having to make my mum travel such a distance, for all that embarrassment I'd caused her when people asked where I was and she had to tell them her daughter was in prison. I'd let her down. I was adding to her illness.

Fuck the world, I thought. Don't ask for me for shit. But even then, that was all me, me, me. Seeing Mum and Yusuf walk out of that door made me realise, perhaps for the first time, that my actions have got consequences for other people too.

Even then, it wasn't that that was worrying me. My fear was this: as soon as I stepped back out into the world I would be thrown back out into the dragon's den.

I'd created a monster, and monster I was going to have to stay. Once you come out of prison, the stakes are higher. My name would be bigger. I would be a sitting target, open to all sorts. I was open to being killed. Open to being hurt by whoever wanted to take a pop and raise their own status.

My release was surely only a few weeks away, and I wasn't ready. I wasn't feeling quite so brave. As bad as I was, I was still only a girl, and there were plenty characters out there who thought girls were easy pickings.

I steeled myself for release. I felt like a girl condemned. The problem wasn't that I wasn't going to get out of prison; it was that I couldn't stay in.

Sooner or later, I knew I would be back amongst the wolves.

On my way back to the dorm, I did some room-hopping, stopping in to pop my head round the door of the married ladies dorm, as I called it.

"Hi love, come in and shut the door."

Sally was a married black lady in her 40s. Real beautiful. I didn't know her as well as the others, but there was no one else around and I was feeling sociable after seeing my family, so I closed the door behind me and sat down on her bed.

She spoke about family, and showed me pictures of her husband and two sons. The faces of her toddler and a cute little boy in a brand new school uniform beamed out from framed photographs by her bed.

She had always been friendly, Sally. Always the first to ask if I needed anything. How naïve.

"Aw, is that your youngest?" I asked, picking up one of the photographs. She leaned over, kissed the glass with a delicate peck and let her finger linger over the frame.

"Yes, he's coming to see me next week."

"And this one?"

"Nate. He's five. It's his birthday next week. I miss them, you know. I miss them so much."

She looked up at me. She was now sitting quite close.

"You've done your hair?"

"Well, visitors here, innit. Wanted to –"

"Looks nice."

She reached over and gently tucked a ringlet behind my ear. Something in the way she did it made me feel uncomfortable.

Slowly, she took the photo frame from my hand, and placed it gently on the bed beside me. I felt tense.

"So many things I miss …"

Clasping my hand in hers, she leaned over and tried to kiss me.

"Whoah!"

I shot up off of that bed like a girl possessed. Shit, I practically left a Sour-shaped hole in the wall.

I was freaked out, man. Live and let live and all that, but coming on to a young girl like that? It just ain't right. That woman was a predator, man. Probably ain't even her kids. Just cuts pictures out of a magazine and puts them up there to lure people in.

I rushed back to my room, angry and agitated.

Got nothing against lesbians, but keep it behind closed doors, you know what I'm saying? And stay away from me. No thank you.

I'd give the wardens grief. They were giving us the shitty jobs. Why didn't they do it themselves? I didn't come from South London for this!

I requested a change of duty.

Dr Chris asked if I liked animals. With the exception of Maverick, Roupell Park had hardly been a menagerie. I said I did, all the same. Anything had to be better than planting cabbage.

"Then why don't you go and work on the farm?"

Now, I'm a city girl. All those cows with their long eyelashes and stupid faces fascinated me. But as soon as I saw all those piglets running around, knowing they were going to be some-one's dinner? No way, man.

Besides, it stank. And I mean properly stank, in a way I've never smelled before. You had to have a strong stomach to muck them out all day, and I just couldn't take it. I hated it. I didn't flinch stabbing someone in the thigh, but I wasn't cut out for helping kill piggies.

I went back to Dr Chris the next day, having tried to scrub the smell off, even more miserable than before.

What about the kitchen? he suggested.

Now you're talking. I liked food more than I liked animals, and much more than I liked digging mud.

"OK," he agreed. "Go downstairs tomorrow at 7am, and introduce yourself."

Excellent. You're on.

Lesley, who led the kitchen shifts, was blonde, smiley and very, very fat. It was just me and her in our part of the kitchen. She ran me through everything, and gave me my gloves and hair net. Happy days. This beat Wellies and waterproofs, I thought, triumphantly.

This, my dear, was definitely an upgrade. Maybe they'd let me do some cooking.

As a kid I'd loved baking. I was a dab hand at the old Victoria sponge. I could make egg custard, biscuits, flapjacks, the lot. There was always someone at the mosque having an event that required cake, so I'd learned a lot from Mum.

Mum even had a Kenwood blender. A powerful thing too. It was always on the go in our house, and I used to love coming home from school and hearing it buzzing away. The sound always came with the smell of nutmeg and cinnamon, and when she finished mixing she used to let us lick bowls and pour the mixture into heart-shaped baking tins.

For all her manic-ness, she never burned the food either. She might have been mental, but she was a good cook, my mum. Used to pack lots into the freezer. Corn beef – I knew how to make that. Maybe that would go down well. I made a mental note to suggest it to Dr Chris.

Our job, explained Lesley, was to clean the pots. OK, I reckoned. Sounds simple enough. I was shocked to see vats bigger than me. And plenty of them.

This was going to keep me busy. But at least it wasn't cold, and Lesley was cool. We would chat away while washing the never-ending pile, which never seemed to get any smaller. I soon got into the rhythm of things. Move too slow, I learned, and you'd get a pile-up which would stress you out.

Sour

Once Lesley showed me her scrub and rinse technique, soon I was flying along. I learned how to keep up, and for the first time in my life got a strange satisfaction from working hard.

I nicknamed Lesley "Miss Piggy" – not to her face, obviously. She was big and blubbery but she was the most pleasant woman in there, and I soon started looking forward to our kitchen shifts, tiefing food together and nibbling on the biscuits.

After our shifts, we treated ourselves to extra puddings. I've never had such good puddings as I had at East Sutton Park. I realised this was probably the happiest I'd ever been.

After a few shifts together, I waited for the right moment to ask her how long she got. It was always a sensitive subject. Some inmates volunteered it, but others – the long-timers – you knew it was best not to ask. But I was curious about Lesley and she seemed pretty open about everything else.

The moment came at the end of a particularly tedious shift, once we'd eaten all the food we could, and there was nothing to do but chat.

"You'll probably be out soon," she said, brightly.

Tell the truth, I knew there was an appeal but I hadn't given it much thought. I didn't like to think about it, but she was probably right.

"How long you got?"

"10 years," she shrugged.

"You serious?! What for?"

The moment I'd blurted it out, I regretted it. I fidgeted. The same soft, smiling, stupid-looking woman who I'd been chatting happily with all week looked me right in the eye. When she said the word, it was like I saw the devil in her.

"Murder."

I'll be honest. She freaked me out.

I couldn't be sure, but I thought I read something in her eyes that said she enjoyed seeing me squirm. Suddenly, I started imagining a cruelty I hadn't picked up on before.

I had felt safe around her, comfortable, you know? She threw me off kilter. How I could get it so wrong, even after all that time on the road, made me anxious. Perhaps it ain't so easy after all. Suddenly chopping veg lost its appeal.

I went back to digging up the cabbages in the garden soon after that. Still, on the plus side, at least she didn't try to kiss me.

"Get your stuff packed up," said Dr Chris. "You're going home."

Everyone had looked out for me. The inmates, the screws … I'd been mothered for the first time in my life. There were no fights, no tensions, just camaraderie and support.

Most liberating of all, there was no need to be aggressive or make my mark. You don't swagger into HMP Holloway, aged 16, and expect to shake things up. *Duppy know who fe frighten*.

Yeah, prison had been a good experience. I could breathe. Exhale and inhale. I didn't have to play a role or worry about nothing. And I understood for the first time why my dad didn't want to come out. It's comfortable when you're institutionalised. There were no worries about food or gas meters or electricity getting cut off. In prison, it was easy living.

I had never felt free in life. But inside, in those dorms, it was easy to cope. I could let my guard down and be myself. The only problem was that I'd forgotten who that was.

Don't get me wrong, part of me was excited about the prospect of causing a stir, going back on the road as a postcode celebrity. Serving a sentence gave you status. I wanted that feeling of having been missed. I wanted the welcome.

But the other part? I wanted to stay just where I was. I had time to reflect. Prison, in its own way, had been a blessing from God. It gave me peace and quiet like I'd never had before. No sirens, no functions, no pressure. All my stresses had been put on hold. But now it was time to confront them again.

So that was me, the tomboy who couldn't handle the dirt, the brand-name who had heart but couldn't be kissed and the gangster girl weary of murderers. Yeah, prison had taught me a few things about myself.

When the day came to leave, I knew I wasn't the same person as before.

I left East Sutton Park, if not reborn, then at least refreshed. I collected my see-through bag of stuff and promised Dr Chris one day I would show him Brixton. And I thought of Klaire doing the same, waiting to be picked up in some shiny new car and being driven back to her huge house with its automatic gates and double garages and swimming pool.

Above all, I left prison having learned my lesson. Petty crime and foolishness gets you nowhere. If you want to make real money, deal drugs.

Change of Occupation

I came out of prison a reformed character. I was prepared to work. I was ready for my first job.

The only problem: nobody told me starting out was such hard work.

I wasn't interested in looking up the old faces. Many of them weren't even there no more. Drex, Badman and Stimpy were still in prison.

This was a fresh start, of sorts.

When you're around so many hotheads, you notice the quiet ones. In the days and weeks following my release, one new face had caught my attention. For the sake of a name, let's call him Winston. Winston was a much older guy, discreet. I liked that.

Furthermore, I had eyes. I'd see him on the estate. I watched how people reacted differently to him.

He didn't seem like just another one of the elders. His was a different kind of power. Not the chest-puffing knife-wielding of the brand-names. People seemed to defer to him. They needed him.

He used to wear a lot of animal skin – some kind of fur – and I knew that wasn't cheap. I started to watch what he was doing. He would stop and speak to people. He had a hand-shake. Unless he's a particularly sociable type, greeting the

Sour

whole world, he's up to something. Something about his way, his routine, told me it was something big, something organised.

I'd look out for him from my window and time my visits to the Pen to make sure he saw me.

One day, we got chatting.

I told him, whatever it was he was running here, I wanted in.

He laughed. "Come on, girl. What makes you think you're cut out for that?"

"Don't mock me, Winston. I mean it. I want in."

He said he'd think about it.

Next time he saw me, he slipped me a mobile phone and some pebbles of brown and white, wrapped up real tight in cling film.

The phone was so big it was like a Dom Joly brick. With a gold-coloured aerial. I thought he was taking the piss.

"Don't fuck up my p's," he snarled. I told him his "p's" – his money – was safe with me.

"People ain't loyal," he warned. "If you don't pick up that phone every single time it rings and give them what they've asked for, you lose money. Correction," he said, "you lose *my* money. So what do you do the moment that phone makes a sound?"

"Pick it up," I repeated.

"Then what?"

"Give them what they asked for."

"Correct," he nodded, satisfied I'd understood the basics of supply and demand, at least for now.

"Miss a call and those people go elsewhere, me and you gonna have problems. OK?"

I nodded.

"Don't fuck up my line."

So, after some gentle persuasion, Winston let me take care of his line. He handed me a plastic bag, which I pressed down deep into the central pocket of my hoodie. If I did well, he said, he'd let me carry on doing my thing from these street corners and stairwells around the estate. Roupell Park would be my patch.

What I didn't anticipate was that this phone would ring every fucking minute – bearing in mind I'm someone who likes to take my time getting up in the morning, this was tough. That bloody gold phone rang day and night.

What was I supposed to do? I couldn't keep up.

The phone started to ring almost immediately, barely minutes after I'd got in the door. The people were hungry.

My first dilemma was where do I keep this shit? The wardrobe seemed as good a place as any, so I stretched up to the top shelf and shoved the bag inside an empty Babyliss box, behind some handbags.

The second dilemma was more pressing. People kept calling. The order list was already adding up. How was I going to give them what they wanted? Do I move back and forth? Do I take it all out in one go? Doing it one by one meant running in and out of the house all bloody day. It's two flights of stairs up to my mum's house. I ain't doing that, I decided.

Clever thing to do here is consolidate. Economies of scale, ain't that what they call it?

I started bunching them up together, saving myself a few journeys up and down to the Pen, lining up half a dozen people in one spot to save time, handing over plastic bags of fuckery with one hand, taking the money with the other.

Sour

By the second or third time, I was beginning to get looks. I began to feel jumpy. This was too bait, too stupid.

The Feds were gonna get suspicious. I racked my brain. What had Winston done? He was always on the move. Not going anywhere quickly, but never stopping anywhere for too long. But doing it that way meant it was gonna be a long day. Why should I be hanging outside in the cold, when I could be inside, on the sofa?

Yeah, that was that decided. The people are hungry enough. I wasn't going to go to them. I ain't Avon Calling. If they're hungry, they can come to me. My new job would involve working from home – business would take place, specifically, through my bedroom window.

People knocked and slipped their cash through the gap above the sill, and we'd make the exchange. Quick, simple and completely out of sight of my mum cooking in the kitchen. They were just people, after all. They don't hang around for conversation. All these characters cared about was getting their fix. So what was a little extra traffic along the gangway?

The phone kept ringing, like a screaming baby that just wouldn't shut up. A few days into my new career, and already I was feeling overwhelmed. I toyed with the idea of jacking it all. But then I started to see the money rolling in. Twenties, fifties, hundreds. The notes came flooding in quicker than I could count.

Yeah, once I started getting into the swing of it I began to love my new lifestyle. Klaire had been right. I was self-employed and moving up in the world. I wasn't out doing bullshit no more. The risk was less, but the respect was greater. I was still top dog.

Yusuf soon cottoned on. "Bring me in, sis," he'd say. "Bring me in." I could see why. You've got them all lined up, handing

217

something over and getting money back. To kids that seems glamorous. I was getting established.

Yusuf had ambitions of his own. For his 16th birthday he persuaded a friend's big brother to give him a tattoo.

He pretended it hadn't hurt, but hours later he was still trembling. He looked like he was going to pass out. Some blood stained the shirt fabric from his freshly tattooed chest.

"Thug Life" was scrawled across his skinny frame, Tupac-style. He had also started going out with a girl aged 20, with two kids.

I worried about him.

The world ain't your friend. Trust no one. I'd learned that much. But that was Yusuf's problem. He trusted too many people, too easily.

The dynamic had changed. Drex and I were no longer a couple but that didn't mean I got cast aside. Hell no, my name was strong enough.

I was an entrepreneur now. I got a phone that won't stop ringing. I was establishing myself. I had something people needed. That gave me power.

Somewhere, at the back of my head, it had worried me the older heads might have targeted me, unhappy that a new face was manoeuvring on their patch. Had I been a big, bulky character, maybe. But no one seemed to take much notice of the new girl on the block. The block had always been mine. Now I was running my own show. I was just marking my territory.

Real talk, I was missing life inside. I wanted the world to leave me alone. The whole situation with the Man Dem and being a brand-name was fun before I went to prison, but I'd grown up, innit. I was moving over to the other side.

Sour

What I was doing required a different kind of postcode celebrity and I was stepping up, and minding my own business. I didn't need no one to come troubling me.

That applied to the Man Dem too.

From now on, I'd be picking and choosing who I'm socialising with. I liked that mystery. I wanted to be exclusive. I wanted to be the girl that not everyone can get hold of.

So who were my new customers? The mix surprised me. Many were normal men and women who you wouldn't blink twice at if they passed you in Brixton Market. Sure, some were straight outta central casting – death mask faces and that anxious, arm-jangling walk I call the junkie shuffle. But honestly? Most of them made no impression at all. They came and went, no questions asked. Only one woman pricked my conscience.

She looked like death on legs. She was gaunt, Scottish and looked like somebody's granny. Her voice was loud and croaky.

She lived upstairs in the same block, and always used to come knocking at my window late at night. Of all the cats, she was the one who woke me up the most.

"Sour, Sour," she'd hiss, "can you fix me up?" I'd be in bed, or watching TV, or having a bath, when I'd hear that same knock of skinny knuckles on glass, followed by the same croaky voice. "Can you fix me up?"

She always dragged with her a beautiful little kid, man. Red hair and freckles. Seriously cute. Others calling at that time, I'd tell to go away, but this one? I worried if I didn't help her out, she'd be dragging that boy around in the cold all night. I'd sort her out, and watch her drag him back along the landing and up the stairs, and hoped he was being taken home.

At least that child could go back up somewhere warm and safe. Maybe.

I was lying in bed when I heard the croak.

"Sour …"

I popped my head outside. The child stood quietly beneath the window.

"Fix me up … Don't have the money this time, luv, but getting it soon, I promise. I can give you these?"

She offered a skanky pair of earrings. Books, jewellery, freshly stolen CDs – there was always something she wanted to trade off.

"No cash, go home."

"OK, OK," she fussed, finally pulling out a note from tight jeans. Her clothes were so small, they could have been child-sized.

I leaned over and winked at the kid.

"Alright?"

He nodded slightly, but didn't say a thing. In fact, don't think I ever heard him say a word.

I knew she was giving me her last notes. Sometimes I'd made the mistake of giving it to her for free, because I knew that kid was hungry. But it only meant she came more often.

On the bad days, she'd leave her giro book with me as a guarantee. Sometimes took her a whole week to pick it up. If she was giving me this, how could she be feeding that little boy?

Sooner or later, she'd return, poking crumpled rolls of cash through my window, dragging the same silent boy behind her.

Tyrone was the only old face who came to visit. He was doing well. He had studied hard for his exams and was one of the few people I knew who was staying on for sixth form.

"So engineering, yeah? Is that, like, building bridges and shit?"

He explained patiently which courses he was going to apply for, and which universities had the best departments. He was determined, I'll give him that. Good luck to him, I thought.

That afternoon he came over with some R'n'B CDs and we were listening to them in my room. Post-prison present, he called it.

He'd got a part-time job too, working week nights and Saturdays at a printing shop, and going on holiday to Ayia Napa.

"You should see it, Sour. The music, the honeys, man don't know what to do. You should come. Big crew of us going out there again next summer. You'd love it."

"Yeah, I'll bear that in mind."

"Ain't cheap but worth every penny," he said, his eyes glazing over with memories of all-nighters at Black & White and Insomnia.

Money was the one thing I wasn't worrying about, thanks to my new lifestyle. If I carry on at this rate, I thought, I could pay for the whole crew. I made a mental note to book me and Tyrone's flights to party island.

I checked my phone again, for the millionth time.

"What's wrong wit you, girl? Keep checking that phone every second. Expecting Tupac to call?"

The phone rang.

"I'll just be a sec."

I scurried out to the landing and took the order. I sat back down on the bed. Minutes later, another call.

Tyrone looked confused.

"What's going on here? How come your phone's ringing all the time?"

He was looking at me suspiciously.

"Nothing. Wrong number."

"Both of them?"

Sometimes, in these situations, it's better just to act like you can't hear what's being asked.

"You hungry?"

"Man's always hungry."

"Good," I said, jumping off the bed. "Let's go to the pizza shop. I'm buying."

That afternoon, after I'd said bye to Tyrone, I had Winston on my back. I had no choice. It was time to chase up some debts. First on the list was the croaky witch. The thought of having to go upstairs and chase her down made my skin crawl.

I quickly raided the kitchen and headed up the stairwell. She lived three floors up. The flat was easy to spot: it was the one with the cracked, broken-down door and the blinds pulled down in daylight.

When that front door opened, whoof! The smell punched you in the face. It was like the smell of plastic burning. Like someone had set a match to the CD collection, and set alight a bag of rubbish while they were at it. Animal, mineral, vegetable, I had no idea, but it stank. Yeah, you didn't want to hang around up there.

I knocked on the splintered door but needn't have bothered. It wasn't locked. She shouted me through to the living room where she was sitting on a burst sofa with the vagrant bunch of heroin guests who happened to be visiting at the time.

"Alright doll, come and take a seat."

"Nah, I'll just stand."

Occupational hazard. If I wanted to see any money, I knew this had to be done.

The sofa was always full of bodies.

"Sit down, kid," she'd fuss, as she made a theatrical attempt to look for notes that both of us knew she didn't have.

Sour

There was another reason I wanted to go up there. The little boy wandered down the hallway, barefoot. His hair was matted and filthy, and he clung to a dirty blanket.

"You hungry?" I whispered.

He nodded. Always nodding, never speaking.

If I keep your mum cool, I thought, she'll keep you indoors.

I pressed the treats from Mum's kitchen into his hands. Ginger cake, and a packet of salt and vinegar crisps. His eyes lit up. He grabbed the food and ran back down the hall.

"It's just here, somewhere," she shouted, kicking her comatose guests out of the way as she searched around the remaining furniture.

"Bingo!"

She stuffed the note into my hand. This game had plenty of perks, but whenever I saw her I felt bad. Then one day, she stopped coming completely. The flat was empty. I still wonder what happened to that little boy.

The other cats were enough to keep me busy. Yeah, all sorts started arriving at my doorstep. One guy, a Scouser known as Ankles, on account of his missing foot, used to crack me up. Always coming up with designer perfumes and things he'd tiefed from music stores. One day he arrived with a bike.

His entrepeneurship impressed me. Here was a guy with character. It just went to show, if you applied your energy to something you could get your hands on whatever you liked.

"Have this," he said one afternoon, offering up some discount box of perfumes he'd tiefed from Boots. "Take this and a tenner."

"Are you for real? I can buy my own perfumes, my friend."

I pulled down the window, laughing to myself.

I must have dozed off for a few hours because it was dark when the phone woke me up.

223

It was a lady's voice. A new voice I didn't recognise. She sounded Caribbean.

"Are you around?"

As a matter of fact I was.

"Can I come meet you? By the bins at the entrance?"

I occasionally went down there when the house was too hot.

I looked at the clock. It was late, and I really didn't feel like it, but the cash would make up for the money the croaky witch still owed me.

"OK, 10 minutes, yeah?"

The woman hung up.

I pulled the bag from the Babyliss box. There wasn't much left. I wondered whether to take everything or just a couple bags. I hesitated before stuffing all of it in my hoodie. Then I went downstairs.

It was dark but as I was walking down the last flight of stairs I saw a figure heading towards the caged area where they keep the big communal bins, and disappearing out of sight.

Good, I thought. A punctual chick for a change. At least I wouldn't be hanging about.

I turned the corner, but there was no woman waiting for me. Just a guy in a ski-jacket, holding a gun to my face.

"Man don't want to do nuffink serious, understand? Where's the stuff?"

I was looking down the barrel of a handgun. I felt angry. He could at least have had the decency to press it by my temple. Staring down the nozzle at point blank range, darling, that's a different threat entirely.

The blocks were well lit, but there were no lights by the bins. I'd never seen him before in my life. He was wearing dark colours, a dark tracksuit, dark hoodie – you know how it goes.

Blood racing, I pulled out the bag and slowly offered it over. He swiped it out of my hand. I didn't even have time to miss my knife, which was still sitting on my chest of drawers.

"How much is there?"

"About 12 wraps, give or take."

He seemed to hesitate, as if wondering whether to believe me.

"I don't have any more. That's all I got left."

Then he bolted. I lost him pretty quickly in the dark as he darted through the estate. I ran back up to the house, locked the door behind me and pulled the blind tight, all the way down my bedroom window, until not even a flicker of street-light could seep over the sill.

I was still shaking when I lay down on my bed.

I replayed the situation over and over in my head. I couldn't have done anything differently. But this was a serious situation and I was getting into some serious shit. First thing, Winston could never know. He had to believe I was up to the job, that I could protect his lines, just like I said I would. There was no time for amateurishness now.

At first, it was a relief I'd taken it all with me. What would he have done had I only brought two wraps down? He could have marched me all the way into my house.

But the more I thought about all the money I was going to have to work even harder to pay off, the more it made me furious. That chick had fucking stolen from me! I don't suffer that behaviour rightly.

I could have died! Sour or no Sour, it wouldn't have stopped me from getting a bullet in the head. I'm not made of metal.

Even worse, now I owed money. I felt deeply disrespected. Having a gun pulled on you does something to you. You lose something. You've had the worst threatened and you've come out the other side. Some might think it makes you more fearful. I felt the opposite. I'd looked down the barrel of a gun and held my nerve. That gave me confidence.

That's when I realised I need to tool myself up. I needed weaponry. That way I knew if anyone dared threaten my life again, I was in my rights to threaten theirs.

Going Professional

I was always taught round my endz it was the white guys who have the weaponry and ammunition. If you wanted to place an order, you needed to go to one of the older heads, who in turn would make the calls. This was way above the 28s of my age. The Man Dem who were left on the road weren't ready for this kind of behaviour.

I needed to go higher. Every estate has a postcode celebrity from back in the day, an older head who's done the crime, served the time and still got fingers in all the right pies.

Badman used to boast about an ex-serviceman he knew in Brixton who offered to take anyone out for £5,000. That was probably beyond my requirements. No, I decided I would ask someone to put me in touch with the right guys – refraining from telling them the reasons why, of course.

All they needed to know was that I was in some serious trouble. They bought it, and through a guy who knew a guy arranged a meeting. It was as if you needed to be OKed by a serious character. Once someone OKed you, that was the Blue Peter badge right there.

Without being vouched for, forget it. It's like trying to book an appointment with Peter Andre. How you got the money, well, that was up to you.

You place your order, hand over the money, and wait for the call to confirm a time and a place. Of course, the older player holds all the power. They always do.

If you hand over the cash and never hear back, then you've been skanked.

Luckily, doing my own thing had proved pretty lucrative – even despite robbery at gunpoint.

Soon enough, I was given the message.

"It's on. He'll call you."

There was only one type of call I received on the gold phone. So I knew straight away when the phone rang a few days later that this one was different.

"Hi," said the man's voice. The accent sounded different. Not Cockney, but one of them faraway accents. Manchester, maybe? "I'm going on a shopping spree. Heard you wanted to come. Meet me in the Burberry store on Regent Street on Thursday afternoon. I'll ring you three times when I'm there."

Then he hung up. I'd been told to expect to meet anywhere, any time – a café, a nightclub, a designer store. Burberry suited me fine. It sounded like a suitably stylish place to meet up.

I jumped on the bus that afternoon with a spring in my Reebok'd step. I had a wad of notes in my pocket and I was going shopping. I was going to buy something new.

I hung around outside for a long time before going in. Didn't want to be inside too long, else the snotty assistants would start getting suspicious. In the end I timed it just right.

I was admiring a pair of snakeskin shoes, which were looking lonely on an empty, spotlit shelf when the phone rang. I didn't need to answer it, because the man who had just made the call was standing a few metres away from me.

Sour

He wore blue dad jeans and a pink Ralph Lauren shirt, with the navy polo player on his pocket. He was pot-bellied and reminded me of Grant Mitchell – exactly the kind of guy, in other words, who could have been Klaire's husband.

We walked out together, the cute black girl and the loaded white guy who, worst case scenario, appeared nothing more than escort and client. Yeah, we know the story there.

I followed him round the back of Regent Street, and hopped into his shiny black Range Rover which was parked in a back street in Mayfair.

"So, what you after?"

Some might have been intimidated at that point, but thing is, I've always been a demanding girl, yeah. If you don't ask, you don't get.

"It's gotta be light, fresh, chrome-plated, feminine-looking. Something James Bond would like. Miss Moneypenny shit. Get what I'm saying? And I'd like it to sit well in my palm. Something dainty, yeah?"

OK, so I might have got a bit carried away.

There was no flirting. He just smiled.

"What's your budget?"

Now this I had done a bit of research on.

"£500?"

"Right. OK, we'll get back to you," he said.

I'd never met a guy of this calibre before. He looked like a businessman on a casual day. I could smell money. Maybe he wasn't the villain, he just got connections.

Either way, it was almost like meeting royalty. You just automatically assume these people have got a swimming pool.

There I was sitting in the back of a shiny Range Rover in a street in Mayfair, with a man who smelled faintly of cigars. I was moving with the big cats. I felt like I'd upgraded. I smiled inside. I was going up in the world.

I'd seen guns before, of course. Once, Tyrone and I found one discarded in the hedge on the estate. Shit, I remember going to a rave and seeing this guy pull out a Mac-10. It even had a strap so he could carry it around like a tennis bag. And of course there were the young, dumb kids who'd take up the offer from an elder who needed to get rid of one, quick. The idiots thought they'd hit the big time. I used to laugh at them thinking these serious characters suddenly found it in the goodness of their hearts to start giving presents.

But this was like buying a new car. I was going to be getting a piece of my own.

I handed over my £500.

"I'll be in touch."

He waited for me to get out of the car, and drove off, looking like any other swimming-pool-owning, Ranger Rover-driving, tax-avoiding businessman around Mayfair.

I went home on a high that afternoon, thinking about the order I'd placed, and counting down the days and weeks for my James Bond shit to arrive.

Man, I thought it would never come. I was like a kid waiting for Santa Claus.

Way I saw it, I would be a responsible owner. I would not be getting in the devil's way. I wasn't going to go out, flashing my cash and making myself bait. I needed it so that, if disrespect did come to me, I would be within my rights to protect myself.

Defence is the best line of offence, innit?

Three weeks later the call came, and I was told the Brixton address I needed to collect it from.

Sour

I'd been expecting a box of some sort for my luxury item, packaging, like you'd get with an expensive TV or a fancy necklace. So I was a bit disappointed when this unknown elder just handed it to me as it was. I didn't want his mucky hands all over my new toy.

I slipped it into the Head bag I'd brought especially, and couldn't get home quick enough to inspect it.

When I did get home, I could hear the music blaring from across the Pen. I walked in the door to find my mum was hysterical.

"My boy! They took my boy. He no hurt a fly, dat child."

"Mum! What are you talking about? What's happened? Where's Yusuf?"

It took some time to get any sense out of her.

Yusuf had been arrested.

He had done a steam and he got caught for it. He was still an innocent kid.

Boydem had him in custody. I hated police. I hated the system. I hated this whole fucking place.

They could do what they liked to me. I was serious enough to handle it, but my little brother? That was going too far. He was just a kid.

I stormed straight up to my room, leaving Mum wailing and howling in the living room.

I laid the bag on the bed, and opened it up. Grant Mitchell had come up with the goods. The piece fit snugly into the palm of my hand. I got used to the weight, and the feel of the chrome against my palm.

Prison had been fine for me – hell, I'll tell no lies, I was still missing it. But I knew, for all his bravado and new tattoos, Yusuf was still a sensitive soul. I worried how he would cope.

I didn't think being locked up would be good for him, and my first visit proved me right.

When he sent his first VO, I didn't know what to expect.

Feltham ain't no East Sutton Park. Feltham was where it all happened, everyone knew that. If you weren't a gangster when you went in, you sure as hell were when you came out.

What do they expect? When you keep all the Man Dem from different gangs across London all cooped up in the same hardass units, you're asking for trouble. Feltham was a big man's prison for kids. It was known.

Being a visitor there for an afternoon was more daunting than a month at Her Majesty's Service in the luxury of ESP.

Just getting in, you're searched like you're a criminal, dogs sniffing you, fingerprints scanned by a machine. The corridors smelled of bleach. This was serious shit. This was not a place for my little brother to be.

Yusuf appeared behind the glass, and sat down. I wanted to hug him but couldn't. His eyes were wide and frightened, and flickered around the room. He sat on the edge of his seat, checking over his shoulder and fidgeting.

"Alright, sis," he mumbled.

I felt responsible for him. I wanted to help him, to hug him, to tell him he was going to be OK, but I couldn't. That hurt.

They had given him clothes to wear – a burgundy tracksuit – but it was too big, and his skinny frame looked lost. He had lost weight. He seemed lost behind the eyes.

I didn't know what to say.

"Do you need any money?"

He shrugged.

"I've been writing to you. Just keep looking out for stuff."

"Yeah," he mumbled. "Got 'em. Thanks."

Sour

"Gonna be OK, Yusuf. Just gotta keep your head down."

He told me he'd been on 23-hour bang-up. Didn't have much choice.

A year, I thought again. A year is a long time for a child.

Sitting on the other side of the glass brought back memories of visiting my dad, only this time it felt serious. This time there was someone I actually cared about on the other side. The only person I cared about.

It felt like only a few minutes had passed when I was being ushered out of the door and through the security checks again. I turned to wave goodbye, but Yusuf was staring at the ground, head hung. He didn't look up.

Anger was boiling inside me. I wanted to go out onto the streets and cause some mayhem. I needed to cause trouble in his honour. Back home, Tyrone tried to reassure me. Everything happens for a reason, he said. What kind of fucking reason could there be for keeping a boy in prison for a year?

God was trying to fuck with me.

As for Mum, she'd always expected this from me – said a lot that she seemed to sail through my sentence – but Yusuf was her baby. He was the apple of her eye. So it was little surprise that when he was sent down, she broke down.

When I saw the flashing lights at our door, my first instinct was to turn off my phone. Everyone would have to wait. Mum was being carted off in an ambulance. She'd been walking up and down the street, swinging around her baseball bat, threatening to hit people, and was now struggling with the paramedics, yelling Koranic quotations at the top of her voice.

Some neighbours stuck their heads out of windows. Others stopped in the street to watch the commotion as Mum was taken away.

"Salwa!" she yelled from the stretcher. "Call the police! They're trying to kill me! Get your hands offa me …"

I went inside, slammed the door behind me and drew the curtains shut.

So, that was that. Three family members incarcerated. I had my own space and my own money. I would only have myself to worry about.

I went from room to room, pulling shut all the curtains. I wanted to shut the whole world out.

"Datter of darkness," that's what Mum used to call me when I insisted on lying in my darkened room, wishing I was back in prison. Daughter of darkness, damn-straight. Pack up the sun and shut out the world, that's what I wanted to do.

The house was quiet. I missed Yusuf's music. I went in to his room, pressed play on his stereo and took his favourite Dolce & Gabbana blazer out of his wardrobe and into my room. Biggie's "Mo Money Mo Problems" reverberated through the empty house. I collapsed on the bed, cuddling Yusuf's blazer like a blanket, smelling its familiar smell.

I could still hear my mum's reaction when she first heard Yusuf had been arrested. Her words rattled in my ears.

"This is a test from Allah! It's his will. If you kids had not rejected Islam, none of this woulda happened."

I wondered if Yusuf was thinking the same.

Losing It

"Think you're bringing disrespect to my mum's door? Take one more step, just one."

"Wooah, relax, Sour."

I was pointing the ting at him. A baby 8mm. It was really nice-looking in my hand. Real feminine. And I was holding it point blank range at this blood's face, totally prepared to use it face straight, if I had to.

Tyrone had brought some friends over. Having free run of an empty house meant a lot more traffic through the door. They were sitting on the settee, playing the PlayStation. Some were Youngers, others just kids from the estate.

He had been telling us about a run in with some boy from Deptford, at one of the nightclubs he used to go to every weekend. There had been an altercation. Or at least, there nearly had been.

"He tried to offer me out!"

"Did you go ahead with it?"

"Hell no! Stimpy knows him. He's a Ghetto Boy. Proper mental case. I was out with my girl."

He and Keziah were now officially a couple. I was glad things were going well, and felt pride in my Cilla Black role in their relationship.

"We were just there getting a drink. I wasn't in the mood for no nonsense."

"So what did you say?"

"I pointed at his Gucci loafers, and asked him if he felt a bit overdressed, innit."

The settee rugrats laughed. Bouncers came over and threw him out. They said he'd been starting trouble all night.

Yeah, for Badman and the rest of the Man Dem that would have spelt war. But Tyrone had never been one for an altercation.

"You were lucky, bruv."

He laughed.

"You're always gonna have haters," he said. "Shit!" He threw down his keypad in frustration as his PlayStation character was killed by an opponent's lucky punch. "You can't let them get you down."

I was only half-listening to his story about the club.

I'd missed the action the week before. A yout from East had been linked with a Samurai sword. Nearly died. Rumour was a Younger yout from around my way had been involved. The young bucks knew to expect a retaliation.

East youts had their own grievances, and I understood that. But I hadn't expected it here. Not on my doorstep.

I was upstairs when I heard the knock on the door. I didn't recognise the guy as anyone I knew. As he waited for the door to open, he was shifting his weight from one side to another, with a couple of his crew at his back. I got the vibe he was there for trouble, but there were codes and I wasn't prepared to argue. He was bringing disrespect to my mum's front door.

My welcome was not the kind he had been expecting.

As soon as they saw that I wasn't playing, the rest of his crew fell back. I held the ting, steadily, closely, at head height.

Sour

"Take your grievances elsewhere, you hear me? Any of you think you're going to bring trouble to my mum's door, I'm going to lay you out."

Tyrone, ever the peacemaker, jumped off the settee.

"Sour, what you doing?! Leave it alone. Blood's just gonna back off, and we're all going to calm down, yeah?"

He put a soothing hand on my shoulder, and nodded to the guy to step back.

"Just need to pass on a message to your people dem ... what happened won't be taken lightly."

Tyrone tried to reason. "We ain't got nothing to do with last w—"

I wasn't in the mood for reasoning. I had a new motto, and it was called "Leave Me the Fuck Alone".

"Message received, now back off."

"What she's trying to say is you've got the wrong house, yeah? Ain't no one here who was there."

The East youts backed off slowly.

"Just tell your peeps this ain't over. Dunno who these kids are running around on some hype."

Tyrone nodded and squeezed past me to shut the door. It slammed shut, and he pulled across the chain.

He looked upset.

"What the fuck?"

I had power, but this situation had got my back up. Things had moved on to a different scale, and I was struggling to keep it together. The elders on the estate controlled the drugs and the guns.

Some girls liked make-up, some liked fashion; being serious, that was my new passion. I was clever about it, though. Wasn't baiting myself up, showing off when I didn't need to. I ain't no Robocop.

237

Yeah, burners had wiped out that primary power of knives. Suddenly my collection of flick-knives and kitchen knives and other blades looked childish. I had a higher power.

Five bills could get you a nice little hand ting; but don't get it twisted, things also floated by for free. I came across some serious shit. Kinda worries me now the things that can easily fall into young hands.

Once you'd been vouched for, there was always an ex-marine, traveller or retired bad boy from Essex or Tottenham or wherever, willing to do you a deal.

I'd heard of too many deals going wrong, of young idiots taking their bricks of hard-stolen cash to the old boys, exchanging it for their new toy only for the old boys to follow them back to their house, robbing the youngers of their new piece and bare more besides.

Or, worse, you could be buying from the police without even knowing it. That was the biggest gang you want to stay away from: the Feds.

If someone came to try to take my life, they had to take what they got. There was only one problem: that was meant to make me feel safer, but I'd never felt so on edge.

I was living in no man's land. I felt like a soldier with a lost cause. What the cause was, I didn't know. The road had got my back up alright, and I was tense and anxious. I was losing control.

The youts waited some time before daring to leave the house that night, in case East youts were waiting to link them.

Tyrone was the last to leave. He seemed pretty disgusted.

"That was bat-shit crazy stuff back there."

"Fuck you, Ty. Man brought disrespect to my door. I'm moving on a different level now. I have to defend my home."

Tyrone zipped up his hoodie, shaking his head.

"You need to sort yourself out. Gonna give you a bit of space to clear your head, yeah. Call me when you've cut that shit out."

He walked briskly down the stairwell.

"Don't bother. I'll give you all the space you need!"

I slammed the door shut.

I knew Tyrone was right. I'd acted crazy and I knew it. For what? For coming to my door? I had been genuinely prepared to switch on that boy, and it scared me. What if he had stepped one more step? What then?

I was a lone soldier, damn straight. Who was there to help me when I needed it?

Since the rape, I knew I was on my own. That I could handle. My anger was at something bigger. I'd been dealt a bad hand. Why had I been given a rapist as a dad and a manic depressive as a mum?

Was I meant to be grateful for some shitty job, stacking shelves, or cleaning toilets, just because I was born into life on the estates? That was demeaning. I knew I was smarter than that, but prison meant it was already too late to get a proper job. I could rule that out, instantly.

When I thought of the outside world, of GCSEs and sixth form and Tyrone and his engineering, it only made me angrier. I was no longer part of it. I was only 16, and suddenly all those avenues had already been closed off. I'd missed the turnings. There was nothing to do now but thrive and survive.

Way I saw it, the outside world had done nothing for me. So it shouldn't ask me for shit. I'd been to Holloway, I'd done the time. There was nothing else left to aspire to.

Well, not entirely. The phone kept ringing, not with calls from friends. Now it was older heads, trying to recruit me.

Voices I didn't recognise would start to introduce themselves. I never knew how they got my number.

"Come and meet here," they'd ask. "Come and meet me there."

The one who rang moments after Tyrone had left was typical. He called himself Shaquille. I didn't know no one by that name, but he insisted he knew me.

"Come and meet me. I want to run something by you."

"Well, if you've got something to say, you might as well say it on the phone. That's what phones are for."

"I know you're about this ting."

He was letting me know the stripes I'd earned. He told me he had been watching me.

"I know you've got heart. I know no one will fuck with you. How about you come and work for me?"

"Why would I want to do that?"

"Why not? You're acting like you don't know me," said the voice. "I've watched you grow. I've heard your name around."

I told him straight. I wasn't prepared to make another older man rich. If I wanted a pimp, I'd go out on the streets.

"Look, it's not going to happen. Thanks but no thanks. I'm not anyone's sendout."

He sounded almost offended.

"If you come and work for me you'll be earning crazy Ks ..."

"No disrespect intended, man, but I'm going to do my own thing. Laters, yeah."

I hung up.

It was in the fug of this dark cloud of a mood that I went upstairs and took the letter out of my bedside drawer. It was crumpled and faded from re-reading.

"Yo bloodtype, what's popping?" Yusuf wrote. "I've bucked

into a couple Man Dem in here from the road. I'm cool. I've got peeps around me. We're good. We've been jamming on the wing, chilling out, playing pool. Am getting used to tings. Ain't that bad, once man gets into the rithim, innit."

The rest of the letter asked about faces from Roupell Park.

"Send Mum love from her boy. Hope she's not giving you too much shit."

I hadn't told him about Mum. Thought it best if he didn't know. He probably had enough things to be thinking about in there. I knew how unhelpful it was hearing news from home, which you could do nothing about.

"Later, sis. Yusuf."

He had drawn a doodle of a skinny boy, smoking a doobie.

I folded the letter up and put it back into its place in the corner of the drawer.

Maybe I was worrying too much? After all, he sounded in the letter like he was holding up OK. Perhaps he wasn't quite as innocent as I'd like to think. Better. Maybe he'd come out stronger, harder, less naïve.

If he truly was becoming a bit of a bad boy, he should be safe. I corrected myself. No one was ever safe in Feltham – that was well known. It was a pressure cooker for grievances across the city. No one was ever safe from harm – from rivals or themselves.

No matter how hard I tried to look at the positives, I kept on coming back to the same feeling. This was my worst nightmare. For the first time in my life, I was heartbroken.

David

Shotting was proving lucrative, I couldn't deny that, but all that activity round my house was getting bait. I'd bought myself some nice threads and a car – a sweet, sporty thing that made me feel like Brixton's answer to Penelope Pitstop.

As time went on, I began to think it might not do any harm, when someone asks me what I do, to have an alternative response to 'road chick'.

I remembered how much I'd liked doing the girls' hair at East Sutton Park. I was master at applying false eyelashes in a hurry, and could do Sixties' streaks of black liquid eyeliner with my eyes shut. It was decided: I enrolled on a hair and beauty course at college.

With the help of some of Dr Chris's contacts, I applied to college and got a place. The beginning of term, I put on my best tartan blazer and short skirt, and backcombed my beehive till it was standing tall and triumphant. Hell yeah, Amy Winehouse ain't got nothing on me.

"First day?"

I nodded.

"Me too."

The class had finished and I was hanging back, trying to avoid all the excited first-day chat among all the eager beavers trying to make friends.

Sour

I assumed another class must have just finished next door at the same time, on account of all the boys hanging around in the corridor, but found out later they had come especially to sniff around the beauty students. Apparently, it's well known that all the nice chicks study beauty therapy.

David was studying business and computing. I'll be honest with you, he was not my cup of tea, but over those first few weeks of college that boy grew on me like a rash.

I mean, for starters, he had sideburns shaped like the Versace symbol. Oh my days, I couldn't believe what I was seeing. Big square things that must have taken him ages every morning. But the boy had style, you had to give him that. He was freshly dressed with his designer gear, Moschino trousers and the latest trainers.

There was one big difference between David and all the other boys I knew. All his gear was legitimately worked for, darling. A normal kid. He was the only person I knew who went to a cash machine to get money.

His mother was a primary school teacher, his stepfather a first-aider at St Johns, and they lived in a house with a garden in Dulwich. A proper family. I had never known anyone like that before. His was like legitimate money from a legitimate family.

Yeah, he knew some of the Ghetto Boys from New Cross and Deptford, but he was from good stock.

Even the good boys can't avoid the bad boys sometimes, you know.

Maybe that was the problem. Did I fall in love with the boy or his background? Sometimes it was hard to tell.

There was no need to be Sour with David. That didn't impress him. I had to learn how to be myself.

"You should come and roll with me one day," he said one afternoon after college. He had a car. It was his mum's, which she let him borrow.

"Yeah, go on, come for a drive. Come and see my endz. You don't know my endz."

So, I took him up on the offer. I switched the phone on silent, and crossed into SE22.

His house was on a proper road. There were no estates nearby and the door had a number with a bell on the outside.

There was a wheelie bin outside in the front garden, and a couple steps leading to an outer door with a stained-glass window.

Wow.

The hallway smelled of very fresh laundry. Everything smelled clean. There were fresh flowers in a vase, and a big open-plan kitchen led out to a patio at the back.

The bathroom even had a shower cubicle *and* a bath.

"Hello."

His mum was a very swanky, stylish-looking lady from the Dominican Republic. She was the kind of mum who cooked food, and froze it and stored it. It was thanks to her he knew how to make spaghetti Bolognese, and chicken and rice, and was trained in how to keep a house perfect.

Yeah, he was raised well, man. He was neat and tidy, and knew how to fold things. You could see from their house that everything had a place.

"Who do we have here?"

She seemed relaxed.

"Mum, this is my new yat."

"And what is a yat?" she laughed, washing her hands under the tap, and wiping them on a floral dishcloth.

"My new girl."

"Pleased to meet you."

I smiled my sweetest smile and shook her hand. I wondered what she was thinking, of the jewel piercing in my lip, or the swirls of black Islamic script I'd just had tattooed on my cheekbones.

But if she was disapproving, she had the good manners not to show it.

I could feel my phone vibrating in my bag, and wished it would stop.

"What's for dinner?"

"What do you want?"

"Any preference," he asked me, picking up the remote control and getting comfy on the sofa.

I shook my head.

"Any of that chicken stew left?"

"Yes," his mum called through. "In the pot. Help yourselves."

"Sweet."

I couldn't imagine him being rude to his mum. In fact, I got the feeling he was very protective of her, the way she was protective of him. That evening, watching TV together and finishing the stew, followed by ice cream, I managed to avoid most of his questions about my family.

From then on, I was always round his way. I took pleasure in switching off my phone in the evenings, adopting his life and pretending it was my own. I was craving legitimacy, and if it was too late to get it myself, I'd just have to channel it through someone else.

David seemed proud of his family. He talked a lot about his stepdad training the local football team at the weekends, and doing his first-aid shifts. In my world, first aid meant trying not to panic while pressing your hand on some yout's wound. Or, more often than not, taking them to hospital and dumping them in the parking bay.

We even walked down the street holding hands – I'd never done that with anyone. He introduced me to people who cared less about being a brand-name, and more what course you studied.

If he said, let's go out to get some food, he didn't mean the kebab shop, he meant an actual restaurant. When he bought me presents, I knew he hadn't tiefed them.

If we walked past a new café or restaurant, he'd say things like "Should we go and try it?"

Things like that thrilled me. I had other top drug-dealers who use to think they could woo me. Legitimacy was much more exciting.

So I began college with two lives: the one at home, with the phone always ringing in an empty house, and the other with David. For the first few months, at least, I managed to prevent the sour bits from meeting the sweet.

One night, I asked David to drop me off on Brixton Hill. I was about to get out, when he reached for my wrist, pulled me towards him, and kissed me. I liked the way he kissed – like he meant it.

He stroked my face, and smiled his stupid smile. "You're beautiful," he said.

"Shut your mouth!" I shot back.

It was so much easier to respond with an insult than just accept the compliment. As soon as I said it, I wished I could take it back and replace it with something less hostile, something softer. But softness didn't come naturally. It made me nervous.

He stroked my cheek again, studying the tattoo.

"When did you get that done?"

I'd made a promise to myself I would get the tattoo on my cheekbone as soon as I got out of prison but I wasn't about to tell Mr Legitimate about that colourful part of his new girl-friend's past. Not yet.

"A few months ago."

"And what does it mean?"

"It says God in Arabic. Allah."

He ran his finger over the dark script, which swirled subtly against my skin.

"It makes you look sexy."

This boy was confusing me. It was meant to make me look fierce.

"It ain't there for sexiness," I growled.

He kissed the other cheek. "Well, I like them."

I flinched but he pulled me into another kiss, until my guard dropped.

"See you tomorrow."

I didn't know whether to smile or scowl, but in the end I mustered just a strange combination of the two.

I wasn't in the mood for going straight home into the empty house, so decided to check out the road, to see who was rolling.

I was pleased to spot Wayne, a character I knew from a nearby estate, and a few others hanging on Coldharbour Lane.

"OK, stranger, how are you?"

Our mums had known each other back in the day, but it had been a long time since I seen his face. He was as big and cuddly as ever. That's why they called him Blobby. Most boys would be uncomfortable with this, but not Wayne. He wore it with pride.

"So you out now? When did you get out?"

"Few months back, innit. It wasn't so bad. How's your mum?"

"Yeah, she's good, man, busy with the church, y'know how it is, innit."

"So what's a good mama's boy doing out here so late?" I teased.

"Man bored, innit. Nuttin ain't going on. You got something going?"

He flashed a cheeky smile.

"You always got something going on, girl. Bet you do. Got some friends for us?" he teased back.

His friends were now paying attention, sniggering.

"No, I'm rolling by myself. That's how I'm doing it right now. This is the new me. I don't need no friends."

His older friend cut in.

"So who's the chick, Blobby?"

"This is Sour, from Brixton Hill."

Why did guys always do that? Introduce you like you weren't there?

"Sour? But you look so cute and innocent," he laughed. I could feel it coming. I took a deep breath and waited.

"Why do they call you Sour? Is it coz you got a sour pussy?"

And there it was.

"You're hilarious. Chris Rock ain't got nothing on you, man."

He was still cracking up at his own joke.

Yeah, I wasn't missing anything on the road.

My phone was buzzing again. These people were getting anxious.

"You gonna be OK getting home?" asked Wayne. "Young girl like you shouldn't be out this late, man. It's dark."

He was a nice guy, Wayne.

Sour

"I can look after myself, don't worry about me. More to the point, it's you guys who should be worried. Why don't you guys come off the road, before the Feds come pick you up, and start bothering you?"

Wayne shook his head, unconcerned.

"Feds ain't gonna bother us. We ain't doing nuttin."

"OK, say no more. Make sure you roll safe."

"You too, see you round."

And I didn't think anything more of it until I switched on the news several weeks later.

Inshallah

Salaam Alaikum,

Here's hoping all is well with you, sis. I'm fine, honest. How's Mum? I'm missing her chicken and rice, but tell her I'll be home soon. I've been training at the gym a lot, and been praying. There's a chaplaincy here, and the other Muslim boys are teaching me lots of things about Islam.

We got it so wrong before, but I understand it now.

I can just imagine Mum's face when you tell that. She's gonna be so proud! I'm gonna know the Qur'an as well as her.

Seriously though, I'm in good spirits. I'm hopeful about the appeal. Allah knows best. Nothing can happen without Allah's say-so.

It was tough at first, but since I've been praying, things have been making a lot of sense. Have you been fasting? Maybe you should consider coming back to Islam? Life will be better for you. We had it all wrong before. We weren't taking it serious back then.

They also give you courses in here. They do brick-laying, motor mechanics, painting and decorating. I'm doing mechanics. It's going well.

Thanks for your letter. I think a beauty salon sounds like a great idea!

I'll send you another VO soon.

See when you come, Insh'allah,

Yusuf

He had signed off with something in Arabic that I didn't understand.

I lay back on my bed and put the folded letter with the rest. On my bed was a toy sausage dog, a present from David. Along the length of the dog's body was a shiny satin slogan: *I love you thiiiiiiiiiiis much*. I pulled it out from behind my back, where it was making me uncomfortable, and chucked it across the room.

I read the letter again.

I was proud of my little brother. I'd noticed a change in his letters. He was writing more eloquently for a start, and clearly reading a lot. He had never been the strongest at school, but it seemed like he was trying hard. He was looking on life more seriously. His praise of my beauty salon white lie felt like advice from a big man.

It sounded like he had found peace.

Yeah, I liked receiving his letters. They reassured me. Maybe I had been wrong? Maybe Feltham was capable of doing some good, after all?

Say what you like about the regime inside, but my little brother didn't want to be a gangster no more. That was something.

The letters that followed reassured me even more. He had started doing talks at the prison mosques, and volunteering to do readings. He was finding a new role for himself.

Even when his appeal failed, and his parole got knocked back, his strength of character surprised me. He said he had prayed a lot, and that the anger was fading. Even when I wrote to tell him about Mum, his reply impressed me, and suggested, once more, that returning to the religion of our childhood had brought him the peace and comfort that I was now craving.

On the real, on some level, I envied him.

I put away his letter, and busied myself, looking for a spare space to store Winston's latest delivery.

The phone rang. My lifestyle was tiring me out. Not so much the work itself, but keeping it hidden from David. People were getting annoyed. Some had already gone elsewhere. It was only a matter of time before Winston started to complain.

I looked at the clock. Where was he? David had looked at the fridge and complained it was bare. He was always complaining these days. He was spoiled, that was his trouble. I had told him, this ain't his house. If he wanted Masterchef, he could go back to his mum's.

He had stormed out, real angry.

That was at 2pm. It was almost 9pm now. The phone rang again. I couldn't ignore it any longer.

"Yeah? Depends. How much do you want?"

At that moment the door opened. It was David, standing with his hands full of shopping.

I ducked into the hallway and up the stairs so he couldn't hear.

"Come round in 10."

I hung up, and put the phone down.

David stared me up and down. "You look skinny. You never used to be so skinny."

"That's coz man been waiting on you to fill up the fridge for days."

He started unpacking the shopping and slamming the packets of microwave food into the shelves, not saying a word. The silence hung like a black cloud between us. He was angry. Even angrier than when he left.

"Met Jal when I was out, a friend of someone called Stimpy … Said he knew you."

Sour

The name rang a vague bell, but it was the mention of Stimpy that got me worried. I pretended I didn't care.

"Oh yeah? There's a lot of big talk on the road. Wouldn't go believing it …"

"Not much," he said, chucking a bumper packet of crisps into the cupboard with venom. "Just told me my girlfriend was a gangster. That she was knife-happy. That she hurt people."

"Man Dem talk lies, don't they."

"Mmm."

It scared me more when he went quiet. I preferred it when he was shouting. Scream, yell, throw the microwave through the bloody window. Do anything, just don't be silent.

Truth was, I'd fallen for this boy, and it tormented me. Just when I'd worked out who I was, or at least what I was going to be, and how I was going to do it alone, along came this nice legitimate boy who confused me, until nothing made sense any more.

Being in love is meant to make you feel safe, innit? Being loved is meant to make you happy. So why did I feel so unsure? I couldn't understand how another person could have me in tears so easily. No one else had that power over me. Only David.

He didn't need knives and Glocks to hurt me; all he had to do was say the right thing. All he had to do was open his mouth, and say something hurtful, and it felt like the end of the world.

I had heart but I couldn't fight back when it came to feelings. This boy made me feel the one thing I'd sworn I'd never be: he made me feel vulnerable.

"Jal said that you'd been in Holloway for robbery, and that you stabbed a boy from summer school. Obviously, I told him he'd got it wrong, that my girlfriend was sweet and kind and would never hurt someone like that. I told him it must be a different Sour. But he seemed pretty sure it was the same Sour."

David was laughing bitterly and shaking his head, punishing himself for being so trusting.

"Then, you know what he said?"

I hated him at that moment. Why was he tormenting me?

"You know what he said? Same thing you said to me, first night we went out. He said, 'That's why she's Sour; opposite of sweet.'"

Tears burned behind my eyes. Something seared my gut like acid, and stole the breath from my lungs. I think it was shame.

"You know how to make a man feel like a fool, don't you?"

"So what?" I screamed. "You gonna trust some stranger in the street over me? You just think you're better than me, always have, that's your problem. He's not the problem in our relationship, David. Wanna know the problem? You think you're too good for me."

"Yeah, well, I'm beginning to think that maybe I am."

The phone rang. I could see a shadow shuffling by the landing. I ran up to my room, grabbed two boxes of perfume, and slipped outside to exchange them with a pair of sore, chapped hands for £60.

When I came back David was sitting at the table, with his head in his hands.

"If you don't like it you can fuck off, I'm not bothered."

I could see a new look in his eyes. He was ashamed of me.

"So that's it now?" I screamed, voice cracking. "Are you embarrassed to be seen with me?"

The fight had gone out of him.

"No, don't be stupid. You're being paranoid."

"Paranoid? Well, if I'm such a gangster, why shouldn't you be?"

Truth was there was only one person ashamed of me in that room and it wasn't him.

"I ain't wasting my time with some yout who can't even defend his girl against some stranger in the street. If you're not interested in me, I'll go out and get somebody else."

He looked up sharply. He looked hurt. I was on a roll. I could feel tears rising up but I was fucked if I was going to let him see me cry. That was not an option.

"If you want to fuck off, do it. Fuck off. Who cares? Actually, you know what …" I said, gathering up his coat and his stuff and shoving them into his chest. "Go home and cry to your mum. Get out, before I give your stepdad some injuries to patch up."

David shook his head in disbelief.

"What a bitch you can be."

"Damn straight. And you're a pussy. Man don't need you in my life."

He was fuming now. He kicked the chair from the table.

"I'm not scared of you, Sour, if that's what you're trying to do. Jal's right. You're just a girl at the end of the day. You might think you're tough on the road, but I ain't buying it. You're a fake. I can see right through it."

I flew at him. Why did he always say those things, the things that hurt me most? He fell back against the kitchen units. I was throwing punches now, I was mad.

David grabbed my wrists and swung me round till I was pressed against the kitchen counter, arms restrained. I bit him on the shoulder and he squealed with pain, releasing one of my arms.

"Get – off – me!"

I reached out for something to grab. My hand connected with the kettle. I slammed it into his face, and lukewarm water spilled onto his chest.

He was stunned. He heaved for breath and staggered backwards, fumbling for his inhaler.

David was having an asthma attack.

He sounded like he was dying. Good, I thought. I slid down the kitchen units, crouching on the floor. I was glad he couldn't speak. All I wanted was for him to be quiet, to stop saying those words.

When he finally got his breath back, he pushed himself up and walked out that door, calling me all the names under the sun. I leaned over the balcony, watching him go, unsure whether to run after him or scream as loud as I could. Not for the first time, I looked down at the concrete slabs below and thought about pressing my weight over the wall, and just letting myself fall.

I don't know how long I'd been there when the couple from upstairs appeared at the stairwell. You'd see him in the early mornings, swaggering along the walkways, with a can of lager in his hand. I didn't see her much. But I could see she was dressed up for a night out – cheap earrings jangled at her jaw, and her hair was pulled into a tight ponytail. They'd been arguing. He was drunk, so was she, staggering behind him in high heels, with make-up smeared across her face.

They hadn't seen me. Or maybe they had, and didn't care. "Fucking bastard," she screamed, halting like a child mid-tantrum, and throwing her bag at him. He spun round, grabbed her by throat and pressed her up against the harled wall. Her legs nearly gave way underneath her, as she stumbled backwards over a bag of rubbish lying by the door.

I knew I should go indoors, ignore it, but I was in no mood

to mind my own business – my own business being in the state it was. She was trying to spit on him, through squashed cheeks. He slapped her, spitting back at her, and saying something I couldn't hear.

"Why don't you leave her alone?"

He looked around in astonishment.

"I'll fuck you up and all, you black bitch."

Now, I ain't going to tolerate that. Some would say I should never have got involved. Others would hi-five me. But suddenly this ugly bastard had given me the green light. All it took was a little disrespect. He'd obliged. Now I had no choice but to get all Kung-Fu Panda on this fucker.

He was so arrogant, he turned his back on me. Big mistake. I sprinted across the walkway and did a running, flying kick, knocking him off balance.

I'd show him what a black bitch could do.

I must have winded him, or done some damage landing a lucky kick, because now the beer-bellied shit was on his knees on the walkway.

It was his girlfriend who yanked me off, by my hair. The ungrateful bitch. I had come to help her, and now she was protecting her ugly brute of a boyfriend.

"Baby, baby," she said, dropping to her skanky knees to hug him and wipe the hair from his face. She looked up at me through tearful, panda eyes.

"Leave us alone," she spat.

Fine, have it your way. I disappeared, locking the door behind me, and slumped back down on the chair in the kitchen. I didn't have the energy to pick the kettle up off the floor, or clear away the chaos from our fight.

I looked at my reflection in the microwave door.

I didn't know the animal I had become.

No Such Thing as Justice

Yusuf smiled broadly and gave me a big hug.

"Salaam Alaikum, sis."

He looked good. Gone were his tracksuits, designer gear and the bum fluff on his upper lip; in its place was a handsome young man, dressed all in white. It was almost like an angel had appeared.

He chatted away happily on the journey home. I told him about college, or at least what I imagined college life would be like if I turned up more often.

I'd only ever known boys to come out of Feltham meaner, harder, tougher. If they had a fraught relationship with authority before, Feltham tended to turn it into pure hatred.

But Yusuf surprised me. He gave me hope.

He told me about the whole wad of certificates he'd gained inside; one of them was in repairing white goods – air conditioning, tumble dryers, that sort of thing. He was going to become a repair man. He didn't even speak slang no more. He was like a whole new person. I was so proud of him. It was almost like I was picking up my older brother, not my younger one.

"I'm not going on the road no more," he said. "No more buses neither. I'm going to take my driving test and buy myself a car. Saleem said a cousin of his could sort me out with something cheap."

"Have I picked up the right brother?" I joked.

"Honest, Sour. I sorted my head out in there. Met some people who really changed my view of things. I'm going to work. I want to find a job, a wife, earn money to look after her. It's Allah's will."

Wow, I couldn't believe it. I really looked up to him. You could clearly see he had found peace within himself. That aura, sense of being, you were drawn to it.

Truth be told, I was jealous. You know that calmness, that serenity that sometimes oozes out of people? "Emanate". That's the word, innit? I wanted some of that.

While doing deals kept my money rolling in, and David kept my emotions in a constant state of flux, Yusuf kept to his word. He led a quiet, faithful life, going to the mosque every day, and getting an apprenticeship.

He no longer went to the same Brixton mosque where we'd struggled to learn Arabic as kids. Now, he went north, all the way to Regent's Park and Finsbury, where they provided free dinners to encourage the faithful to trek that little bit further.

His new imam even set about introducing him to a nice girl from a good home, and just a few weeks later he married her, just like he said he would.

He soon moved out, and once again I had the house to myself.

David and I were back into our cycle of fighting and making up. I'd come back from his house late. The flat was cold, and quiet, with a flickering light in the front room that I'd forgotten to fix. I switched it off, and went to investigate what food was left in the fridge. Unimpressed, I shut the fridge door, and opened a packet of crisps and can of coke instead.

I must have fallen asleep on the settee, because that's where I was lying down when the phone rang. It was around 6am. I was about to hang up when I recognised the number. Keziah.

I pushed myself upright.

"Hello?"

I didn't immediately recognise Keziah's voice. It sounded high-pitched and fragile.

"Sour?"

"Yeah? What's gwarning?"

"It's Tyrone," she sobbed. She kept on repeating his name, unable to get her words out.

"What? What is it?"

"He's dead."

It didn't compute.

"Kez, stop playing tricks, man. It's too early in the morning for this shit!"

I could hear her crying more clearly.

"He didn't do nothing, Sour. He didn't do nothing ..."

She was speaking rubbish. She had to be.

But the sobs on the end of the line, they were real.

She told me how they'd been out in a club in the West End, celebrating their engagement.

"It was mistaken identity. Some hothead youts thought he was a rival. Everything was going cool. He said he was going to the bar to get us some drinks whilst I went to powder my nose. You know how we get down gyal?

"All I heard was mayhem and screams and all sorts. I went running back looking for him, and then I saw him ..." She started sobbing again. "He was just lying there, on the floor ..."

It was a night I should have attended too, but Tyrone was

still angry at me and I was in no mood to be lectured about my lack of hospitality that night.

All I could say was: "But he doesn't even pack a shank."

As if only those who deserved it were the ones who got hurt. That had been the law of my life – until then. That was the code of the road. Innocent people didn't get hurt. It wasn't meant to work like that.

"He doesn't pack a shank."

I felt sick. I imagined Tyrone having a shower, splashing on his aftershave, putting on one of his fresh shirts, not thinking for a second he wouldn't be returning home.

"Where are you now?"

"Back in Brixton. I've just left the police station. His mum was there, Sour. You should have heard her when they told her …"

It wasn't the reality of death that hit me. It was the surge of love I had for that boy. I didn't have love left for many people. Tyrone was my only true friend. Tyrone was one of the good boys.

When Man Dem died, faces you knew from the road, there was often anger, emptiness sometimes, but never love. Not grief, not really. No one mourned Cyrus. He lived by the shank and he died by it. Same with all the rest who were there one day, rolling with the Man Dem, and being remembered at their funeral the next, with sobbing mums screaming about guns and blaming everyone else.

But if Tyrone could die, anyone could. There truly was no such thing as gang justice. Gang justice was meant to operate within the gangs, not outside. It was all a lie.

"They got 'em on CCTV."

They would say that his killer was known to police, and that they hoped to be bringing him in soon. And so they did.

But the trial would collapse – five witnesses refused to give evidence. They decided that justice for Tyrone wasn't worth their lives, and though I was angry I could understand.

My head was still spinning. I felt dizzy.

I asked Keziah if she wanted me to come round.

"No," she said. She sounded exhausted. "I just want to go to sleep."

Her voice cracked, and suddenly I heard her wailing.

"Keziah? What is it? Speak to me."

It took her a few moments to speak.

"I've still got his blood on my dress."

The Mosque

Mum was released the day after the funeral.

"Wha dis? You're the datter of Darkness, too right," she said, going through the house, pulling open the curtains I liked to keep closed, yanking up the blinds and bathing the house in light.

She went through that house like a Tasmanian devil, wielding a bin liner with yellow rubber gloves, cleaning surfaces until they shone, and chucking the wilting flowers David had brought me as an apology after our last argument into the rubbish.

Yusuf too had come home for the occasion. Naturally, Mum was delighted her baby boy had embraced Islam. She was also pretty psyched he could fix the washing machine too.

Yusuf looked well. Marriage seemed to suit him. He had shot up, and was now quite a few inches taller than me. I tried to put on a happy face, but I could never hide the truth from Yusuf. He knew me better than anyone. I could see the concern in his eyes. When Mum went out of the room, he asked if I was OK.

"You look skinny. Your eyes look puffy."

"Thanks very much, Denzel Washington."

"Nah, I just mean, are you OK? You seem stressed."

"Lot going on, innit," I shrugged.

He clocked my new clothes and my expensive trainers, and shook his head.

"You need to come back to Islam, sister. I mean it, for real." He held up my wrist to get a better look at my flash new watch. "These things," he tutted, "they don't matter, y'know. When you're gone you can't take them with you."

"Yeah, well, while I'm here they help tell me the time," I snapped.

"All I'm saying is God is evident in everything that surrounds us. Everything happens for a reason, innit. Being inside helped me – it was Allah's will. You gotta stop aspiring to this Biggie life. Where's that gonna get you? In the grave or in a jail cell."

The more pious Yusuf became, the more I grew ashamed of myself. He had turned things around. He had turned his back on steaming and money. He was happy.

I looked at my little brother's earnest face. Before I could get annoyed at his lecturing, he winked and flashed a mischievous smile. I couldn't help smiling with him.

"So tell me more about this Muslim brother."

"The authorities, they don't want him there. They've kicked him out into the street, so he's gathering youts there every Friday. You shoulda seen the TV cameras! He says the media is trying to make war with Islam."

"So why do you go?"

"There's some good people there too, innit? It's the brothers' mosque. They're good to lots of proper poor boys from Algeria, Somalia, places like that. They give them food and shelter."

Yusuf's new mosque intrigued me. I worried about him praying with all these characters.

"Don't worry, Sis," he tried to reassure me. "I stay away from the ones I don't like. They're too forceful, man. They invited me paintballing next week – they're going on a trip outside London somewhere."

"Are you going to go?"

"Nah. No way. That's not what Islam's about, innit? These guys, they're not preaching the beauty of Islam, the only true religion. Anyway, I gotta work."

Work's for clowns, I thought. I'd have gone paintballing in a second, but that's what I admired about Yusuf these days. He had discipline.

"So, this Muslim brother, what exactly does he say?"

"The house of Allah should be open. If we don't defend our mosque, who's going to defend it? If we can't liberate our own mosque, how can we liberate Palestine? There is no victory except with the help of Allah …"

"Do ye want some soup?"

Mum was shouting from the kitchen. We shouted back at her that we didn't.

"Anyway," I said, "I'm glad that you're happy, Bro."

He nodded and smiled. "I am. We have to be grateful to Allah for all his blessings. I know I'm going to dedicate my life to dawah."

I remembered that word: spreading the message.

"But stay away from the psychos, yeah?"

He laughed.

"I'm not an idiot. Bye, Mum," he shouted next door. "I gotta go. Said to Amina I'd help her with some boxes. Keep telling her there's plenty time to get a nursery ready, but she wants it done yesterday …"

The phone rang. "Hang on, wait a minute. Just gotta get this."

I jumped up the stairs two at a time, and snuck into my room.

"Can you fix me up?"

I had to check. I hadn't seen Winston for a while. Stocks were running low. I pulled myself up, and looked into the shoeboxes on the top shelf of my wardrobe.

"Nah, I'm out."

They hung up.

By the time I went back downstairs, Yusuf had gone.

The Raid

"He's been arrested."

"What's up?"

It was a bad phone line. David clearly hadn't heard me.

"I *said* he's been arrested!"

"Who has?"

"Yusuf."

Not Yusuf. Not now. Not for this. Life was falling apart. My kid brother ain't no terrorist.

"What happened?"

I told him what Yusuf had told me in his single phone call.

"He said they invited him to a restaurant. He said he didn't want to go but when a brother invites you to dinner you can't say no."

"Who's they?"

"Men from the mosque."

There had been around a dozen of them, he said, all sitting in the private dining room at a Chinese restaurant in Southwark.

"Anyways, before they know it, MI5 are raiding the room, telling them all to put their hands on the table, and that everything will be explained.

"They spun his house and found some kind of book from the mosque."

267

What were the exact words again? "He was found 'in possession of material useful to a terrorist' or some shit like that."

It was only a book. It wasn't an instruction manual or anything like that. It was just a book. It wasn't even his. Boydem had got it wrong – Yusuf was bad once, for real. But he was good now. He'd found peace. Why were they victimising him now? That's not the way it should be.

Turned out some of his new mosque friends had been under surveillance for months, thanks to a nutter in Hackney who liked to call himself Osama Bin London. He'd been brainwashing a ragtag bunch of newly recruited Jamaican boys, recent converts, former crackheads – deluded jihadis of that kind of calibre.

The same person was accused of setting up training camps attended by some of the 21/7 bombers – remember them? The ones who tried to blow up buses and trains three weeks after the 7/7 bombings, with explosives made from hair bleach and chapati flour.

They could have killed hundreds. Thank God they lacked the basic maths to count out the ingredients.

"The paintballing!"

"What you are talking about?" asked David.

"Yusuf told me about them. Said he didn't like the way they talked."

Turned out the paintballing trips he had escaped were actually al-Qaeda training sessions – albeit ones that took place inside a paintballing centre in Berkshire.

In fact, while Yusuf was spending Saturdays working as a repair man, fixing the tumble dryers and washing machines of South London and trying to earn some legitimate money for his family, his brothers at the mosque were visiting Cumbria and the New Forest, organising secret assault courses and playing at jihad.

Boydem even attached cameras to trees and shit, recording this band of brothers in the woods, doing forward rolls with sticks. It was like watching bloody *Carry On Taleban*. Or a really rubbish episode of *The Krypton Factor*.

It was the discovery of that book in his house that did it for Yusuf. His biggest crime was to have the misfortune of being with them that night, tucking into a chicken chow mein.

His lawyer advised him to plead guilty for a reduced sentence. He got two years.

He is a good man, my brother. He's got a good memory for the Qur'an, he understands Islam. But how shall we put it … he's gullible.

I don't believe for a second Yusuf was taken in by that psycho shit. He was simply in the wrong place at the wrong time.

I thought of him back in a police cell, and wanted to give him a hug and a good talking to. I wanted him to look very closely at the friends he had around him. I wanted him to realise that not everyone was as innocent and pious as he was.

Islam had been good for Yusuf.

Me personally, well, I'd jumped out of it as soon as I could. I felt something I didn't understand, or want to understand, was being forced on me against my wishes. What was the point of being bound by a religion, but not understanding its terms? The most troubling part for me was that the people forcing it on me didn't seem to care whether I understood it or not. All I had to do was accept it. That ain't good enough for me.

God had looked out for me. I realised that now. There had been times I should have been dead. But Islam had never given me peace in the way it had Yusuf.

He was a peaceful Muslim. It had changed his life – for the better. And now he was being punished for it. I knew he had done nothing wrong. I couldn't take it in. It made no sense.

As I kept saying down the phone, "It was only a book."

I answered David's questions – about where he was being held, when he'd go to court, and what kind of sentence he was facing – until I could answer no more. How could he possibly understand? His brother was a dentist.

Our relationship had changed since David found out about my past. Yeah, sure, he'd stuck around, which was more than some boys woulda done, but I wasn't sure it was for the right reasons.

Now I wondered whether he was with me just for the thrill. A dark thought niggled. Maybe being with me gave him some street cred. Maybe I was his rebellion against a nice, happy home life of Tupperware and fridges that are always full?

I started to worry he was getting a kick out of having a girlfriend from the wrong side of the tracks. I had given him Sweet. That was the deal. What if he wanted Sour?

I told him I'd call him later. I needed some time alone. I whipped on my poncho, grabbed the house keys and cash, and went out the door.

I walked for hours. Past the empty Pen, where the net-less basketball court stood empty and me and Ty used to hang, past the kids queuing for Chinese chips at Tens takeaway, past the Quaker meeting house, until I reached Brixton Hill.

At the Man Dem meeting spot outside the police station, an old woman was having a rest under the tree, leaning on her tartan trolley while having a fag. Wilting bouquets of flowers had been strung around the trunk, tributes to various dead youngsters whose fading pictures were pinned to the trunk in plastic pocket folders. One included a long, handwritten note, but the words had been long since ruined by rain.

The Man Dem were nowhere to be seen. I wondered who was left. It was a warm summer evening, the kinda evening when the Youngers would hang around the open doors of parked cars, playing music, smoking weed, boasting about the chicks they'd banged and planning the next altercation. There was no one I recognised in Morley's either, or any of the usual Brixton Hill haunts.

Down the hill, the concrete blocks of Angell Town loomed large. I considered heading down there to see Keziah and find out how she was doing and ask after Tyrone's family, but I couldn't face it. The funeral was still too fresh, the suspicious looks from relatives I'd never met still seared on to my memory. You brought this on, they seemed to say. The stench from bad kids like you, their stares said, you are the ones to blame.

I left early, having slipped in silently once the service began. I lingered long enough to see his mum, brother and sisters kiss the coffin, listened to the speech his mum gave from underneath a broad black hat, and watched Keziah sobbing in the front row.

"Don't let the haters get you down." Was that not what Tyrone had said the last night I saw him? Easier said than done.

I turned my back on Angell Town, and headed north. Red buses rumbled along, brakes exhaling like large, metal lungs. Groups of girls in short skirts and heels they could barely walk in giggled out of off-licences, armed with bottles of wine to drink while doing their make-up. *Big Issue* sellers hawked their last copies. Past kebab shops and KFCs, past Ladbrokes and the loan shops. At Windrush Square I turned right, back up

Coldharbour Lane. It was the same walk I'd done with Tyrone a thousand times, up to Myatt's Fields.

The park was closed when I arrived, the gates were shut, the bandstand out of bounds. I didn't care. I just needed to keep on moving. The city had that summer buzz. You could feel it, that delicious freedom that comes from week upon week of glorious, hot weather. That up-for-anything vibe that comes from sunbathing in parks, paddling in fountains and drinking outside.

These were my endz. These were my streets. This was my postcode. For better or worse, this was my home, and I belonged here. I didn't want to go anywhere else. Just as well. There was nowhere else to go.

Riots

I'd always been a follower of news. But when I heard the name Wayne Douglas, it almost passed me by. I was about to change channels when his picture flashed up on screen.

"It's Blobby!" I said to myself. The boy I'd met that night on the way home. "No way."

I called Mum through from the kitchen. She knew his family.

"Oh my. What a loss dat is, what a loss," she said, shaking her head. "That poor woman."

Blobby was 26. He had died in police custody. People were angry.

The news reporter was standing outside the police station, just beside our tree. He said there was going to be a march this evening. I had no plans that day. I considered going to join them, on a cause I supported, but thought better of it.

I said a prayer for him, and for his parents. Hope the march goes well, I thought, but I'm going to sit this one out. The Feds are going to be busy tonight.

By the time the 6pm news came on ITV, it had all kicked off.

The Feds were out in their riot gear. Witnesses were telling the news cameras they had heard shots being fired down by the Ritzy cinema. Hundreds of youts, black and white, had

273

taken to the streets, attacking police, ransacking shops and burning cars.

They were pulling police officers from motorbikes and hurling petrol bombs.

Hearing something, I pulled aside the curtains. A police helicopter was buzzing overhead.

The news reporter was no longer standing in Windrush Square. Now the cameras were on the shops. They showed moneybags hanging out the banks. Places were getting looted big-time. There was a stand-off between people and the police. It was chaos. My eyes started to open up out of my head.

Moneybags. Mmm. Easy pickings.

They're reporting this now, I thought, but it won't be live footage.

Mum came through and recognised the shops.

"Oh wha' gwarn in Brixton?" she exclaimed. "Oh my! Riots in Brixton? That's crazy."

"But Mum, look at what's happening."

She could read what was going through my mind.

"Listen, child, don't you leave this house. Don't go near fucking Brixton! When riot go aff in dis place, oh," she shuddered.

"Why am I going to Brixton? What's wrong with you?" I snapped. "Chill."

Yeah, Brixton could do riots, I knew that much.

I went to my room and tried to listen to some music. I watched some TV, flicking from sitcom to quiz show. I fiddled with my hair, and tidied up my room.

Brixton was calling me.

In the back of my head, all I could think of was the free money. It was all kicking off. It was hardly any work. What's stopping you?

Sour

I wanted part of this. David and I had been fighting again and I needed some light relief.

I could hear Mum watching the news downstairs. More police helicopters zipped over the estate.

I couldn't handle this no more. I was going out.

Let me get dark clothes. I flicked through my wardrobe. They had to be unremarkable, but not too bait.

I went for a black jacket, with two leather panels on the front and back, with dark, woollen sleeves. I put on cream jeans, a tight white top, some trainers and looked in the mirror. Perfect. I looked girly, but if I did happen to get involved in anything, shall we say, unforeseen, I had a black jacket to cover me. I was ready.

My plan was simple. Keep your eyes on the prize. If I happened to pass something that was just there for the taking, well, I would just take it – before somebody else did.

As soon as Mum saw me coming down the stairs, she started shouting.

"I told you not to go anywhere. Hard ears pickney will always feel."

That was Jamaican for: "If you don't listen, you're going to learn the hard way."

"Chill out. Just going to see my friend in Tulse Hill."

"Girl, you ain't got no friends."

I ignored her, took my keys and walked out the door.

"Where you going?" she shouted after me. "Come back here."

I kept walking till I couldn't hear her no more. Then I headed straight for Brixton.

I had barely left the estate when I saw them coming. They were like a pack of zombies, walking slowly down Brixton Hill, coming this direction.

A huge wave of people.

"Killers! Killers!" chanted the mob, as they swept down the hill towards our estate.

I got over-excited. I'd never seen people unite in such a way, in such a number. There were so many! One form makes many. Imagine what we could accomplish.

I guessed they were about five minutes away from where I was standing. I stood still, overwhelmed with anticipation of being swept up with them.

It didn't make sense to go back down to Brixton. Those moneybags will have long gone. These guys were where the action was. That much was clear. They were on a mission. What was to come, I had no idea. The long, hot day was dying. The summer sky was violently pink.

This was going to be quite a night.

All I remember was the sound of feet, sweeping me up. Beyond the chants, there was not even much talking. A lot of noise and chaos but this was no place to chat.

I thought of *I, Robot*. No one was smiling, just a stern, straight-faced, wild-eyed mob.

I knew there were shops that lay ahead. I even knew the shopkeepers. These were the local shops I'd never be naughty in. I'd made it a policy to only ever steam other people's locals. Just like these guys, probably. I hoped Jay had been smart enough to bring down the shutters of his mini-mart early.

We were getting closer. Soon we'd hit the electrical shops, barber shop and fish bar. Further down was the Co-op and a pizza place. You knew there would be money. As soon as the mob hit the parade, so it began. I was in awe. Suddenly, it felt like there were hundreds, ripping off shutters, smashing windows, breaking glass and stealing whatever they could. This was new to me.

Sour

Before you knew it, people were ducking out with grins and PlayStations under their arms. The electrical goods shop took the biggest battering, haemorrhaging TVs and radios and consoles until its shelves were empty.

This was steaming but without the aggression. There was no one around to put up a resistance against the mass.

I was no stranger to badness, but I was used to a ticking clock, counting the seconds from the first smash of glass till the arrival of sirens a few minutes later.

But there was no police.

What the fuck is going on?

People smashed and grabbed, but still no police. They didn't come. Then it dawned. This was just a splinter group. The Feds must be tied up elsewhere. This was a free-for-all!

I was beside myself. You felt like you had some control. When people are in numbers, man, it's amazing what they can do. That vibe, that mass, one form makes many. It was powerful.

And if you can't beat 'em, you join them, right? So who was I not to join in? I didn't know where to start.

Still, I hesitated. This was my territory. I used these shops. Oh nah, this ain't right. I felt like I was betraying them.

But no one was listening. If I said, "Come on, leave that shop alone, that guy's cool, go for that one instead," I knew no one would care. On the other hand, I also understood shops were insured.

I liked that fish shop, I use that Indian restaurant, I thought, wincing as they ripped off the shutters and smashed through the doors, chucking a sandwich board advertising meal deals right through the window, scattering the red tablecloths with glass. Fuck, move on, Sour, I told myself, there's nothing I can do here.

Out of the chaos, I saw this guy running towards me.

"Sour!" he shouted. It was a Jamaican lad from Myatt's Field. We called him Stone.

He hi-fived me.

"You never believe what happened." His nose was burst, with blood spattered over his collar. He was as jittery as a Mexican jumping bean.

"Brandon, innit. He took my console. Just headbutted me and took it away. It's war, man."

I knew Brandon. He lived on Roupell Park. He was a bad boy with a boxer's build. He looked the part – the kind of Asian guy black guys did work with. He had heart. That's why Stone was so shocked. He knew him too. He did business with his uncle. It must have felt like he was turning on his own. Even while chaos reigned, disloyalty would not be tolerated.

"You for real?"

Now I'm angry. I liked Stone. He was a smart kid. Brandon lived just a few blocks away on the other side of the Pen. This was a crime in my jurisdiction.

"He only did that coz he knew I didn't have anything on me," he said. Stone was some years younger than us. "I'm going to hurt him. Have you seen my uncle?"

This boy's uncle was a real postcode celebrity of the day. I'm not overstating it when I say he was known as a fucking nutter.

"He knows who my uncle is. My uncle is going to fuck him up."

I had never seen Stone so psyched. He was usually so chilled. The vibe had got to him too.

"Look, calm yourself down, man."

He touched his face, and saw red.

Sour

"Fuck, I'm bleeding!"

I wasn't packing a shank. It was inquisitiveness that brought me here. I wasn't going out for war and crime. My plan was to do a bit of sneaky tiefing, being an Oliver Twist for the night. And Oliver Twist doesn't carry knives or guns, darling. That was the vibe I was on. So meeting Stone threw me off course.

He was already pumped up, spoiling for a fight, with his hoodie pulled down tight. I felt the flicker of that old buzz.

Brandon had taken a liberty. He knew who Stone was. He knew who his family was. It felt like blatant disrespect. Stone was a kid I would have looked out for.

Brandon was older than us. He made money. He was a name to be known. Why was he headbutting a little boy? It was unnecessary. He had to be put in his place.

Any visions of me being Oliver Twist for the night were now thrown out the window. This was war.

It was getting dark. Police cars were now racing by, but they weren't stopping. They sped right past us.

So, now we're looking for faces in the crowd. Looking for his uncle. Lo and behold, we soon find him. He wasn't tall, but he wasn't hard to spot. He was the man who seemed to be leading a crew of his own through the mob. You could see from the thickness of his neck and the tattooed arms that he was someone who had done a bit of gym, but more than that, he had the swagger of a crazy bastard. He had shot people, people who he shouldn't have shot, and right now he was in his element.

Stone ran over and told him what had happened, showing his own red rags to this crazy bull.

"What the fuck? That fucking Brandon tinks he can fuck abaht, does he?"

The chase was on. One form makes many. Now, there were thirty, maybe forty of us, a swollen splinter group, all looking for the same face. Brandon was a marked man.

This was no longer about making money. This was about getting justice.

This was getting way above me. The mob had drifted along New Park Road. We were following Stone into my estate.

"That's him!" he cried. "Let's get him!"

Brandon ducked out behind a parked car, and over a wall into an alley that led back to the estate. Someone else shouted, then another, and another. We all made chase. We could head him off at the pedestrian underpass that opened out into Roupell Park.

The uncle led from the front. I wasn't far behind. I was so far in front, in fact, that I swore I'd be the first to get this guy. I'd make sure of that. You're in the moment, innit.

I wasn't fearful of no one, least of all an idiot like this boy. As we started to give chase, it sounded like a stampede.

We sprinted through the piss-stinking concrete tunnel of the underpass, and out into the open courtyard of the estate. Then boom. All I know is that the sky lit up. The gunshots sent us all hitting the ground like in the movies.

Hold on. I saw the crazy-arsed uncle diving to the floor. So I dived too. I cowered tight, to keep myself safe. I could smell the earth, and realised my jeans would be stained by grass. I stayed still, unsure whether he was coming forward to shoot again.

No shots came, and I rolled over behind a car. He had disappeared like a ghost.

"Is everyone alright?" the uncle shouted.

All I'm hearing is yeah, yeah, yeah.

I got back up.

Sour

The uncle was livid.

"He's just tried to kill me. That's it. Everyone exit. I'm going to get my mash. Fuck this. Who's in?"

I realised the group was considerably smaller. It was just the hard core left.

"Everyone meet back up here, yeah?"

"Cool," I said. I was going to my house. Someone had just made an attempt on my life. It was time to defend myself properly.

As I started to run, I felt a pain, a slight sting.

I could hear voices behind me. I ain't waiting on them, I thought. I've got my own argument with this Brandon boy now.

Luckily my house wasn't far away. I could see the block beyond the Pen.

I heard more talking from behind.

"Are you OK?"

Actually, that step down on to the pavement didn't feel right.

I tried to walk, but noticed now a numbness in my leg. I was dragging it. Next thing I knew I'd fallen.

Stone spotted me.

"Sour! She's been shot!"

Initially my instinct told me, no, it was a blank. But why couldn't I get up?

I looked at the sky. I didn't want to look down. My mum's warning earlier played back at me: Hard ears pickney always feel.

The pain was so severe, I couldn't cry. I could feel the pain radiating from my leg up my left hip and into my tummy.

I put my hand on my thigh. It felt cold and damp. I imagined a big-arsed hole that I could put my hand right through.

I took a deep breath and looked down. There was bare blood all over my cream jeans. It was the kind of blood that soaked your clothes, instead of staining them. Deep dark, almost black. I'd never seen so much blood in my life.

The ball bearings had sprayed across my thigh. Blood was now seeping down my jeans, and I could feel it soaking the inside of my trainer.

OK, can't be that bad, I lied to myself. Just ride it, you're a soldier, stay firm. You've had worse beatings from your mum. You can take this.

But the pain wouldn't go away. I tried to cry – it seemed like the logical thing to do – but the tears wouldn't come. The pain only got worse.

Stone scooped me up and helped me stagger across the grass, over the tarmac that Tiefing Timmy used as his race-track, and along the path by the bushes, pocked with dog turds and litter.

A few more came to help him.

"We gotta get her to hospital."

He sounded panicky. He was slapping me in the face, telling me not to shut my eyes. Dunno what films he'd been watching.

I was just thinking I've gotta stay awake. If you nod off, you don't come back, ain't that what they say?

No one mentioned ambulance. That made sense. When you're a criminal, the last thing you want to do is deal with police, or any emergency services for that matter. When things go wrong, ambulance ain't your first instinct. There will be questions, and more than likely some comeback.

No! Gotta take her to the hospital. I don't know who brought the car.

Sour

My leg was so stiff, I remember Stone having to forcibly bend it, to fit me in the hatchback. I couldn't breathe properly. Their voices were beginning to blur into one.

"I'm thirsty, I'm thirsty. I want Ribena."

She wants a Ribena.

"Stay awake," Stone shouted from the passenger seat. "We're gonna get you your Ribena, girl."

Once we reached the loading bay there was a moment of panic. I was physically stuck in the car. They tugged and pushed, and finally dragged me out the car like a rag doll. I was slammed on the floor.

Someone, from somewhere, must have got me a wheelchair, because the next thing I knew I was being pushed through the automatic doors of A&E. I rolled into reception. When I turned round, there was no one there. It was like being wheeled in by ghosts.

Staff hurried around, then it went blank.

I came through in a cubicle – just one of the cubicles set up in a special room for riot casualties. It was like a makeshift army hospital. They'd prepared for a busy night. They got one.

They'd cut off my trouser leg.

Beyond the curtains, I could hear someone crying like a bitch. Groggy from fading pain relief, I tried to ride the pain, talking to God, talking to my mum. I should have listened to her.

Was I going to walk again? I thought about this boy Brandon, and how I was going to kill him when I caught him. I was also thinking about the police officer I'd seen circulating. He knew me well. He would know that wasn't the right name on my medical notes. I didn't want him asking questions. I was in the unusual position of being a victim, for once, but I was in no mood to be snitching on anyone.

As he walked past, I shrank beneath the sheets. Not because I felt I'd done something in particular this time, but people in glass houses, innit.

Pain shot up into my hip, and I thought of Brandon and wondered whether they had caught him. If that uncle had found him, he would probably be in here already. Or the morgue.

The X-ray looked like a dot-to-dot. I'd been hit by a sawn-off shotgun. The ball bearings had sprayed across my left thigh.

"Samantha Miller?" she asked, lifting up my notes.

I nodded.

"OK, we have to take some of these out."

She lined up swab pads and starting rubbing solutions along my whole leg. I was trembling, shaking. I wanted to kill her. She picked up tongs.

I cussed her out, and screamed and shouted.

"If you're going to be that way, I'll just leave it, shall I?"

"Just cut the whole thing off!" I yelled.

Later, a doctor came through and told me I was free to go.

"You'll be OK. You had a lucky escape, but I'm afraid there's nothing we can do to remove the rest of them. If we go in and take these out, it will cause you more harm, and possibly ruin more nerves. So we're just going to have to leave them in there."

Like the shards of glass door left in Mum's head.

"You can go."

I hopped out on my crutches, avoiding police and their demands for a statement. I had no desire to be associated with being shot tonight. The Feds would spin my house. I suddenly panicked. What if they had spun it already?

I couldn't check out of hospital quick enough. I got out, hopped home and laid low. I had every intention of killing that boy. It was only his good luck, and my bad, that fate intervened once more before I could find him.

Plus, I needed to get home for another reason. Someone had run round to my mum's and told her I'd been shot. She didn't know if I was alive or dead, so when I went through that door you can imagine the scene.

When I hobbled up to my room, I held my black jacket up to the light. The bottom looked like it had been crocheted. There were holes everywhere.

The doctor was right: I was lucky to be alive.

I laid low. No shotting, no meetings, no nothing. I pulled the curtains down and shut out the world.

Brandon wasn't seen around the estate again. Wise move. He had opened fire on a postcode celebrity; he knew he had to get out.

In the first few days, Stone and his crew came round to reassure me there was a hunt out for him. He had a hit out on him for a while. Soon enough, the visits stopped, the world went silent.

No. Growing up in my world, you have two fears: going to prison and getting shot. Now I'd achieved both. There was nowhere else to go. There was nothing else to aspire to.

Worse, I'd been shot and survived: I became invincible. If I wasn't Teflon before, I was now. If a guy pulls a gun on me, I'm the one who knows what that pain feels like. That gives me the upper hand. I mentally reprogrammed myself. If being shot means a night in hospital and a few weeks in bed, what was there to be scared of?

Once again, almost without even trying, my infamy grew. Getting shot simply confirmed my role as one of the Man Dem. That was it. It wasn't elegant. It wasn't glamorous. But it was getting dizzy near the top. The stakes got bigger, the loss of face even greater. It was like the tiny trapdoor that was an exit to a normal life, with normal hopes and normal fears, was shrinking to a pinprick out of my reach.

Life on the road was consuming me. I was running out of energy to keep running, keep ahead.

Life was cheap. Getting shot simply made me more reckless than ever. There was nothing left to be scared of.

I no longer cared about what I was doing, or who got hurt. I wasn't just a menace to society. I was now a menace to myself.

But before I took the boldest step of my life, there was one more person I had to hurt.

Point of No Return

Is it nature or nurture that makes you bad? In my case, it was hard to tell. Either way, it was a lose-lose situation.

In the months after the shooting, the house went quiet, the phone stopped ringing. There was only one person left in my life.

David, any fool could have realised, was my way out. I could have adopted his life; instead all I did was drag him down into mine. I would do something unforgivable to David, something that leaves my heart cold and chills me with an unfamiliar sensation. I think it's called regret.

Weaponry had lost its wonder. I didn't care what knives and guns could do. They'd lost their glamour, the potency that gave me power. But something else was happening too, and it was down to the volatile and destructive relationship with David. I was losing heart. And David knew it.

"You're nothing but a thug," he'd scream. "You think you're so hot, but really you ain't that nice."

"Shut your mouth. Or Man Dem –"

"What Man Dem, Sour?!" he screeched. "Who are these Man Dem you're always on about? I don't see no one knocking down your door. Wake up. You're living a fantasy. I'm the only one left!"

He was right. My confidence was wavering. A leader needs confidence – and people to lead. To go out on the road without confidence ain't just unwise, it's downright dangerous. I felt trapped.

I had hoped being with David would elevate me to something else. Instead, all he made me feel was shame in being Sour, the chick from Brixton. His words could hurt me more than any gun. Yet every time we fought and finished it, we soon found our way back to each other again.

To have "heart" on the road, you couldn't have emotions. To be fearless meant shutting down, having nothing to care about and no one to care about you. The minute that went, the minute *feelings* came into it, you were compromised.

It was freaking me out. Worst of all, David didn't fear me. He could see behind the bravado, and I didn't like it. It made me feel weak, and I didn't like feeling weak.

He'd been picking all that day, criticising my clothes, my hair, my make-up. I was used to people stopping when I said stop. David never stopped.

To be honest, I was sick of the sight of him. He just kept being negative towards me and was always complaining about something.

"Gimme back the keys," I screamed.

We had been sitting in my car, outside my mum's house. The plan had been to drive to his, but he was annoying me so much I changed my mind. He could walk. I was driving nowhere.

"I'm already late. Mum's waiting for me."

"You got feet. Walk. I ain't going nowhere."

"Stop being a bitch and drive me home."

I'd had enough.

"Get out of my car. No word of a lie, David, I ain't messing."

He made a grab for the car keys, whipping them from the ignition.

"Oh yeah? In that case, neither of us are going anywhere."

"Gimme back those keys, or I swear to God I'm going to hurt you."

"What?" he scoffed. "Like your dad hurts people?"

How dare he?

"Don't say another word about my family, or I swear to God, David …"

"Swear to God what? You gotta look at yourself, girl. Look at what you derive from. Your family is fucked up! No wonder you are the way you are. Look at you. For you as a big sister, no wonder your brother's in jail."

As he said it, he threw the keys across the street. I followed the arc of the furry key ring through the air, and watched as it hit the gutter, and jangled through the bars of the drain.

Even David couldn't believe his shot.

"Face it, Sour, you're just a fuck-up."

I saw red. Before I knew it, I was punching him in the chest and neck, wishing he would have another asthma attack, grabbing for his throat and thumping his ribcage. But something changed in David. He did something he'd never done before. He started fighting back. We tumbled out of the car, lashing at each other like rabid dogs.

I raged, in between jabs to his kidneys.

He grabbed my throat and overpowered me, pressing all his weight down on to my throat. I had finally done it. I'd brought out the devil in him.

I could see the whites in his eyes as he leaned down over me.

I lost it. I wasn't playing no more. I pulled my right hand free, and reached for my belt. My fingers felt for the rabbit foot, and up to the skin holster. I nudged my hip to dislodge the blade from the pocket, and the handle slipped free.

I tried to block out the words, until I just saw his mouth moving. The rest of the world melted away.

A single jab, and suddenly he slumped to the side. His fingers fell from my throat, and soon he too was lying on the pavement, a strange look of disbelief on his face. His hand was pressed to his stomach.

He was saying something, but I couldn't hear. The knife fell from my grasp, as I heaved for breath. His lips were still moving. His eyes were frightened. Gradually, the volume slid back up again …

"You fucking bitch," he was muttering over and over again. "You fucking stabbed me …"

We both looked at the rose of blood blossoming across his shirt. He tried to get up, but fell back down to his knees.

I stepped back, but this time felt none of the power or triumph that usually came from feeling a blade slipping out of a wound of my making.

He had some intentions to harm me. I'd warned him I'd defend myself. Why had he said those things? Why would he do that? It was his fault for bringing out my demonic side.

Only, as I watched the boy who loved me try to push himself up on his hands and knees on the kerb, my usual justifications didn't sound right. They didn't even ring true to me any more.

David, the boy I'd tried to love, the boy who treated me right, took me for dinners and paid for the hairdresser, the first boy who ever treated me like someone who'd got out of the ghetto, was lying in a ball, bleeding on the pavement.

His face was crumpled with confusion. He just kept staring at me in disbelief.

The blood was spreading over his clothes.

"Oh shit."

Sour

I ran to the phone. I didn't care about the consequences this time.

"Send someone quick," I pleaded. "Man's been stabbed." I gave the address. I didn't say who stabbed him.

Then and there, for the first time, as I watched David being stretchered into the back of an ambulance, I realised the badness I was truly capable of. This was no faceless Peckham Boy, or Ghetto Boy, or Junction Boy, making threats or causing harm. This was my boy.

Overdose

David decided to drop the charges in the end.

The police came to my door a few days later to tell me there would be no further action. He had been discharged from hospital. He was going to be OK. Even had he died, I don't think I could have felt much lower than I already did.

Truth be told, when boydem said I could walk free, I didn't feel relief. I felt disappointment. It would have been an escape to get caught. Looking back, prison was the last time I'd felt happy. It was the only time I'd felt happy. I wanted to have that time-out again, that break from reality.

I'd had enough. I didn't want to be demonic no more. And if I couldn't do that, I didn't want to be here at all.

Yeah, waking up to the same story every day becomes annoying after a while.

Nobody came to knock at the door after that. Steaming, shanking, shotting, tiefing. It makes you feel at the top of the tree for a while, but it's a lonely girl's world, you know. Postcode celebrity or not.

I shut myself away, locked the world out, and dared not take another step outside, for fear of what I would do, or who I would harm. Daughter of Darkness indeed.

My life wasn't worth shit. Where exactly had it gone wrong? This was not what being 18 was meant to be like.

Sour

There were other lives out there I would have liked, but this one wasn't one of them.

The phone rang, but the people on the other end of the line only ever asked one question: "Can you fix me up?"

I didn't just withdraw from the road; I withdrew from the world.

Every so often, Mum would come up to air my room, and pull open the curtains, ranting something from the Qur'an. In his letters, Yusuf would urge me to rediscover Islam from his prison cell.

But so much for Allah. I kept asking God questions but he wasn't responding. I asked him why he made the path I was living available to me? Why didn't I have a normal life?

No answer. So I had to come up with my own answers, which frustrated me even further.

My life was no longer anything that I recognised. I'd sold myself a lie. I was not happy with myself, my life or anything I'd accomplished. But there was no one I could tell. They were all dead or in prison. One form makes many. Now I had no one.

Anyone I'd ever trusted was gone. I'd never really thought about anything as grand as a "future". That's what other kids did. The ones who are expected to go on to university, the ones who get certificates and plan nice holidays.

I felt suffocated. I needed to breathe. Inhale, exhale. Why was it so hard to do?

Had I not arrived when I did, maybe my dad wouldn't have made Mum jump through those windows. Had I been a better daughter, maybe she wouldn't be as ill as she was. Maybe, had I been a normal female, a nice girl like all the rest, maybe I could have set a better example to my little brother.

I took each day as it arrived, just wishing for it to pass quickly and then disappear, moving on to the next. In retrospect, being cooped up in a bedroom full of disappointing thoughts probably ain't good for a girl's mental health, but them days I wasn't thinking straight.

All I knew was that I'd had enough. I didn't want to be Sour no more.

For hours on end I sat in my room, staring at that beautiful chrome gun and toyed with all the thoughts racing through my mind. I wanted to cause harm, and if I'd lost heart to do it to other people, I might as well do it to myself.

One night, I left my mum in the front room, came upstairs and locked my door. The TV was still blaring. Fort Boyard.

I sat on the edge of the bed, pointed the ting to my temple, and looked at myself in the long wardrobe mirror. Could I do it here? I thought about the mess, imagining all the JFK gunk all over the duvet. Nah, too messy. Not the ting. Sure, it would be quick, but I just couldn't stomach it.

I wasn't no good at tying knots, and didn't much fancy hanging from my bedroom light.

Eventually, I hit upon an idea. Mum's anti-psychotic tablets. Amitriptyline. That was powerful shit. Anything else would be messy, but if I took the tablets it would look natural, innit. I could just lie there, like Sleeping Beauty.

I unlocked the bedroom door, and hesitated. The gameshow was still blaring. Dirty Den and Melinda Messenger were still bounding about with some screaming contestants. Mum hadn't moved. She was probably asleep on the sofa.

Padding softly over the thick carpet, I snuck through into her room, where the tablets were easily located among the pillboxes on her dresser. There were so many bloody bottles, she'd hardly notice one was gone. I filled a glass of water in the bathroom and slipped back into my bedroom.

Did I need to write a note? I wondered. Nah, the reasons were pretty obvious.

I got under the covers, downed the bottle, lay back and waited.

Shock

"Can you hear me? You're in the ambulance. Can you tell me what you took, sweetheart?"

Lights were being flashed in my eyes. I was trembling violently, covered in sick. I felt a vague sensation of being wired up to things. Machines beeped in total darkness.

The voices faded away. I drifted into blankness.

So much for my fairytale. I ain't never read the one where Sleeping Beauty wakes up in the hospital, feeling like shit, to be told she's up the duff.

"Pregnant? But I can't, I don't …"

My arms felt like lead, and I could barely lift my head from the hospital bed.

"Thirteen weeks. Or thereabouts."

There was a woman's voice talking to me. The pink lips were moving, but I couldn't compute.

"But I can't … I can't have kids …"

After Daggers, I had waited for the consequence, but nothing had happened, so I just assumed I couldn't have kids. That's what I thought would happen with David too. Bloody idiot.

With all the stress with David and Yusuf, I hadn't paid attention to missed periods. I barely paid attention even when I wasn't stressed. The less they came, the better, if you ask me. Just an inconvenience. Police cells don't have sanitary bins.

Sour

It was like I'd woken up in someone else's dream – after what felt like a very good sleep.

When I came round, I had what felt like ten pairs of eyes staring and blinking at me. My bed was surrounded.

Even worse, now all these hospital staff were treating me like I was vulnerable or something. I ain't vulnerable, I wanted to shout at them all. I'm just fucking pissed off to be here. I'd decided to do a job, but the job didn't get done.

I felt like a failure. I couldn't even kill myself properly! How dumb. Worse, I'd managed to wake up with an extra problem.

Pregnant. I couldn't take it in. My first thought was that there must be a way this can be put to an end. But Islam doesn't look too kindly on such things. It was forbidden. Fuck's sake. I had made my bed, and now I had to lie in it. I was 18. I wasn't ready to be a mother.

More than that, I didn't know *how* to be a mother. I'd grown up, watching Mum struggle, unable to cope. Motherhood meant struggling. It meant unhappiness. It meant being alone.

I spent the next few days in hospital, answering questions from a revolving door of health professionals who introduced themselves one moment then disappeared the next. They put me in a room with a shrink! How embarrassing.

Sleeping Beauty didn't have to put up with this shit.

The shrink was nice enough. Young woman, smart shoes. Looked like she shopped in Hobbs. But Lord have mercy, she was boring. Just kept asking the same questions over and over again. Why would such a young person want to die? Why did you take those tablets? What are you unhappy about?

Where do you begin? Bless her, she was only doing her job, but I thought she would never shut up.

Remorse is not an emotion I'm too fond of. But I learned quite quickly in that little box-room, at the end of the ward, that I had to act like I was OK or I would never be leaving that hospital. So I put on my best brave face and convinced this sweet woman in the sensible court shoes and beige tights that it was just my silly, one-off error.

Once I got home, what did I do?

Well, I let time glide. I think it's called denial. Though there was no denying those months of morning sickness, bent over the toilet, too ill to eat, too ill to sleep, too miserable to do anything.

Nope, this chick didn't like being pregnant at all. People speak about blooming and glowing and all that shit. When you're on your own it's a bloody horrible experience. An alien had invaded my body and there was fuck all I could do about it.

I'd spent years struggling for control of my own chaotic life. Now I didn't even have control over my own bloated body. Didn't know what to expect for motherhood.

So, I took every day as it came. Didn't have much choice. No one came to visit.

Eventually, the time came to call David.

"Hope the kid's mine."

"Just look at you, you ugly boy," I snapped. "You were lucky to have ever had a girl like me."

"You nearly killed me, you vicious cow."

I had no response to that one. I hung up. The ball was in his court.

My back ached, my fingers tingled, but despite all the aches and pains and loneliness, a realisation shot through my mind.

I could be an OK mum, you know. Maybe this ain't so bad.

Sour

I got the bus home to Roupell Park that day, if not a new woman, then at least a re-energised one.

I was going to have to reassess some things. First things first, you can't push drugs with a pushchair. It doesn't look good. I needed to cut all that shit out. I'd never been addicted to drugs, but I needed to wean myself off selling them. I'd miss the money. Where I come from, legitimacy means poverty.

Fuck the phone. Fuck the guns. Fuck the lifestyle. The moment that phone rang, I knew I'd be caught in the same old rubbish. I snapped that gold aerial and threw it away. The cats could call someone else.

Everything else I left for the elders to deal with. I went through my room that night like a woman possessed, chucking out trainers and the last bags of brown, sweeping the Moet bottles off the shelf into a bin liner. They smashed into the bag in a cloud of dust.

Next came the clothes. Out went gangster chic, in stayed anything with an elasticated waist.

That night, I collapsed on the bed. Under the duvet, I laid my hands on my belly and felt my baby kick. The somersaults continued till late in the night. I fell asleep quickly for the first time in a long time, with my hand on my tummy and a smile on my lips.

Epilogue

"Montana! Where's my change?"

A tall, slender young girl in a pressed, clean uniform hands me a £10 note.

"Where's your football kit?"

"Washing machine."

"And your schoolbag?"

"My room."

"Homework?"

"Done."

I'm trying to think of another thing to catch her out, but I can't.

"Going to Letitia's. Want me to bring back some food?"

"No, there's stuff in the fridge. Don't be late."

"I won't," she sings, but she's already out the door.

When Montana was born, I couldn't take it all in. It had been a difficult labour. I was glad the pain was over, but the rest I couldn't compute. What was I meant to do? Who was going to tell me?

I didn't know how to be a mum. And I had no one to teach me. You can't anticipate what you don't know. Suddenly this little rugrat was depending on me. I had to step up.

I won't lie. They were dark days. I barely left the house. I lived like a zombie. I was scared. More than that, I felt lost. I didn't feel like I was part of society. This was a whole new kinda isolation.

The first few months passed in a fug. I used to wish the time away. Get her sleeping right through the night, good. Get her on solids, great.

I wished away the days. I wished away the firsts that other, happier parents might celebrate. First footsteps, first words, first potty – these weren't things to be savoured, they were stages of survival. I broke it down into little steps. OK, she's one, I'd tell myself; now let's get to two. Two, now let's get to three. It was a big responsibility. Certain days I was fine. Certain days I was sinking. But I got through.

David stepped up too. Thanks to his mum, mainly. She's a good lady. He's got a good job. He sees Montana a lot, and so does her nan. They go out on educational trips together, to museums, libraries, swimming pools. She gets to sample some fine dining.

She's 16 in March. I was well and truly battle-hardened by then. But 'Tana – I'd like to think she's exactly how a 15 year old should be.

Would you believe, she's friends with some of Drex's children? He's got a few now. Funny how things work out. She knows about my past, most of it, anyway. There wasn't much choice. We live in the same endz – of course it was going to be mentioned to her, at some point – "Your mum used to be this, she used to do that." She would have found out sooner or later, so I'd prefer she heard it from me.

Yeah, me and 'Tana, we're cool. She gets provided for. She says I'm strict. Damn right. I operate a zero tolerance household, make no mistake. It works. She even likes school too. Sometimes I wonder if she really is my daughter.

I would love for her to be a brain surgeon. She says she

wants to be a vet. Or a lawyer. I just hope she can be whatever she wants to be, the best in her field. She wants to see the world. Unlike me at that age, she knows it's out there, beyond prison and a postcode.

It's lonely. I ain't gonna lie. There's no reward for turning over a good leaf. There's no medal for returning from the dark side.

I'm not sure there should be. I don't expect an invitation to Buckingham Palace. I'm just being the best mum I can be. Had Montana not come when she did, I know one thing for sure: I'd be either dead or in jail. Now there's Molly too, my latest little rugrat. She'll soon be three.

She's the spit of her dad, with pale, olive skin and the most unusual-coloured eyes. He's another one that can't figure me out; he's not around, but it's hard work. I know I'm not the easiest of characters. The three of us are a unit. We get by.

What they don't like to tell you is that giving up gangs makes you poor, that's the truth. It's not like there's a choice between good squillah or bad. As a single mum with no qualifications, it was drug money or nothing. It's a choice between thriving on ill-gotten gains, or surviving the endz with benefits.

Do I have regrets? Put it like this: if I'd put as much energy into a business as I did into crime, I'd be on Dragon's Den, darling. I'd be proud and loaded. If I'd studied as much as I steamed, I'd be an architect or a doctor by now.

Instead, I got work at a bookies, took shifts at Greggs. I even tried out a job with some health insurance company, but I'm still searching for the right path.

Funnily enough, the City headhunters didn't beat a path to my doorstep, though I think that's their big mistake – if they want whipsmart kids who can spot a business opportunity when they see one, they could do worse than tap up the shotters on the sink estates. Dealing drugs sure as hell brings out your inner entrepreneur.

Winston got someone else to look after his P's. Brixton was changing. There were whole new tribes of young, white professionals to supply with pills and cocaine. And there was plenty fresh blood to fight over who got to get rich keeping them happy.

Want to hear a coincidence?

At secondary school, my niece became friends with a lovely mixed-race girl. Lovely kid. She was always coming round, and soon saw me as a big auntie.

Turned out her uncle was called Brandon. He was Asian, but no longer a boy.

Imagine that – our nieces became friends. How about that?

She must have gone back home one day, talking about her Aunty Sour, when Brandon made the connection. Next thing I know, I'm getting a phone call from a number I don't recognise.

"Listen, yeah," he said. "I just want to apologise. I know it's a lot of years ago but I didn't know you were part of that crew and I'd never have – Basically, yeah, I'm sorry."

I laughed. None of it mattered. Blood under the bridge.

"It's cool, innit."

"For real?"

"For real. What you done to me was probably payback for something else. Karma, innit."

I found it weird that all these years later he still wanted to apologise.

"Look, me and you, we've never had arguments. It's done. No hard feelings, yeah?"

He sounded stunned.

"Look after yourself."

"You too."

I never heard from him again. Bless him. If I saw him today, I'd go and give him a hug.

And the Man Dem? What happened to all those boys I was prepared to get knifed for? Good question.

A couple made it through, with businesses and jobs of their own. A lot of them haven't. But every now and then I'll hear one of them has done well or found God, and be pleased. It is what it is.

I'd hear about Gadget or Badman or Cruz, as one by one they got out of jail and went back on the road. But they were no longer in my life. One minute someone's there, the next they're not. You get used to that in Gangland.

I feel old. I've been through so much I feel 50, not 35.

Am I completely reformed? It depends. I would like to say so, but put it this way: I trust myself more now, but I don't trust society. I think of myself as a recovering alcoholic who tries to avoid putting themselves in the way of temptation. So I keep myself out of trouble.

If I came across someone in the street who was threatening violence, I couldn't say I would not step in. Not so long ago I tried going clubbing again but realised pretty quick it was not for me. When some women get drunk and lash out, put it this way, I'm not the right girl to be with.

So I just keep myself away from harm. I've become a bit of a house hermit these days. Prevention is better than cure.

Do I feel shame? Of course. I was a horrible, aggressive little bastard.

I used to ask God, why did you let us live the way we did? Why was my mum a manic depressive? Why was my dad a rapist? My life always used to feel determined by someone else's bad decisions.

But I also know God is merciful. He has tested me but he has also looked out for me. I'm not dead. I'm not in jail. I've got a lot to be thankful for. I've lived it. Only now, I've got shit to show for it.

How many people did I stab? Too many, is all I know. All it took was for someone to look the wrong way at me in the street, one glance to make me feel threatened or uncomfortable. Stabbing actions happen fast. There ain't no time for any of that Rocky Balboa shit. Jab in, slip out. *Duppy know who fe frighten*.

Do you think of the consequences? Hell no. When you're 15, surviving one day to the next, there are none.

So who's to blame? Politicians could blame my parents, and perhaps they'd be right. Social workers might blame the poverty, and they'd probably be right too.

But here are the facts. If I went up to any of the black boys I see in Brixton now, slinking round the stairwells, cycling round the estates, they'd all have their stories. They'd all have hard times. Maybe some of their dads were like mine. Maybe their mums suffered the same shit that mine did. But here's the truth. There are no excuses. I had no excuse.

Maybe badness is genetic – I still think it is – but here's what I've learned. Everyone has to be responsible for their own actions, no matter where they come from. I made some bad decisions and I've got to live with it. The devil will always sit on my shoulder; the only difference now is that I try not to listen.

Mum still lives in Roupell Park. We just celebrated her birthday with music and laughter. She cooked a serious dinner, it was nice. I was playing the music. Imagine, I was selecting the same music Mum would play when we were younger. I took her down memory lane to remind her of when she was happy. Lovers' rock and Studio One. I took it old skool.

Mum and I get on much better now. I see life differently now I have children of my own. I see first hand how hard it is to be a parent. She takes her medication to remain stable but still has relapses.

It's hard. Every time I think I've overcome my past, her mental breakdowns take me back to square one, back to that trembling young girl on edge. I don't tell her much as I don't feel she can handle much info without over-worrying. It's always been that way and I don't think it's ever gonna change.

But she does like to laugh. And I love her for doing her best to raise us. I know how hard it is to be a single mum.

I live a few miles away. I still see the youngers prowling. And true enough, they keep getting younger. Now they call themselves the Muslim Boys, Poverty Driven Children. The names change, the problems don't.

Sometimes, when I'm feeling bold, I confront the youts out in Brixton and Tulse Hill looking for trouble. I stop and ask them what they're doing, ask why they are wasting their time.

I don't tell them who I am. I shouldn't laugh, but it confuses them, seeing this fearless black lady approaching. I like to think they might stop and think about it once I'm gone.

Not so long ago a boy was stabbed right outside my mum's home. He was screaming, bleeding bad from two puncture wounds.

It wasn't long after Yusuf got out of prison. He's moved to Dubai now with his family. Says he doesn't like the way Britain is going.

Anyway, we piled this poor boy in the back of the car and I put my foot down. We were a proper urban ambulance, man.

Sour

When we dropped him off, we asked him if we could do anything. He asked me to call his mum. He fumbled for his phone. I found her number.

She had a polite voice.

"You don't know me," I said, "but I've got some bad news you need to hear. Your son has been stabbed."

I'll always remember her first word.

"Again?"

I explained all I could, and wished her and her son good luck, as she dashed to his bedside.

I looked out for him on the news that night, and the night after that. I checked the papers for a few days. I was relieved to see no mention.

Then again, black boys getting stabbed don't much make for news these days.

Do I miss Sour? Hell no.

What did she achieve for me really? Not much. All she did was give me a way to relieve some anger, I guess.

I don't even like people calling me Sour these days.

I was about to get on the tube at Oxford Circus when I last heard it. I'd seen him on the opposite platform and tried to hide, but he saw me first.

He had put on some weight, a bit chunkier round the cheeks, but he was still as short as ever. He was wearing baggy jeans and a lot of jewellery, and had modified the early '90s limp to more of a swagger. It was Stimpy.

"Sour!" he shouted across the platform. "SOUR!" He put two stubby fingers to his lips and whistled. People were looking. I could see the rest of the passengers on the platform inching away from the swaggering hardcase who was starting to make a scene.

"Sour! Can't you hear man calling you? Sour? You gone moist?"

Eyes glazed over, I stared into the middle distance, and prayed for him to stop. I didn't want to be that person no more. The platforms filled up, swallowing me up. Stimpy pushed to the front. I exhaled slowly, concentrating on the sound of the next train to rumble out of the dark.

Brightly lit carriages flashed by, obscuring him in clapper-boards of red and glass. He bounded in, jumped up on the seats, and banged on the dirty window. "Sour," he mouthed, till the doors beeped shut and the carriages carried him off, out of sight. "It's me, Stimps …"

But it wasn't me. I'll never be sweet, but I'm no longer Sour. She was about anger, badness and greed. I'm someone else now. I am Tracey. Tracey Miller. Ex Gang Girl.

A Note From Montana

I've just turned 16. Mum and Dad threw me a party. I had a beautiful dress and did my hair real nice and arrived in a limo. My friends threw away their knives before they came in. They know I don't like that stuff.

I'm friends with people on all sides. They know I'm not going to get involved in that dumbness.

There were some groups I couldn't invite to my party, even though I wanted to. I couldn't have Brixton ones, and I couldn't have New Park ones, because that's when it all gets mad. It wouldn't have been like a party no more; it would have been a death street.

But everything went well, and we all had a good time.

Nowadays most people have knives – usually the pocket ones that flick out – but I'm really not interested. If they didn't carry anything, they would say that they are lacking.

Somebody on one side might ask me for the number of somebody on the other side, but I tell them I'm not going to give it to them. Just leave it, I say. I don't see the point. It's usually silly things, like somebody stepped on your trainers, or gave you the wrong look. And it's never one on one; it's usually the whole group.

"Pagans", that's what they call enemies nowadays. And everyone's got enemies. I was going to my Nan's once with some friends, when they spotted a pagan who'd wandered into their territory. He was on his own. They went after him. He got gang-rushed. I went the other way. I know how that dumbness can end up. My mum and Nan have warned me. Some of my friends have lost close friends or family members.

I want to be a lawyer. Or a vet. My family say I'm good at arguing my case and getting my point across. And Mum let us grow up with lots of pets – birds, dogs and snakes, you name it – so I get on good with animals. I want to earn money, but I want to earn it legitimately. I know a few friends who got a bad reputation, who have done robberies, but there's no point getting a record for that kind of dumbness.

I'd like to go on to Sixth Form College.

I'm mainly a B student, but Mum and Nan tell me not to think about Bs; I've got to aim for the A stars, so that's what I do. I'm studying for sociology and business and maths and English. I know those exams are my last resort – they will follow me for life, so I want to do well.

Mum tells me not to make the same mistakes she did. She's strict, man! We're close. Sure, we have our differences like any mum and daughter, but mostly we get on well. And I'm close with my dad, and Nan and Granddad too. They're good to me.

They try to make sure I get on as well as I can. They support me and buy me stuff and tell me to do my best.

Mum is the toughest, for sure.

"You don't want to end up like me" – that's what she always says.

When I don't pay attention at school, she goes mad. Says she doesn't want me leaving school being dumb, like all these kids on the street doing nothing. Yeah, I know the stories. Some of my friends can't believe it. They ask questions about her, to check if what they've heard is true. Quite a few have told me that they're scared of her.

But she has changed a lot. That was a long time ago. I'm proud of her. She came out of it alive. If I got involved in the same stupidity, she tells me I might not be so lucky.

Everyone can change if they try. She's been able to keep me out of trouble. Even though it's annoying she's so strict, I know it's for good reasons. No one messes with my mum.

Some things never change. South London has its characters. We're all lively, I'll say that much.

Older people see the younger generation as a nuisance. They're scared of them. They don't feel safe, and sometimes they're right to – these kids want to be feared.

I'll jam with my friends round the estate. But I'm not allowed to stay out late, like the rest. Some kids stay out from early in the morning to late, late at night, sometimes not going home till 7am the next day. They see their gang as a family; they do for each other what their own families don't.

I feel sorry for the ones who are escaping domestic violence, but most of them I don't feel sorry for at all. They choose to be like that. They are the ones who want status. They have to take responsibility.

As for the ones who say they've never been taught the difference between right or wrong, they're just lying. How can you not know stabbing someone is bad?

But they keep on fighting – hurting each other over wrong looks across the street, dissing each other in raps, insisting on postcode wars. Soon they'll forget what they're fighting over. It has to get boring eventually, right? Maybe one day they'll realise they're not getting anywhere, that their friends are dying. I hope so.

People can't war forever.

A Note From
Brooke Kinsella

On 29 June 2008 my family and I were left heartbroken when my 16-year-old brother Ben was murdered. He had just finished his GCSE exams and was looking forward to a life filled with promise, but this was snatched away in five seconds by a knife attack that left my family, friends and our community devastated.

After Ben was killed I just wanted to lie down and go to sleep. I was a big sister who had lost a little brother and all I could think about was that I wouldn't be able to buy him a pint on his 18th birthday, that he would never dance at my wedding or meet my future children, that he would never get to fall in love or have children of his own.

But I also wanted to make sure that Ben was never forgotten. I loved him too much for him to fade away at 16 and I was determined to try and stop this happening to somebody else's brother. I wasn't naïve enough to think I could put a complete stop to knife crime, but it seemed to have become a much bigger problem in our society and I wanted to make our streets safer in any way that I could.

My family and I started off by campaigning for tougher sentences for those who carried or used a knife, and our hard work finally paid off in 2010 when the tariff for murder with a knife was raised to a starting point of 25 years.

Sour

But I believe prevention is better than cure and I wanted to get through to young people before they were ever faced with the decision of whether to pick up a weapon. My family and I decided that we wanted to create a legacy for Ben, and so we built The Ben Kinsella Exhibition, which uses Ben's story amongst others to educate young people and create awareness around knife crime and its consequences.

It was while researching stories to include in our exhibition that I came across Tracey Miller. Her story immediately stood out to me as not only was it exceptional to hear of a young girl committing such terrible acts but to then have completely turned her life around in the way that she did seemed to me an incredibly brave and inspirational thing. We wanted to reach out to young people and show them they could have a better life if they made better choices, and Tracey was a prime example of how you could do this – no matter how caught up in a lifestyle you were.

As soon as I met Tracey I knew she would be an incredible asset – not only to our exhibition but to anybody who is trying to put an end to this problem. She speaks quietly and passionately, but above all she speaks honestly about her life, the mistakes she has made and what helped her to stop making them. You can't help but listen in awe to her story and the life she has lived – from hurting people violently to being shot herself – but it is when she talks about learning she would soon become a mum and how she decided then and there to change her life around that you sit up and take notice. On the surface it could be easy to dislike Tracey, given the things she has done in her life, but she is now so determined to make up for those things and to prevent others from doing as she did that you cannot help but admire her.

Tracey Miller

It is so important to hear stories such as Tracey's as there are many young people out there who believe that it is not possible to change their lives, that they are too caught up in this world or that gang to ever get out. Tracey shows them that it is indeed possible and for them – and us – sparks hope that it doesn't have to be that way.

I am delighted Tracey is sharing her story as I believe strongly it is one that needs to be told.

http://www.benkinsella.org.uk/